THE FIRST BOOK

Published by Princeton University Press,
41 William Street, Princeton, New Jersey 08540
In the United Kingdom: Princeton University Press,
6 Oxford Street, Woodstock, Oxfordshire OX20 1TW
press.princeton.edu

"Two Scenes" is from *Some Trees* by John Ashbery. Copyright © 1956, 1978 by John
Ashbery. Reprinted by permission of Georges Borchardt, Inc. and Carcanet Press (UK),
on behalf of the author.
Excerpt from "A Wave" is from *A Wave* by John Ashbery. Copyright © 1981, 1982, 1983,
1984 by John Ashbery. Reprinted by permission of Georges Borchardt, Inc. and
Carcanet Press (UK), on behalf of the author.
Excerpt from "Education of the Poet" is from *Proofs And Theories: Essays On Poetry* by
Louise Glück. Copyright © 1994 by Louise Glück. Reprinted by permission of
HarperCollins Publishers.
Excerpt from "Recent Poetry" by Randall Jarrell is from the *Yale Review*. Copyright
© 1956 by Yale University. Reprinted by permission of John Wiley & Sons, Inc.
"Diligence Is to Magic as Progress Is to Flight" and "To an Intra-Mural Rat" from
Observations by Marianne Moore are reprinted by permission of the Special Collections
Library, Pennsylvania State University Libraries.
"Its Form" is from *The Lion Bridge* by Michael Palmer, copyright © 1998 by Michael
Palmer. Reprinted by permission of New Directions Publishing Corp.

All Rights Reserved

ISBN 978-0-691-16447-2

Library of Congress Control Number: 2015934756

British Library Cataloging-in-Publication Data is available

This book has been composed in Granjon LT Std

Printed on acid-free paper. ∞

Printed in the United States of America

1 3 5 7 9 10 8 6 4 2

To my family

Contents

Acknowledgments

I am deeply grateful to my teachers, friends, and family for help that has come in so many forms that the distinctions between teachers and friends, friends and family, family and teachers seem irrelevant. This book began as a dissertation at Yale University. My advisers, Langdon Hammer and Amy Hungerford, have been extraordinarily encouraging and supportive throughout every stage of my work: there isn't a word in these pages that doesn't owe something to their advice and examples as teachers and scholars. Paul Fry offered generous responses to each chapter of my first draft and provided me with a detailed report on the whole that I have returned to time and again throughout the revision process. I am indebted to Leslie Brisman and Wes Davis for insightful responses to an earlier version of the manuscript, to Linda Peterson for guiding me through the dissertation process, and to Wai Chee Dimock, Lawrence Manley, and Claude Rawson for helping me to think about literary vocation outside of the context of twentieth-century American poetry. Chapter 2 benefited from a thoughtful reading by Ala Alryyes, Jill Campbell, and John Muse. Harold Bloom deserves more thanks than I could possibly express here—for guidance, encouragement, and especially the gift of his time.

Stephen Burt and James Longenbach provided unbelievably detailed and insightful responses to the manuscript for Princeton University Press. I thank Alison MacKeen, who first took the project on, both for believing in it and for finding such sympathetic readers. Anne Savarese is everything one could ask for in an editor: would that every writer's work could be read so carefully and improved so much. Ellen Foos deftly guided the manuscript through the production process, Juliana Fidler helped with permissions, and Brittany Ericksen provided expert copyediting. Theresa Liu cheered me on and helped me out as the project approached completion.

I would like to thank anonymous readers for *American Literature* and *Twentieth-Century Literature*, where earlier versions of chapters 2 and 3 first appeared, for their helpful comments and suggestions. I am also grateful for the opportunity to present my work in progress to audiences at Delaware State University, the New School for Social Research, and New York University.

Several trains of thought that inform this book began in conversations with teachers at Princeton, including Michael Wood, who introduced me to modern poetry. William Howarth introduced me to Emerson and Whitman, and it was with him that I first developed the idea of studying poetic debuts. James Richardson introduced me to contemporary poetry; for that, and also for his encouragement and friendship, I am hugely grateful.

While working on this book, it has been my good fortune to have taught alongside Tanya Clark, Joe Coulombe, Theresa Craig, Bill Freind, Zena Meadowsong, Cathy Parrish, Bruce Plourde, Lee Talley, and Tim Viator at Rowan University and Joe Amoako, Amanda Anderson, Fidelis Odun Balogun, Natalie Belcher, Andrew Blake, Dawn Bordley, Adenike Davidson, Ed Dawley, Joseph Fees, Tina George, Victor Gomia, Myrna Nurse, Susmita Roye, Ladji Sacko, Sandra Sokowski, and Angmoor Teye at Delaware State University. Students too many to name have inspired me and refreshed my interest in poetry over the years; still, I have to mention Kristen Brozina Angelucci in order to return the favor of mentioning me in the acknowledgments to her best-selling first book, *The Reading Promise*. Michael and Mary Pat Robertson encouraged and supported me throughout my work. I would also like to thank Provost Alton Thompson at Delaware State for an Academic Enrichment Award that helped me to see the book through to publication.

Stuart Watson and Samuel Arkin challenged and inspired me during my first semester as a teaching fellow at Yale, and they have continued to do so by making time in their own evolving literary careers to read versions of several of these chapters. Christopher van den Berg and Brett Foster provided good company as well as intellectual and moral support during our time together in New Haven and afterward. Brooke Conti gave me helpful advice on navigating the publication process.

My parents, Monica and Philip Zuba, have provided every kind of support since day one: it would be impossible to ever thank them enough. Conversations with Scarlett Lovell helped me clarify my thinking, and Bruce Burgess helped me stay the course with the interest he took in my work. My brothers, Colter, Andrew, and Morgan, helped me take breaks from my work even as they pushed me to finish it. Sarah Zuba has been patiently reading drafts of this book for years: her love and encouragement mean everything to me. It is to her, and to our children, Luke and Sadie, that I dedicate this book.

Earlier versions of chapters 2 and 3 appeared in *American Literature* 82.4 (December 2010) and *Twentieth-Century Literature* 59.2 (Summer 2013), respectively. I am grateful to Duke University Press and the editors of both journals for permission to reprint material from those sources.

Abbreviations

BMM   Marianne Moore, *Becoming Marianne Moore: The Early Poems, 1907–1924*. Edited by Robin G. Schulze. Berkeley: University of California Press, 2002.

FCP   Pierre Bourdieu, *The Field of Cultural Production*. Edited by Randal Johnson. New York: Columbia University Press, 1993.

HCCP   Hart Crane, *Complete Poems and Selected Letters*. Edited by Langdon Hammer. New York: Library of America, 2006.

HCL   Hart Crane, *O My Land, My Friends: The Selected Letters of Hart Crane*. Edited by Langdon Hammer and Brom Weber. New York: Four Walls Eight Windows, 1997.

JACP   John Ashbery, *Collected Poems, 1956–1987*. Edited by Mark Ford. New York: Library of America, 2008.

LH   Sylvia Plath, *Letters Home: Correspondence, 1950–1963*. Edited by Aurelia Schober Plath. New York: HarperCollins, 1992.

MML   Marianne Moore, *The Selected Letters of Marianne Moore*. Edited by Bonnie Costello. New York: Knopf, 1997.

PT   Louise Glück, *Proofs and Theories*. Hopewell, NJ: Ecco Press, 1994.

SP   Wallace Stevens, *Souvenirs and Prophecies: The Young Wallace Stevens*. Edited by Holly Stevens. New York: Knopf, 1977.

UJSP   Sylvia Plath, *The Unabridged Journals of Sylvia Plath*. Edited by Karen V. Kukil. New York: Anchor Books, 2000.

WSCP   Wallace Stevens, *Collected Poetry and Prose*. Edited by Frank Kermode and Joan Richardson. New York: Library of America, 1997.

WSL   Wallace Stevens, *Letters of Wallace Stevens*. Edited by Holly Stevens. Berkeley: University of California Press, 1996.

THE FIRST BOOK

Introduction

The History of the Poetic Career

So all the slightly more than young
Get moved up whether they like it or not, and only
The very old or the very young have any say in the matter,
Whether they are a train or a boat or just a road leading
Across a plain, from nowhere to nowhere.
—John Ashbery, "A Wave"

In the winter of 1901 Wallace Stevens wrote to his father, Garrett, to propose leaving the *New York Tribune* so he could take up writing full time. The response he received was unequivocal: "This morning I heard from him &, of course, found my suggestion torn to pieces" (*SP* 101). Stevens's experience is hardly exceptional: Hart Crane argued with his father, Clarence, about devoting himself to poetry, and Ezra Pound unsuccessfully tried to persuade T. S. Eliot's father, Henry, to support his son's move to London to make his way as a poet. When Langston Hughes showed his father a copy of *The Crisis* magazine featuring "The Negro Speaks of Rivers," Jim Hughes asked only how long the poem had taken to write and how much money it had brought in.[1] Though Marianne Moore enjoyed more encouragement from her mother than Stevens, Crane, Eliot, or Hughes received from their fathers, Mary Warner Moore's support for her daughter's literary career was nevertheless complicated by their different perspectives on how such a career should be conducted.

Poetry offers so little in the way of such traditional occupational values as security and remuneration that the notion of the "poetic career" in this chapter title is apt to seem inherently contradictory.[2] Pursuing a career as an American poet during the twentieth century has typically meant pursuing a career as something else: Stevens worked for an insurance company, Crane for an advertising agency, Eliot for a bank, and Moore for a library. Hughes worked at a variety of jobs and wrote prolifically in other genres to

1

support himself, well after the popular and critical acclaim of his debut had established him as a central figure of the Harlem Renaissance. In the years since World War II, poets have often taken jobs teaching literature and creative writing in colleges and universities. While the challenges of cutting a path as a poet have obscured the importance of the poetic career to critics, among whom it still remains "largely unexplored," those same challenges have made it a central preoccupation for poets.[3] That preoccupation registers with special force in the first book, since the difficulties of conducting a poetic career are exacerbated by doubts about vocation that tend to plague even the most self-assured and ambitious poets prior to any substantial achievement or public recognition. The representation of career offers a powerful way to dramatize the construction of poetic authority, even though that authority traditionally derives in large part precisely from the difference between poetry and those forms of work that lend themselves more readily to the normative progress of the conventional occupational trajectory.[4] In fact, imagining "the shape of life," as John Ashbery puts it, is so far from being irrelevant to poets that it can, on occasion, seem difficult to evade. No matter how he conceptualizes it in poem after poem devoted to "finding metaphors for life," he discovers that "still the 'career' notion intervenes," and "all the slightly more than young" in the epigraph quoted above get "moved up whether they like it or not" (*JACP* 323, 292, 799).[5]

The First Book examines the twentieth-century obsession with career in the context of the poetic debut, a unique form of literary production that comes to be endowed with its own tradition, conventions, and prestige as it assumes an increasingly prominent role in the way poetry is written, published, marketed, and read. Surveying the ways in which career has been represented by American poets from Wallace Stevens to Louise Glück, I trace a shift from the emphatically indeterminate paths projected in first books of the 1920s to the emergence of trajectories that evoke various kinds of progress after World War II. That shift reflects a tension already in place at the beginning of the century, when the rise of professionalism put in crisis a romantic conception of the writer that emphasized untutored genius and spontaneity. The broken, errant, or halting trajectories often evoked in modernist debuts defy the ideology of professionalism, in which authority grows through the pursuit of a unified course of regular development.

With the institutionalization of poetry in the academy in the post-1945 period and the concurrent proliferation of first-book prizes for poetry, poets adopted new strategies of self-definition that struck a balance between the conflicting imperatives of professionalism and romanticism. The often strikingly explicit theme of beginning that typifies first books of the last half century is writ large in the titles of such debuts as *A Beginning* (Robert Horan, 1948), *The Arrivistes* (Louis Simpson, 1949), *First Poems* (James Merrill, 1951), *A Mask for Janus* (W. S. Merwin, 1952), *Birthdays from the Ocean* (Isabella Gardner, 1955), *The Hatch* (Norma Farber, 1955), *A Primer of Kinetics* (James L. Rosenberg, 1961), *Preface to a Twenty Volume Suicide Note* (LeRoi Jones, 1961), *Birth of a Shark* (David Wevill, 1964), *The Breaking of the Day* (Peter Davison, 1964), *Preambles and Other Poems* (Alvin Feinman, 1964), *The Broken Ground* (Wendell Berry, 1964), *Fits of Dawn* (Joseph Ceravolo, 1965), *The First Cities* (Audre Lorde, 1968), *Learning the Way* (James Den Boer, 1968), *January: A Book of Poems* (David Shapiro, 1968), *Firstborn* (Louise Glück, 1968), *Breaking Camp* (Marge Piercy, 1968), *Official Entry Blank* (Ted Kooser, 1969), and *First Practice* (Gary Gildner, 1969), among others. Such titles project forms of normative development adapted to an increasingly institutionalized poetry scene. At the same time, they cast the poet as a kind of amateur whose art remains uncorrupted by the rationalizing ethos of modern professionalism.

Recent work in the developing field of "career criticism" has shown that the literary career demands further investigation, and it has laid out a variety of questions and contexts relevant to the topic. Inaugurated in the early 1980s in a pair of studies by Richard Helgerson and Lawrence Lipking, career criticism was developed through Patrick Cheney's several books on early modern authorship from the 1990s and 2000s and promoted in two recent volumes of essays, *European Literary Careers: The Author from Antiquity to the Renaissance* and *Classical Literary Careers and Their Reception.* " 'Career criticism,' " as Cheney remarks, "emerged almost exclusively in English Renaissance studies, and primarily in studies of Edmund Spenser," and it is still primarily concerned with preromantic literature.[6] Since this book deals mainly with modern and contemporary poetry, I adopt an approach adapted specifically, though not exclusively, to cultural and literary analysis in an era of increasingly autonomous artistic production, with the result that it departs from career criticism in several significant ways. The received definition of the literary career in the field, for example, stresses the "writer's self-conscious inscription of a pattern of genres."[7] Rather than focus exclusively on the Virgilian progression from pastoral to georgic to epic and its variations in the work of poets who respond to it by scrambling, reversing, or suppressing its pattern of development, I follow the twentieth-century poets discussed here in engaging career from a variety of angles. Drawing on Pierre Bourdieu's influential sociology of cultural production, I take as a basic premise the idea that poets' trajectories generally lead across the field of production from a dominated position to a dominant one through the accumulation of recognition in the forms of publications, honors, and profits. This gradually intensifying alignment with the establishment comes at a cost, and a particularly significant one for poets, insofar as poetry defines "the most perfectly autonomous sector of the field of cultural production," where "the economy of practices is based, as in a generalized game of 'loser wins,' on a systematic inversion of the fundamental principles of all ordinary economies" (*FCP* 39). In other words, what Bourdieu calls the "autonomization of intellectual and artistic production" creates an environment in which upward mobility, even on the relatively limited scale available to most contemporary poets, entails a kind of tragic fall, one that is no less damaging for being inevitable for any poet with an audience.[8] The perceived decline in autonomy attendant upon recognition generates a sense of vocational crisis that is embodied in and negotiated through the representation of career.

This negotiation demands everything of a poet, not least because the creation of poetic authority itself crucially depends on pursuing a condition of relative autonomy through the elaboration of career.[9] That this pursuit involves playing a "game of 'loser wins'" doesn't make things any easier: success both corroborates and corrodes artistic legitimacy, with the result that any claim to disinterestedness can always also be construed as a covert expression of self-promotion. Moreover, this negotiation is bedeviled throughout by what Bourdieu describes as "the hectic rhythm of aesthetic revolutions," a defining attribute of the field of poetic production, which ensures that even the most effective forms of self-presentation have a half-life dictated by ongoing intergenerational struggles for legitimacy (*FCP* 52–53).

As important as the "self-conscious inscription of a pattern of genres" is to the history of the literary career, the poetry discussed here calls for a perspective in which career permeates every aspect of a poet's work, not just genre. Anyone studying literary careers would do well to remember Stephen Greenblatt's claim that "self-fashioning is always, though not exclusively, in language."[10] A poet's every gesture and reference, including those that are less than self-conscious and those only obliquely related to genre, index more or less specific relations to one or more of the practices, norms, values, figures, schools, subjects, and styles that define the field of production, and in this way they participate in the process of career making. On this view, those texts that overtly invoke career, which Cheney terms "career documents" and which Philip Hardie and Helen Moore describe as specific "statements or hints, explicit or implicit, in an oeuvre that point to a developmental relationship between the individual works in the oeuvre," are no more important to the negotiation of vocational crisis than those in which career is represented indirectly or runs against the grain of a "developmental" plot. Even a poet's silences signify—indeed, are particularly likely to signify—in an arena in which independence from the market, from political power, and from institutional authority carry a great deal of value.[11]

Such an approach implies that career is not only or even primarily a means of self-promotion, deliberate or otherwise. The poets I focus on in the following chapters, including Stevens, Moore, Crane, Sylvia Plath, Ashbery, and Glück, among others, bear witness in their different ways to the impoverishments of career, which always entails seeing "under private aspects," as Emerson puts it in a well-known passage from "Experience," with a corollary sense of estrangement and isolation. As each of the following chapters will show, in the twentieth and twenty-first centuries career tends to be suffused with pathos in still greater measure than it is steeped in triumph, and it is often treated as a sign of separation, a form of imprisonment, or a species of self-betrayal that is no less devastating for being inescapable.[12] If the representation of career has sometimes served to propel poets on the very developmental courses inscribed in their verse and thus to operate as an effective strategy of self-advancement, it has also figured as a way of coming to grips with a variety of threats to poets' sense of artistic freedom and relationship to the greater human community. As the readings elaborated here show, to lament the upward fall into official honors and privilege as the telltale sign of a contemptible careerism is only to oversimplify and reiterate a point that poets themselves have been making with no little passion and sophistication for a long time.[13] Moreover, in placing the blame for selling out on particular individuals, such a view misses the crucial fact that career, and thus the appearance of careerism, are inherent in the very structure of the field itself, insofar as the "space of positions and the space of the position-takings" that constitute the field inevitably change around a poet as struggles for legitimacy unfold. These changes endow even putatively stationary figures with a kind of virtual mobility, and they render even the inactive poet vulnerable to the charge of that sort of crypto-careerism in which self-interest takes cover in a calculated exhibition of disinterestedness.[14]

Such accusations apply not only to poets, but also to the field of poetic production as a whole, which, it may be argued, evolved the culture of the debut as a means of elevating its status within the hierarchy of artistic subfields by advertising its willingness to welcome challenges to the status quo from new generations of poets. The broad applicability of this sort of critique, however, makes it not only tiresomely repetitive, but also misleadingly reductive, because it simplifies the complexity of art's resistance to economic determination. While the freedom of the artist for Bourdieu is not a "godlike freedom" from rational self-interest and market demand, neither is that freedom "unreal," as John Guillory observes.[15]

Consider as a ready example of the poet's position both in and out of the game a letter Plath sent home from Smith College to her mother in which she provides "a list of prizes and writing awards" for the year (*LH* 176). The list includes a range of honors and publications (not all of them "prizes" or "awards") along with the money brought in by each—"$5 *Alumnae Quarterly* article on Alfred Kazin," "$100 Academy of American Poets Prize (10 poems)," "$50 Marjorie Hope Nicholson Prize (tie) for thesis," and so on—and ends with a summing up: "$470 TOTAL, plus much joy!" Plainly, Plath writes for money, though her sensible plan to "pay all debts and work toward coats and luggage," which she notes in closing, can serve as a reminder that even the kind of blatant self-interest evident here, though it runs against the grain of the art-for-art's-sake ideal, doesn't seem all that embarrassing or depraved once we see it in context.[16] There are certainly more expeditious ways to amass wealth and prestige than writing an article on Alfred Kazin for an alumnae magazine. And even if Plath does, to an extent, write for these reasons, by themselves they cannot account fully for her motives, even if we assume that her "joy" may have as much to do with her sense of successful accomplishment as her pleasure in writing poetry.

As Guillory goes on to explain, "Playing the literary game to win in no way cancels the work of making art as an expression of 'the love of art'" for its own sake.[17] In other words, economic self-interest accounts for only part of a complex literary practice that incorporates a wide range of motives, strategies, and forms of production. In my view, neither Plath nor the other poets discussed in these pages would play the game so hard if they were playing only for economic rewards, though such rewards, which confirm vocation even as they undermine it, can scarcely be ignored. So it is that I draw on Bourdieuian sociology in conjunction with formal analysis, biographical criticism, cultural history, and paratextual studies in order to offer an account of twentieth-century careers and the rise of the first book that tries to do justice to the complexity of poets' efforts to invent their writing lives at a historical moment in which assurance of artistic election is particularly hard to come by.

As the focus on the first book in my title suggests, I also diverge from Cheney's view that "holistic commentary" ought to serve as a foundation of career criticism. The trajectories on which poets develop and decline exhibit an anarchic variety that ought to unsettle the conventional assumption that steady maturation endows a series of works with a developmental arc that should be understood as a whole. To insist that career criticism try always "to come to terms with the total oeuvre of a writer" is to concede a great deal to that assumption, for it implies that the logic of the career path can be discerned only when a poet writes her last poem. In this regard my approach turns still more radically from that of Lipking, who claims not only that the careers of "great" poets progress, but that they progress in the same way: "The same patterns recur again and again; the same excited discoveries lead to the same sense of achievement. We cannot ignore the evidence that the development of a great many poets follows a consistent internal logic."[18] More recently, wondering whether "the real story of any career" is "no grand design but only one thing after another," Lipking suggests that "career critics do not think so."[19]

Granting that a poetic career might well exemplify a "grand design," one inscribed by an author conceived not as a Foucauldian "function," but in the more traditional sense of the gifted individual who writes with the intention of ordering his oeuvre in a particular way, I think there are still good reasons to make room for alternative, less totalizing conceptualizations of career alongside the ambitiously organized developmental narratives that Cheney, Lipking, Hardie, Moore, and others tend to prioritize. At virtually every turn in the stories of the lives and works discussed here, we see how career takes shape amid a wide range of unstable circumstances and shifting modes of response. Marianne Moore had two first books published under her name; Hart Crane evoked career as both a "constant harmony" and a "record of rage and partial appetites"; W. H. Auden went out on a limb to publish Ashbery's debut, gave the book a new title, and then used his introduction to sound off on its faults; Glück's rebirths manifest not a "grand design" but the mixed excitement and frustration of starting over and over; Matthew Dickman thanks forty-five individuals by name, the Vermont Studio Center, the Michener Center for Writers, the Fine Arts Work Center, the *American Poetry Review*, the Honickman Foundation, and Copper Canyon Press for being "a part of this book" in the acknowledgments to *All-American Poem*. Such examples could be multiplied indefinitely. They collectively suggest that the questions Michel Foucault raised in "What Is an Author?"—questions that challenge the unity of "the work" and deprive the writing subject "of its role as [sole] originator"—remain pressing ones even now, despite their familiarity.[20] The examples also stress the point that the representation of career, like the notion of the poetic debut, varies according to its contexts, in ways that both complicate the notion of an oeuvre as a unified whole and forestall the inscription (and perception) of grand designs without, however, diminishing the relevance of career to the interpretation of the text at hand. In focusing intensively, though not exclusively, on first books, I argue for treating the representation of career as the product of a diverse set of practices geared toward the affirmation of vocation and the construction of authority at every step of the way.

By tracing the rise of the twentieth-century poetic debut as a special type of literary production, I follow a number of critics in ascribing a special importance to literary beginnings.[21] The axiomatic importance of making a good first impression places acute pressure on the debut: if, as Edward Said suggests, succeeding books settle doubts about whether an author can "keep appearing," the first settles the question of whether the poetic career will exist at all.[22] In fact, career is never more at issue than in the first book, a work positioned at a moment in which the writing life is not only highly precarious, but also uniquely (though not totally) unfettered, insofar as the debut and its reception inevitably affect prospects for self-definition moving forward.[23] As Magali Sarfatti Larson observes, "While biography is looking backward over one's life, an after-the-fact search for order and meaning, career is looking forward, with a sense of order to come."[24] Career assumes special urgency for anyone on the threshold of one, for it offers a way of laying claim to authority in the present by projecting an image of a self in the making.

The lack of an established reputation can count as a threat to the debut author's prospects, then, but also as an advantage, particularly in the almost purely autonomous subfield of production occupied by poetry. The rise of the first book of poetry to special prominence in the twentieth century is propelled in large part by "the primacy the field of cultural production accords to youth," which can be "traced back to the disavowal of power and of 'economy' which lies at the field's foundation." As Bourdieu puts it: "the opposition between the 'old' and the 'young' is homologous with the opposition between power and 'bourgeois' seriousness on the one hand, and indifference to power or money and the 'intellectual' refusal of the 'spirit of seriousness' on the other hand." In other words, youth—understood here not biologically but as a phase in the process of what Bourdieu calls "social aging"—registers as a key virtue in the upside-down economy of cultural production insofar as it is usually assumed to be opposed to establishment values (*FCP* 105, 59). Of course first-book poets are in many ways at the mercy of the literary system: who more likely than the aspiring unknown to follow current trends and ape the manners of prominent practitioners? But in an arena in which autonomy counts for so much, youth also functions as a form of symbolic capital with substantial value in the literary market. As we will see in more detail later in this book, Bourdieu's claim about the "primacy" of youth in the poetry scene is evident in the rapid proliferation of first-book prizes for poetry, which afford a unique opportunity for poets, judges, teachers, institutions, magazines, and publishers alike to capitalize on identification with the debut poet and take part in mediating relations between artistic generations.

Youth wasn't always such a selling point. The "current sense of vocation" is not the "lineal descendant of some original discourse," as Guillory puts it, "but the fossil record of successive upheavals," having passed from classical usage through "the medieval ecclesiastical lexicon," the "radical Protestant concept of election," and the discourse of modern professionalism.[25] So it is that my account of the rise of the first book narrates and interprets a recent episode in a complex evolution that began many centuries earlier: the literary career originates in the same external sources of legitimacy that it is often used to hold at various distances later on. "For later ages," Joseph Farrell writes, "Virgil's gradual ascent from humbler to grander genres was generally regarded as defining the ideal poetic career."[26] John of Garland represented Virgil's three-phase career pattern as the *rota Virgilii*, the "Wheel of Virgil," a diagram that linked pastoral, georgic, and epic to the settings, characters, tools, animals, and plants appropriate to each.[27] The *rota* assumes the close correspondence between a poet's work and his character that is conventional among the biographies of Greek poets, but the distinctive "rising generic trajectory of Virgil's career" emerges from "within a specifically Roman cultural milieu," not the Greek *vita* tradition.[28] It was in that milieu during the second century BCE that politicians began to enlist the services of poets as a way of promoting their progress through the hierarchical sequence of political offices known as the *cursus honorum*. As a result, Farrell explains, "the interdependence of poets and their politically ambitious patrons came to be institutionalized."[29]

Modeling their careers on Virgil's, European authors made modifications to accommodate their particular gifts and goals, and they adapted their careers to contexts other than the story of the Roman Empire. A few centuries after Virgil, for example, "St. Augustine relied on the literary *cursus* of Virgil and his Roman heirs to form the subsequent pattern of Christian development."[30] Spenser's representation of career from *The Shepheardes Calendar* to *The Faerie Queene* draws on both religious and political contexts, and it is overtly based on the Virgilian *gradus*, which prompts him to give up his pastoral "Oaten reeds" for the "trumpets sterne" of epic:

> Lo I the man, whose Muse whilome did maske,
> As time her taught in lowly Shepheards weeds,
> Am now enforst a far unfitter taske,
> For trumpets sterne to change mine Oaten reeds,
> And sing of Knights and Ladies gentle deeds.[31]

Milton's carefully presented debut collection, the 1645 *Poems*, looks forward to a Virgilian progress that culminates in *Paradise Lost*, a poetic career that manifests a self-conscious orderliness that is in keeping with his famous claim that "he who would not be frustrate of his hope to write hearafter in laudable things, ought himselfe to bee a true Poem, that is, a composition and patterne of the best and honourablest things."[32] A little more than a century later, Alexander Pope continued the tradition of imitating Virgil by publishing a first book of *Pastorals*, to which was affixed, by way of introduction, "A Discourse on Pastoral Poetry" in which Pope placed himself explicitly within the tradition of Virgil, Milton, and Spenser.[33]

Not all poets imitated or varied Virgil's model: the criticism collected in *European Literary Careers* and *Classical Literary Careers and Their Reception* usefully testifies to the presence of alternative paradigms and to many oeuvres that seem to resist patterning altogether.[34] But its persistence as an ideal generally defines the era before the autonomization of art began in earnest. Gradually freed from dependence on state, church, and patron as sources of legitimacy, "the idea of a poetic or authorial vocation as a common cultural myth" underwent "severe change" during the nineteenth century, writes Said. "The poetic *vocation*," he goes on, "in the classical sense, had come to be replaced by the poetic *career*. Whereas the former required taking certain memorial steps and imitating a ritual progress, in the latter the writer had to create not only his art but also the very course of his writings."[35]

In Raymond Williams's classic account, that "severe change" is driven by the "institution of 'the market' as the type of a writer's actual relations with society" in the wake of industrialization, urbanization, new intellectual property laws, rising middle-class literacy, and the replacement of the patronage system, first by subscription-publishing and then by "commercial publishing of the modern kind." The resulting "subjection of art to the laws of the market" threatens the integrity of the poetic vocation. "Never pursue literature as a trade," Coleridge declares in *Biographia Literaria*, perhaps with an ironic awareness that disavowing literature as a trade was quickly becoming something of a trade in itself.[36] Robin Valenza sums up the problem for Coleridge and the other poets of the romantic era succinctly: "Coleridge worries that a poet's dependence on a regular poetic output for income" will require him "to pander to the taste of the market rather than to intellectual or moral standards." The notion of poetry as an object whose value inheres in its originality, and of the poet as the untutored genius who sporadically produces it, is prompted, Valenza continues, by the "need to dissociate the poetic career from other, especially scientific, professions, whose productions might be assigned financial value."[37] Framed by the rapid emergence of the commercial literary market as "just one more producer of a commodity," and pressured to justify and define his role in a field of increasingly specialized and rationalized intellectual disciplines, the romantic poet presents himself as a "specially endowed person" whose labors generally tend to resist the routinizing imperatives of commercial production and the "memorial steps" of the traditional *gradus* alike.[38]

In England this reaction against the role of the commodity-producer began earlier than in the United States, where the conditions necessary to make a living by writing, including the establishment of copyright law, the improvement of technologies supporting efficient manufacture and distribution of print materials, and the development of effective marketing techniques arose later.[39] Linda Zionkowski describes how the representation of the figure of the poet changes with the evolution of the literary market over the course of the eighteenth century. The "Distressed Poet," as William Hogarth's iconic engraving implies, is originally the object of satire—a man who only has himself to blame for his hardships, since common sense held that "poetry made a nice hobby, but a poor livelihood." "Eventually, though, the target of this satire shifts," Zionkowski continues, so that the figure of the impoverished poet focuses a "critique of the entire system of literary production and reception," a critique in which the poet becomes "the repository of heroic values and sentiments that have lost ground in England's increasingly mercantile society." The rising interest in the figure of the bard and oral culture in general—evident in such poems as Thomas Gray's "The Bard" (1757) and James Beattie's *The Minstrel* (1771; 1774), as well as such popular anthologies as Thomas Percy's *Reliques of Ancient English Poetry* (1765) and Walter Scott's *The Minstrelsy of the Scottish Border* (1802)—testify in Zionkowski's account to pervasive uneasiness about the contradictory situation of mid- and late eighteenth-century British poets, for whom literary authority could only be cultivated by engaging with the same print market that threatened to undermine vocational integrity.[40] In Edwin, the protagonist of *The Minstrel*, for example, we see a "visionary boy" averse to money and conventional ambitions, living and working beyond the pale of the patronage system and the print market alike, and endowed with a providential gift for song that is all the more noble for its artless spontaneity.[41]

This highly influential model of organic growth, based on the paradoxically deliberate cultivation of what Wordsworth called a "wise passiveness" to nature's influences, is correlated to a trajectory defined by the intermittency of the privileged moment of perception. The moment serves as the source of romantic poetic inspiration par excellence—the "Pulsation of the Artery," as William Blake puts it in *Milton*, when "the Poet's Work is done." This "Pulsation" epitomizes the romantic myth of poetic production, which privileges a conception of career whose erratic quality—represented, for example, in the recurrent figure of the wanderer—runs counter to the imperative for "regular output" demanded by the market. Harking back to the conversion experiences described in Augustine's *Confessions*, as M. H. Abrams shows, the "unsustainable moment" serves a redemptive function, enabling a transient sense of liberation, communion, insight, appreciation, or transformation in various contexts in romantic poetry and beyond. In Wordsworth's *Prelude,* such moments govern the "plot of mental growth" that "moves in leaps of discovery"; in Walter Pater's "Conclusion" to *The Renaissance*, they center a vision of the tragic division of experience, even as they represent the only means available for redemption, however limited; in Stevens's "Notes toward a Supreme Fiction," they are "occasions in which the poet as-if-reborn looks out upon a world as-if-renewed"; and in Jack Kerouac's *The Dharma Bums*, which ends with an "epiphany on a mountain," the narrator experiences the "revelation of a new world."[42]

Percy Shelley's "Hymn to Intellectual Beauty" illustrates the myth of production predicated on the privileged moment. "Unseen," "inconstant," "uncertain," and "unknown," the "Power" of "Intellectual Beauty" would elevate "Man" so that he "were immortal, and omnipotent," if that "Power" would only keep "firm state within his heart." But it remains the cause of "Doubt, chance, and mutability" insofar as it comes and goes at random, immune to the "Frail spells" of the "sage" and "poet."[43] The poem displays Shelley's yearning for a redeemed state of perpetual fluency even as it evokes his sober acceptance of the fallen world in which manifestations of "Intellectual Beauty" are both fitful and fleeting. In this way it sheds light on the enduring power of this myth, which endows the indeterminate career path with particular resilience as a fiction of autonomy, despite the tendency for such fictions to lapse into formula over time, and despite the changing contexts in which the integrity of the poetic vocation has come under pressure. "Regular output" is aligned with the idea of capitulation to market norms, but here, rooted in the "firm state" the poet might yet learn to sustain, it can also be seen to embody a quasi-religious ideal linked to immortality and omnipotence. The integrity of the poetic vocation is thus doubly affirmed: the indeterminacy of the trajectory attests to the poet's disinterestedness by distinguishing the writing of poetry from routine commodity production; that indeterminacy is in turn certified through its appearance as the result of an agonized failure, rather than a deliberate accomplishment.[44] The poet's autonomy from the literary market is presented not as an option but as a painful necessity to which he cannot help but submit.

The poet's ambiguous relation to the literary market, reflected in the way the normative career is apt to appear as both a lofty ideal and a sign of fallen commercialism, premises a number of studies that date the professionalization of authorship to the romantic period. On this view, professions, like poets, are oriented away from the market insofar as the value of their work is based on an ethic of disinterestedness; disinterestedness can be leveraged, however, as a competitive advantage, so that autonomy from the market, for the poet and professional alike, becomes a roundabout form of participation in it. Larson follows H. Jamous and B. Peloille in proposing a definition that captures the essence of the contradictory logic of professionalism. Her definition features a "ratio" between "technicality," which represents skills that can be systematically mastered and applied, and "indetermination," which represents non-standardized capabilities that cannot be taught.[45] Drawing on this definition, Clifford Siskin contends that Wordsworth's *Prelude* is "both a 'masterpiece' of indetermination" and also "a document of technicality detailing the training necessary to master a required body of knowledge." To see "*The Prelude* now as both" is in Siskin's view to identify it as the very "embodiment of professional behavior."[46] Similarly, discussing late nineteenth-century literature, Jonathan Freedman argues that "aestheticism itself can be seen as the highest form of professionalism," because the aesthete's knowledge is something that can be systematically imparted to the public, even as its "esoteric" character suggests the challenges of doing so—challenges that themselves form a rationale for professional intervention.[47] A number of critics have seen the specialized language of modernist literature as a prime example of the hermetic discourse that accompanies the formal knowledge on which professional authority essentially depends.[48]

Such arguments usefully illuminate the presence of the logic of professionalism in a variety of literary endeavors and, still more intriguingly, often bring to light the ways in which literature has itself contributed to the evolution of that logic. They also raise the question, though, of how to reconcile this view, in which literature from the late eighteenth century onward embodies the very apotheosis of professionalism, with the intuitive sense that "the 'profession' of writer or artist" is "one of the least professionalized there is, despite all the efforts of 'writers' associations,' 'Pen Clubs,' etc.," as Bourdieu observes (*FCP* 43).[49] As tempting as it is to frame this question solely as one of degree—just how professionalized is the literary writer?—I think the persuasiveness with which nineteenth- and twentieth-century literature can be described as both the epitome of professionalism and its antithesis demands an approach that, in keeping with Guillory's sense of vocation as a "fossil record of successive upheavals," employs distinctions of kind as well as those of degree.

As Bruce Kimball has demonstrated, the meaning of "profession" has "changed episodically" since the time of the Puritans, when the "profession" of faith demanded a "fundamentally dialectical" perspective on salvation: "This was the constant message of Puritan preachers: in order to be sure [of salvation] one must be unsure."[50] The uncertain certainty that informs the Calvinist theology of vocation is recapitulated in the ratio between technicality and indetermination that informs contemporary definitions of professionalism, just as the reward of self-realization through modern professional work over the course of a career harks back to the promise of spiritual redemption afforded by signs of election. As Kimball makes clear, the spiritual assurance afforded by successful work in a calling is always partial in that it is ultimately limited by the fundamental human ignorance of divine purposes.[51] If the Calvinist conception of vocation (which underpins that of both the romantic poets and their descendants) privileges indetermination, later conceptions increasingly tend to privilege the standardization imperative that goes by the name of "technicality" in the definition quoted above.[52]

The poets I focus on here tend to resist the rational imperatives of twentieth-century professionalism—systematic training, regular production, the normative career—though the terms of that resistance, as we have already begun to see, are often considerably complex: the wandering path of the autonomous genius of one generation, for example, lapses into the routine protocol of the hack writer in the next, necessitating new strategies of self-presentation. In this study, the late eighteenth-century rise of the print market, the establishment at the turn of the twentieth century of the ideology of professionalism as "one of the facts of life," as Menand puts it, and the post-1945 institutionalization of poetry in colleges and universities represent a series of parallel threats to vocational integrity that poets respond to in different ways. Nevertheless, poets never more than roughly resemble their peers in other professions. If, as Charvat suggests, the defining attribute of professional writing is making a "living for the author, like any other job," then the fact that "no American poet has ever made a living from his work except, in a few cases, late in life," renders the professional status of the poet questionable on a fundamental level.[53]

It may help to clarify the idea that nineteenth- and twentieth-century poets contend with, even as they are shaped by, several different forms of professionalism to show how the poet's progress toward professional status in the more fully rationalized, secularized modern sense unfolds more slowly than Siskin, Freedman, and other like-minded critics often seem to suggest. Williams cites a passage from John Keats's letter to J. A. Hessey as evidence of the romantic resistance to system and method: "The Genius of Poetry must work out its own salvation in a man: It cannot be matured by law and precept, but by sensation and watchfulness in itself. That which is creative must create itself."[54] The "formal knowledge" that typifies modern professionalism is evoked as the codifying discourse of "law and precept," which figures here as virtually useless to the aspiring poet; "salvation" depends instead on a passive discipline of "sensation and watchfulness" that recalls the habit of vigilant introspection encouraged by Calvinism.[55] Tellingly, not much appears to have changed in the century between Keats and Stevens. Wondering if literature was "really a profession," Stevens asked his journal in June of 1900 whether "you [could] single it out" or "let it decide in you for itself" (*WSL* 39). That the same issue is being confronted in both cases and in virtually the same terms reflects the persistence of the question of imagining career in an era defined by an ongoing crisis of artistic autonomy. But the differences are also revealing. The presence of the word "profession" (and the absence of the word "Genius") in Stevens's journal entry suggests that the ideology of professionalism had become much more fully established by the end of the nineteenth century.

The prospects of a stable career path, financial security, social prestige, and self-realization promised in that ideology must have appealed powerfully to Stevens, who had just graduated from Harvard and was looking for work as an entry-level journalist in New York City when he posed these questions. Furthermore, he belonged to a generation that had seen for itself that poetry could, in exceptional cases, make money: poets such as Alfred, Lord Tennyson, Elizabeth Barrett Browning, Henry Wadsworth Longfellow, and Rudyard Kipling, among others, had won both financial success and critical acclaim, while Francis Palgrave's *Golden Treasury of the Best Songs and Lyrical Poems in the English Language*—"the rarest of things poetic," as Frank Lentricchia puts it, "an actual best seller in the United States"—showed that timeless art and economic reward were not necessarily mutually exclusive.[56] These success stories lent substance to the fantasy of a normative career that would combine vocation and avocation, an imaginary formation anchored in the Puritan ideal of life as a series of "good works combined into a unified system" in which artistic election and economic rewards converge.[57] The dominance of the ideology of professionalism is reflected in the fantasy of an ideal professional career encoded in Stevens's question, a fantasy that Keats magisterially dismisses. Stevens's willingness to meet the desire for such a career halfway shows in his promotion to the august category of "literature" the routine journalism he would do as a cub reporter before enrolling in law school. But the word "really" in his question—"Is literature really a profession?"—conveys a measure of skepticism in which, on the evidence of the representation of career in *Harmonium*, he was to be confirmed.

In my first chapter, "Apprentices to Chance Event: First Books of the 1920s," I explore representations of career in *Harmonium*, *Observations*, and *White Buildings* that resist the normative course of development that underpins the professional ideal of regular production. The indeterminacy of representations of career in nineteenth-century poetry is pressed to an extreme in modernist debuts, which are burdened not only with evoking the uncertainty that confirms vocational integrity and the intermittency that signals autonomy from the market, but also with evoking those ideas in new ways. This last challenge, necessitated by the demand that every artistic generation make it new, is made still more daunting by the rise of a culture of professionalism in which writing poetry was apt to appear as childish, effeminate, escapist, elitist, and generally absurd. The irony, outlandishness, and obscurity that characterize the paths projected by Stevens, Moore, and Crane in their first books define their attempts to recuperate the romantic myth of poetic production and the disinterestedness that it dramatizes. So it is that Stevens's "times of inherent excellence" represent "incalculable balances" that are "extreme, fortuitous, personal," as he was to put it in "Notes toward a Supreme Fiction" (*WSCP* 334); in "Nomad Exquisite" from *Harmonium*, he presents his writing as the work of a Paterian "Exquisite" whose fidelity to what "come[s] flinging" in him, as if out of nature itself, dictates the wandering path of a "Nomad" (*WSCP* 77). Stevens's "fortuitous" moments resemble Moore's. "With me it's always some fortuity that traps me," she remarked in response to Donald Hall's question about poetic inspiration in an interview. This emphasis on accident marks the perspective from which she offers her complex critique of "ambition without understanding," as she puts it in "Critics and Connoisseurs" in *Observations* (*BMM* 77).[58] Crane is ambivalent about privileged moments: the lyrics of *White Buildings* admit their destructuring randomness even as they struggle to project their containment in an image of continuity. "Account such moments to an hour: / Account the total of this trembling tabulation," he declares in "Possessions": amass them as he may, "such moments" seem never to yield the heroic whole that is more than the sum of its parts (*HCCP* 13).

If Stevens, Moore, and Crane evoked careers that stressed indetermination, their mid-century heirs were increasingly obliged to balance strategies of indetermination with strategies of rationalization—in effect, to combine the imperatives of the professionalist "ratio"—in order to accommodate an expanding culture of professionalism. In my second chapter, "'Poets of the First Book, Writers of Promise': Beginning in the Era of the First-Book Prize," I examine the professionalization of the poetic vocation in the wake of the expansion of the American system of higher education during the post-1945 era. The teaching of poetry writing in colleges and universities redefined poetry as something that could, at least in some sense, be taught, and it rendered the traditional image of the poet as an "untutored genius" highly problematic. First-book prizes for poetry proliferated in this new literary environment largely because they served to reinforce its central values. For the institutions to which they were in many cases linked, such prizes functioned as an assertion of cultural authority. They strengthened poetry's status as a profession by presenting its hierarchy as a meritocracy, open, like other professions, to anyone with talent and drive. Prizes also affirmed the authority of contest judges, who like professors—and in many cases the judges were themselves professors— were supposed to evaluate work with an objectivity that in turn supported the notion of poetry as an increasingly rationalized discipline.

First-book prizes isolate and formalize the initial moment in the poetic career, which they construe through a kind of synecdoche as a rising sequence of books in which the "first" prefigures others yet to come. In this way these prizes can be seen both to symbolize and advance the claim of the culture of professionalism on the life of the poet: the poet starting out during the era of the first-book prize will likely have more difficulty rejecting the normative progress of the modern professional career, since that progress is often stamped on the writing life from the beginning. The special emphasis on beginning in post-1945 debuts signifies, on the one hand, poets' capitulation to a culture of professionalism demanding career development from the start: the radically indeterminate paths evoked by Stevens, Moore, and Crane would clearly be ill-suited to poets making their way in a poetry scene dominated by the university. On the other hand, thematizing beginning may be read as a strategy of defense, for it allows poets to present themselves as if they had yet to embark on professional careers. As we will see through readings of poems by poets ranging from Richard Howard and Robert Pack to Amiri Baraka and Michael Palmer, among others, this emphasis informs debuts by poets positioned both inside and outside of the literary mainstream.

The first two chapters offer surveys of poetry from periods defined by complex forms of vocational crisis to provide a sense of the terms in which the crises manifested themselves. The third and fourth chapters are case studies, each focused on an individual poet, that explore the ways in which poetic responses to vocational crisis unfold in the course of a book-length collection and a poetic career, respectively. In my third chapter, "'Everything Has a Schedule': John Ashbery's *Some Trees*," I offer an interpretation of one of the most remarkable debut collections ever selected for the Yale Series of Younger Poets award. The reputation of the book as an unconventional debut has dominated the critical response to it, from the early, largely negative judgments by critics such as William Arrowsmith and Donald Hall, to more recent attempts to revalue it by Marjorie Perloff, Vernon Shetley, David Lehman, and others. I argue that *Some Trees* has been misread both by its detractors and defenders, who tend to stress the ways in which the poems resist interpretation while ignoring many of the ways in which they encourage and support it. Ashbery's poetic is much more in keeping with the literary mainstream of the 1950s than has yet been allowed: much like the other poets of the era of the first-book prize, he elaborates in *Some Trees* a conflicted embrace of the career, balancing the dueling imperatives of an increasingly professionalized poetry scene through an emphatic thematization of beginning. By situating the book in the context of its literary and cultural moment, I propose a way of appreciating Ashbery's achievement that resists isolating its anti-establishment energies as its sole source of appeal, and I explore the various ways the book evokes the idea of the "mooring of starting out," as he would put it in "Soonest Mended" from *The Double Dream of Spring*, that was to become one of his central preoccupations (*JACP* 186).

In my fourth chapter, "From *Firstborn* to *Vita Nova*: Louise Glück's Born-Again Professionalism," I turn to a poet whose work lies at the opposite end of the spectrum, in several respects, from Ashbery's, and I expand my focus on first books to consider subsequent volumes from Glück's oeuvre. The differences between Ashbery and Glück are meant to stress the pervasiveness of the fascination with the vocational trajectory that they share: the same conflicted embrace of career is as legible in the serene disorders of *Some Trees* as it is in the fierce analyses of *Firstborn* and throughout the seven collections Glück published leading up to *Vita Nova*. The logic of Glück's career, I argue, illustrates the double bind of literary professionalism with radical severity. Wholly "bent on personal distinction," as she avows in "The Education of the Poet," she is drawn to plot her career as a rational course of artistic advancement, but she is also drawn to strategies of indetermination that devalue steady development as the sign of a discreditable motive of self-interest (*PT* 5). So powerful is the conflict produced by these rival impulses that the theme of vocational initiation that they tend to produce in post-1945 debuts is not only evoked in her first book, but is revisited throughout her career. As my chapter title suggests, the explicitness and regularity of the pattern recall the origins of contemporary professionalism in the never-ending, soul-racking self-examinations of the Puritans. Focusing in particular on the poems with which her collections begin, from "The Chicago Train" in *Firstborn* through "Vita Nova," the title poem of her eighth book, I show how the theme of rebirth in her poems reflects the opposition that typically marks the representation of the career in post-1945 poetry, just as that opposition impels in turn the serial resumption of the beginner's stance elaborated in her first book. The interest that Glück's work continues to command indicates the limits of the critique of the professionalization of poetry and mass production of prize-winning first books. Her example suggests that to privilege the moment of beginning is to practice a resistance to career and institutional routine that is well worth valuing, even if it is bound, in time, to take on the appearance of a form of careerism in itself.

I conclude in "Making Introductions" by bringing up to date the history of first-book prizes begun in chapter 2. Supplementing the interpretation of poems with the interpretation of debut paratexts, I show how the prize-winning debut—framed by lyrical prefaces, elaborate acknowledgments, and other, often tellingly overwrought, textual devices and conventions—continues at the turn of the millennium to legitimate virtually all the figures and institutions operating in the field of poetic production. I highlight the ways in which debut paratexts evoke the ideal of poetic autonomy even as they call it into question, and I look at recent poems that illustrate poets' ongoing engagement with the complex issue of imagining careers at the moment before their careers have properly begun.

1

Apprentices to Chance Event
First Books of the 1920s

After three years at Harvard, Wallace Stevens moved to New York to find work as a newspaper reporter. He arrived in the city on June 14, 1900. Hoping to hit the ground running, he immediately called at the *Commercial-Advertiser* and the *Evening Sun* with letters of introduction. But within a few days Stevens had already begun to feel overwhelmed by the hectic getting and spending of the New York business world. "All New York, as I have seen it, is for sale," he wrote in his journal: "It is dominated by necessity. Everything has its price—from Vice to Virtue" (*SP* 72). How, he wanted to know, could he pursue a career in "literature" in such a place? To what extent could the work of writing be adapted to the calculating procedures of a rapidly expanding market in which a "price" could be assigned to "everything"? The daunting scale and pace of the New York economy drove Stevens to question his choice of vocation and to wonder whether a literary vocation could properly be considered a matter of choice in the first place. Two days later, in his journal he describes spending an afternoon alone in his room, beset with doubts about his calling: "Have been wondering whether I am going into the right thing after all. Is literature really a profession? Can you single it out, or must you let it decide in you for itself?" (*SP* 74).

The problem of whether or not literature could be deliberately "single[d] . . . out" and thus pursued professionally was to preoccupy Stevens during the years leading up to the publication of *Harmonium* in 1923. That he frames it as a question of "profession" reflects the rise of professionalism, which was fully underway in the United States at the turn of the century. As James Longenbach observes, "The moment of Stevens's birth, 1879, coincided with the moment when professionalism began to transform American working habits, and by the time Stevens left Harvard the entrepreneurial spirit of his youth had been swallowed by bureaucratic capitalism."[1] Because the Civil War "dominated the attention of men, absorbing their energies and wealth," Burton J. Bledstein writes, "the first really successful efforts at the professionalization of American life often waited until the later 1860s and 1870s." Professionalism entailed an emphasis on willpower: "In a calculated manner, [the professional] actively willed his action in order to satisfy a drive for self-distinction and self-assertion."[2] This "calculated" approach to self-fashioning is the corollary of the "rationalization and standardization" of skills and knowledge that distinguish "the modern guild-like professions from their *ancien régime* predecessors," as Magali Sarfatti Larson suggests.[3] Refusing to "leave life to chance," modern professionals "aspired to schedule its development in ascending stages" that marked increasing responsibility, prestige, and authority. In Stevens's terms, pursuing a professional career would mean singling literature out: to "let it decide in you for itself" would jeopardize "the coherence of an intellectually defined and goal-oriented life" that signaled the deep vocational commitment of the true professional.[4]

In exchange for the competitive anxiety and delayed gratification that professionalism entails, the normative career promises certain rewards. It holds out the assurance of success on the basis of talent and hard work—for merit, rather than wealth and connections, stands at the center of professionalist ideology. It also provides the psychological, social, and financial security of occupational stability. This stability "effects a particularly strong identification of the person with the role, both subjectively and for others; popular novel, films, and TV serials emphasize this permanence—you cannot *really* unfrock a priest, unmake a doctor, or disbar a lawyer. Occupational stability immediately evokes *career*," which Larson concisely calls "a pattern of organization of the self." Thus career promises control over the process of self-definition—a process just as crucial for the poet as for the priest, doctor, or lawyer, since authority is staked in each case to a particular idea of character that the career "pattern" is supposed to represent.[5]

Stevens's father made sure that the value of such incentives was not lost on his son. As Longenbach suggests, "Stevens enrolled in a correspondence course when he went off to Harvard," and the "course," conducted by his father, had much to do with the choice of a profession that would allow Stevens to support himself financially.[6] On November 1, 1898, Garrett Stevens wrote to Wallace to extinguish in advance any fantasies of pursuing poetry as a career by stressing the importance of knowing his place as a middle-class American:

Our young folks would of course all prefer to be born like English noblemen with Entailed estates, income guaranteed and in choosing a profession they would simply say—"How shall I amuse myself"— but young America understands that the question is—"*Starting with nothing, how shall I sustain myself and perhaps a wife and family—and send my boys to College and live* comfortably in my old age." Young fellows must all come to that question for unless they inherit money, marry money, find money, steal money or somebody presents it to them, they must *earn it.* . . . How best can he earn a sufficiency! What talent does he possess which carefully nurtured will produce something which people want and therefore will pay for. This is the whole problem! and to Know Thyself! (*SP* 71)

The passage presents the "whole problem" of the conduct of life in the precise terms that the newly dominant culture of professionalism had set. The extent of that culture's influence is reflected in the assumption that its norms apply to many "young folks," to all "young fellows," and even to "young America" in its entirety. Garrett elaborates the importance of the career as a means of improvement, rather than amusement, and drives the point home with a hyperbolic emphasis on the prospect of "*starting with nothing.*" The culture of professionalism thrived in conjunction with the expansion of higher education in America, so it is notable that he projects a future in which Wallace is able to bequeath to his sons the advantage of the college degree with which he will have begun his own career. Even Garrett's anxious tone (visible in his italics) is over-determined by that element of professional ideology that constructs the choice of career as a moment of personal crisis, for the "crisis of a career decision" is "in its fullest stature a crisis of identity," as Bledstein suggests.[7]

For all its emphasis on the rational necessity of earning a "sufficiency," Garrett Stevens's letter, like Wallace Stevens's journal entry of June 16, 1900, reflects *both* terms of the ratio between technicality and indetermination that sociologists use to characterize professions.[8] So it is that Garrett's letter, which focuses on choosing an adequately remunerative "profession," closes with an abrupt turn away from economic imperatives to quote a moral imperative: "Know Thyself!" In Stevens's journal entry, the contradictory impulses of professionalism appear in the division between the sort of calling that might be "single[d] . . . out" and the sort that must "decide in you for itself." While Garrett combines the two simply by adding a piece of conventional wisdom to his letter, Wallace, on the evidence of the fairly strict separation between business and art he maintained throughout his life, found them more difficult to synthesize. The difference, of course, is that Garrett is describing an ideal "profession," while Wallace is considering a form of work—"literature"—that "resisted professionalization more strongly than any other field."[9] Menand elaborates the reasons for this resistance. While "late-nineteenth-century aestheticism . . . seems in some respects more compatible with the values of professionalism," he claims, "there were still certain items in the package that art could not afford." To make a profession of literature would mean "sacrificing all the advantages derived from the general perception of its essential *difference* from respectable kinds of work. Spontaneity, originality, inspiration—qualities viewed with increasing suspicion in the world of practical affairs—were among the very things that seemed to define the artistic," he explains, and "they are things that defy prescription."[10]

The problem that Stevens faced was not unlike the one confronted a half century earlier by the Fireside poets—William Cullen Bryant, Ralph Waldo Emerson, Henry Wadsworth Longfellow, John Greenleaf Whittier, and Oliver Wendell Holmes—who also had to find ways to pursue non-remunerative work under circumstances demanding that money be made. Also like Stevens, they sought ways of imagining and presenting careers that would preserve a kind of authority rooted in precisely those "qualities viewed with increasing suspicion in the world of practical affairs." In fact, Garrett Stevens's letter echoes sentiments expressed by another lawyer-father to a poet-son who would soon graduate from college: "A literary life," Steven Longfellow wrote to his son Henry in 1824, "to one who has the means of support, must be very pleasant. But there is not wealth enough in this country to afford encouragement and patronage to merely literary men. And as you have not had the fortune (I will not say whether good or ill) to be born rich, you must adopt a profession which will afford you subsistence as well as reputation."[11] Eventually the Longfellows worked out a compromise in which Henry would take up the study of law in accordance with his father's wishes, so long as he was allowed to devote a year to graduate study of language and literature at Harvard first. When Bowdoin College offered the eighteen-year-old graduate a newly created professorship in Modern Languages, plans for the year at Harvard and career in law were scrapped, and Longfellow began an academic career that carried on for nearly thirty years.

This stroke of good fortune immediately gave Longfellow the security that, for Stevens, would take years to develop, and it provided for a closer fit between vocation and avocation—Longfellow's debut, *Voices of the Night* (1839), featured more translations than original poems—than Stevens's notoriously bifurcated life as a lawyer and poet did. Still, the evocations of career in Longfellow's first book are marked by signs of vocational crisis similar in kind to the more extreme forms of indetermination that pervade the work of Stevens and his contemporaries. These poets all grapple with not only the perennial problem of supporting themselves while writing poetry, but also the interrelated challenges bound up with poetry's ambiguous relation to the literary market: maintaining an aura of disinterestedness while profiting from book and poem sales; casting poetry as a properly masculine activity without turning it into a species of merely mechanical production; and presenting a privileged vision without losing touch with the common reader. *Voices of the Night* is shot through with evidence of the various balancing acts required to negotiate the double binds implicit in pursuing a poetic career even under relatively favorable circumstances. The similarities between Longfellow's and Stevens's representations of career in their first books illuminate the extent to which crisis is a defining feature of the discourse of vocation. The differences accentuate the embeddedness of that discourse in particular historical situations that renew the sense of crisis by introducing it in distinctive contexts, while also saddling the belated poet with the burden of responding to it in new ways.

Matthew Gartner explains how "Prelude," the opening poem in *Voices of the Night*, "takes as its subject the poet's quest for themes congruous with the social obligations of manhood": "Pleasant it was," the poem begins (one notes that "pleasant" is also Steven Longfellow's word for describing a "literary life" enabled by inherited wealth), to "lay upon the ground" in pastoral retreat from the world and indulge in youthful fancies. But "distant voices" direct the poet toward other, more serious subjects, for he is "no more a child!" And yet, as Gartner suggests, the "final injunction of the stern paternal voice obscures what Longfellow's themes should be, even as it purports to define them," urging the poet not to discipline his perspective in accordance with the imperatives of his newly achieved manhood, but instead to "Look, then, into thine heart, and write!" about "All forms of sorrow and delight." This representation of career evokes maturation and masculinity in conjunction with realism and responsibility, but it ultimately promotes a model of poetic production in which the poet, schooled in the literary tradition (as the allusion to Philip Sidney's *Astrophil and Stella* suggests), is held accountable to a standard of sincerity that puts even those childish "forms" of "delight" so recently renounced back on the table as potential topics.

The same contradictory strategies of self-representation animate "The Psalm of Life," which had already caused a sensation upon appearing in the *Knickerbocker* prior to the publication of *Voices of the Night*. As Gartner observes, the poem "alternates between inclusive first-person plural pronouncements ('Not enjoyment and not sorrow / Is our destined end or way' [1:21]) and lofty imperatives ('Be not like dumb, driven cattle! / Be a hero in the strife!' [1:21]). The alternation suggests the poet is both one of 'us' and not one of 'us,'" at once the privileged possessor of special authority and also a relatable everyman figure with plenty still to learn. In a related discussion, Jill Anderson shows how the poem's evocation of a Puritan work ethic, in which work is pursued for its own sake rather than as a means of achieving specific goals, serves to diffuse the motive of self-interest while also assigning the poet a place in a conventionally masculine arena of utility and production. "The imperatives stack up: Act! Be up and doing! Live! Labor! Toil! But Longfellow rarely offered a direct object for these imperative verbs, an absence which lends a hysterical note" to his representation of poetic labor in "The Psalm of Life" and elsewhere. Such contradictions, as Anderson rightly observes, inhere in the poet's contradictory relation to the literary market, a relation that renders the poetic calling acutely problematic: "For Longfellow, the title 'poet' was a kind of dream identity, something to be wished for and worked toward, but also to be disclaimed even as he began to achieve it in the late 1830s and 1840s."[12]

In Stevens's debut, the "hysterical note" that arises from Longfellow's attempt to reconcile masculine agency with a romantic "wise passiveness" in his imagining of vocation recurs in the impression of aberration that haunts the representation of career in *Harmonium*. For Stevens, the "apprenticeship to chance event" is "grotesque" in proportion to its divergence from the rationalized norms for the conduct of life derived from the ideology of professionalism. "Poet" functions as "a kind of dream identity" for Stevens also, and for similar reasons. But as we will see, the different social and historical circumstances under which Stevens pursued that identity a century after Longfellow required that it be "disclaimed" in much different and more forceful terms.

Though the Fireside poets' bridging of the divide between art and commerce may have momentarily framed that "dream identity" as a potentially realizable goal, that same success also helped to make the poetic career seem all but impossible to poets coming of age in the 1890s and 1900s. In *Would Poetry Disappear? American Verse and the Crisis of Modernity*, John Timberman Newcomb skillfully elaborates the many factors that contributed to the pervasive sense that poetry at the turn of the last century was done for, beginning with the very fact of the extraordinary popular and critical achievement of the Fireside group. Trading on readers' appetite for a powerfully nostalgic vision of American life in a time of accelerating modernization, the Fireside poets "paradoxically remained so dominant in the nation's literary culture" during the 1890s and 1900s "that their great age registered as the obsolescence of the entire genre of poetry." Their canonical status was attested to by their dissemination in textbooks (they are also the "Schoolroom poets"), their ubiquitous presence in personal libraries, and the celebrity that made their birthdays occasions for public celebration and their portraits common decorations for the home. Thus, they effectively arrested the process of aesthetic revolution that typically defines the field of poetry according to Bourdieu. As a result, an "impasse" developed, as Newcomb puts it, based on the "conviction that the forms, attitudes, and canons dominating the genre were obsolete or exhausted," which was coupled with a "reflexive distrust of efforts to rejuvenate poetry through innovation in form or iconoclasm of attitude."[13]

But the daunting achievement of the previous generation of poets was only one obstacle to pursuing a poetic career for Stevens and his peers. As Newcomb goes on to demonstrate, the pervasive sense of crisis was also precipitated by a confluence of pressures arising from the cultural ascendancy of professional values, which Newcomb terms "the capitalist-realist managerial ideology." To pursue the writing of poetry in this context was to encounter "an insistent chorus of male commentators" who "worried that contemporary poetry had become not only emotionally soft and intellectually slack, but also sexually suspect." As an 1899 letter to the *Dial* put it: "Men (manly men, I mean) are growing more and more shy of writing poetry" and tend to "feel that a man making verses is more or less a ridiculous object." It was also considered a sign of immaturity, since some saw writing "poetry as disqualifying its aspirants from a productive adult life in the modern world." Attacks on the figure of the poet were corroborated by attacks on poetry itself, which made it seem out of place in a secular and empirically oriented society in which "analysis, examination, research, and exact expression are needed," and in which poetry had lost ground to prose genres, including the novel, which were ostensibly better suited to representing the "exact thought and exact statement" that the modern world seemed to demand. Furthermore, the emergence of "mass-magazine verse and million-selling popular songs" vitiated poetry's traditional claim to authority based on autonomy from the market, and it also paved the way to a "damaging state of overproduction" that made the fundamental "economic unviability of verse" a "truism throughout the publishing industry."[14]

Perhaps it is not surprising, then, that Stevens's attempt to pursue "literature" as a career was so short-lived: he enrolled in New York University

Law School in October 1901, a little more than a year after his arrival in the city. Making money by writing—even of a commercially viable kind—failed to provide a solution to the "problem" that Garrett had set before him. Once he gave up "the literary life," as he liked to refer to his career in journalism, Stevens took legendary pains to separate his work as an insurance man from his work as a poet (*SP* 102). The two parts of his day correspond to antithetical approaches to experience—one that plotted upon it a steady, vertical advance, and another that waited for it to yield unlooked-for moments of vision. Moreover, the two approaches threatened one another. "Reason," for Stevens, was a "jealous mistress," and the calculating habits of mind he relied upon in business might, he feared, stifle his creativity.[15] Likewise, Stevens saw his poetic activities—all too readily identified in the context sketched by Newcomb as emasculating, childish, unprofitable, illogical, and ultimately "ridiculous"—as a liability to his professional reputation. But while it has been frequently shown that Stevens went to great lengths to play down poetry in his professional career, it has not been much noted that he also went to great lengths to play down the normative professional career in his poetry.

Turning now to Stevens's debut, I examine some of the ways in which the book resists the logic of the conventional occupational trajectory promoted by the culture of professionalism at the turn of the last century. That resistance is epitomized by Stevens's indirect self-portrait as Crispin in "The Comedian as the Letter C," a "profitless philosopher" for whom "Life . . . was not a straight course," and who therefore appears as a "clown" (*WSL* 293). I read the implicitly deprecatory judgments that frequently inform Stevens's representations of the poetic career in "Comedian" and elsewhere in *Harmonium* as a gesture through which he submits to the newly consolidated values of professionalism, demonstrating the kind of maturity of judgment exemplified by the "manly men" who knew poetry to be a "ridiculous" pursuit. Through this negative self-judgment Stevens puts poetry in its properly subordinate place, but the gesture also carries the ironic effect of licensing his poetic practice, which proceeds under the sign of comedy, but proceeds nonetheless.

This is to read Stevens's self-authorization project in much the same way that John Guillory reads T. S. Eliot's in *Cultural Capital*, where he suggests that Eliot's complex "valuation of the minor stance" provides an index to Eliot's literary ambitions. In Guillory's account, Eliot's idealization of literary tradition "enjoins a strategic modesty upon practicing poets," for "the new poet must present himself or herself with a demeanor of conformity if there is to be any chance of altering the existing order of [literary] monuments, that is, of joining the company of the canonical writers."[16] On this view, only the self-consciously minor poet has any hope of writing major verse, since more straightforwardly sincere aspirants to major status can only have fatally underestimated the strength of the tradition in which they hope to find a place. In this way, the partial or provisional renunciation of ambition—the adoption of what Guillory terms a "demeanor of conformity"—implies the full knowledge of literary tradition that might yet enable major achievement after all, and the trivialization of the figure of the poet is the means by which high ambition is recuperated. So it is that Crispin is a "clown, perhaps, but an aspiring clown" (*WSCP* 32). I interpret the resistance to the orderly professional career exemplified in *Harmonium* not only as an instance of "strategic modesty" prompted by the splendors of the literary tradition—that is, as a sign of the humility or embarrassment of the belated poet—but also as a maneuver through which Stevens accommodates the predominantly rational values of the modern culture of professionalism. This ironic scheme enables him to pursue poetry on the margins of his workday, and it invests the poetic career—however bizarre or absurd it appears to be in its immediate context—with the authority that derives from the romantic myth of poetic production that it dramatizes.[17] As Harold Bloom suggests, the "Comedian" "shares fully in the obsessive quest that it only ostensibly mocks."[18]

The size alone of Stevens's first book runs against the grain of the measured advance of the professional career. William W. Bevis remarks that, because so many of the poems (66 out of nearly 120) had appeared in print prior to its publication, "The 1923 *Harmonium* was not a first book of new poems. It was rather a first collected poems, made mostly of old material previously published in magazines."[19] Stevens's hesitation must be understood, at least in part, as a by-product of his internalization of an ideology in which poetry held no value: to publish a book sooner rather than later would risk implying that writing verse was something more than a casual pastime. The result of the hesitation was a first collection whose enormity reflects both Stevens's embarrassment regarding writing poetry and the proportionately large ambitions that his embarrassment enabled. A comparison with the debuts of some of Stevens's peers helps to put the sheer heft of *Harmonium* into perspective. Ezra Pound's *A Lume Spento* (1908) had seventy-two pages, Robert Frost's *A Boy's Will* (1913) had fifty, Eliot's *Prufrock and Other Observations* (1917) had forty, Edna St. Vincent Millay's *Renascence and Other Poems* (1917) had seventy-three, and Hart Crane's

White Buildings (1926) had fifty-eight, but *Harmonium*, published by Alfred A. Knopf in 1923, was 140 pages in length—more than double that of the average first volume.

Stevens proposed to call the collection "The Grand Poem: Preliminary Minutiae," a title that would have drawn attention to the book's massive size by presenting it, almost absurdly, as merely the initial installment of a still larger "Grand Poem." The original title captures the ironic logic of Stevens's sense of vocation: writing off even such unquestionably substantial achievements as "Sunday Morning," "Le Monocle de Mon Oncle," and the "Comedian" as mere "Minutiae" is precisely what makes projecting a "Grand Poem" possible. That Stevens ultimately rejected the title is also significant. For one thing, it risks making the self-deprecatory thrust of "Minutiae" seem disingenuous by invoking his long-term aspirations too explicitly. "Harmonium" differs from the title it replaced precisely in its effacement of the linear, premeditated plot that inheres in the evocation of an ambitious progress from mere preliminaries to finished grandeur. However, "Harmonium" also retains that sense of both modesty and ambition on a lower frequency, as at least one early reviewer understood. Paul Rosenfeld notes that the title refers to a small reed organ made for domestic use: "mysteriously, disconcertingly faithful to it," Stevens seems "invariably buffoon-like" to Rosenfeld, and yet since performing on such an instrument can give "no indication" of his "real limits," his powers come to seem limitless, and his identity takes shape in the book review as that of the artist "born . . . for the grand piano."[20]

"Well a book of poems is a damned serious affair," exclaimed Stevens in a letter to William Carlos Williams—particularly so, one imagines, for a poet so anxious about the divide between his serious career in law and his "absurd," "lady-like" habit of writing verses that he asked his wife Elsie to keep the latter "a great secret" (*WSL* 180).[21] Having published dozens of poems in little magazines between 1914, when "Carnet de Voyage" and "Two Poems" appeared in *Trend*, and the summer of 1922, when he "came to the substance of an agreement with Mr. [Alfred A.] Knopf for the publication of a book in the fall of 1923," Stevens took pains to figure out an order for his poems that suited him. He allotted himself a considerable amount of time—about three months—to select and arrange them. He describes the editorial process as particularly difficult work: "Knopf has my book, the contract is signed and that's done. I have omitted many things, exercising the most fastidious choice, so far as that was possible among my witherlings. To pick a crisp salad from the garbage of the past is no snap."[22] As Frank Lentricchia has noted, reviewers of *Harmonium* who said that Stevens "was a precious aesthete—that he had nothing to say and, worse, that his poems were, on principle, mindless" were only repeating "what he was telling his friends in letters during the months when he was deciding on the contents of *Harmonium*," where they are not only "witherlings," but also "horrid cocoons from which later abortive insects had sprung," "debilitated," and mostly "garbage" (*WSL* 231).[23] This low estimation of his own poetry, and more particularly, of the potential for his poetry to develop over time, is reflected in the very arrangement of the poems in *Harmonium*, which seems deliberately designed to confuse any attempt to read it as a document of the growth of the poet's mind.

It will help to provide a sense of the strategies Stevens applies throughout the book to note that in placing "To the Roaring Wind" last (in both the 1923 collection and the expanded 1931 edition of *Harmonium*), he directly reverses convention. "Invocations usually come at the beginning of a major literary work," Eleanor Cook explains, but "Stevens places his at the end." Similarly, John Hollander calls it a "misplaced epic opening" that "addresses its Shelleyan inquiry to the wind of poetry to come."[24] Just four lines long, the poem consists of a question and a command addressed to the roaring wind invoked in the title. First the wind—figured as "Vocalissimus"—is asked what "syllable" it is "seeking" in "the distances of sleep"; it is then directed to "speak" that "syllable" (*WSCP* 77). "The roaring wind is here nature's poem," as B. J. Leggett puts it, "but it is also Stevens's poem, insofar as "To the Roaring Wind" may be read as an invocation to the muse to speak through the poet, particularly given that "Vocalissimus," as Cook notes, is a form of the Latin adjective *vocalis*, which has a "rare poetic use" as a word for inspiration.[25] As "misplaced epic opening," then, the poem reflects the same interest in mock-epic self-presentation evident in "Comedian." To invoke the wind as the traditional source of poetic inspiration at the beginning of the collection would have endowed it with a story, a quest pursued by the poet for a special kind of speech, but placed at the end, the poem defers that narrative and suggests instead that the object of the quest still remains to be identified, let alone spoken. And yet this deflection of epic ambition subtly suggests that Stevens has made a kind of progress after all. Like Charles Altieri, I see the placement of the poem as a daring choice, one that evokes "a certain kind of self-sufficiency earned by the book," an "accept[ance] of the practical world, a finality crucially free from straining after lyrical effects" and evident in the poem's very brevity.[26] The reward of the self-satirizing gesture here is a renewal of the authority that derives from the indeterminacy inherent in the traditional myth of poetry as naturally inspired speech.

The arrangement of the poems with which *Harmonium* opens is guided by the same motive. "Stevens is such a master of openings that we expect the first poems of *Harmonium* to entice us, and we are a little baffled when they do not."[27] Cook's remark echoes the sentiments of many Stevens critics, who tend to agree that the arrangement of the poems reflects a conscious effort to resist conventional forms of order. Bevis usefully emphasizes the care Stevens took in arranging his poems by noting that when he began to assemble the collection in 1922, many of the poems eligible for inclusion had already appeared in groups that brought out thematic and symbolic continuities between them: "Why did Stevens in 1922 strike a new pose, making his poems more obscure and complicating his relation to his readers, and what happened to the old groups, to their continuity and homogeneity?" What happened, as Bevis goes on to show, is that Stevens "systematically dispersed" the groups, and did so, moreover, in such a way as to scramble the chronology of the poems: "If the dates of first publication of the first eight poems, for instance, are written into the *Harmonium* table of contents, the shuffling of dates is apparent: 1918, 1921, 1917, 1919, 1917, 1921, 1916, 1921." "*Harmonium*," he concludes, "covered Stevens's tracks."[28] Robert Buttel observes that the "discontinuities . . . reflect the accidental and fortuitous in life itself and upset any preconceived, rigidly-fixed notions of reality or order."[29]

"Earthy Anecdote," the first poem in Stevens's first book, powerfully reinforces the emphasis on "the accidental and fortuitous in life itself" evoked by the arrangement of the volume's opening poems. As we will see repeatedly in the pages to follow, the vocational anxiety and accompanying discourse of career that generally comes to typify the first book goes double for the poems with which debut collections themselves begin, though modernist leadoff poems tend to render that message with considerable obliquity, burying concerns about the authenticity of the poetic calling well below the surface. The poem tells of a repeated encounter between "bucks" and a "firecat":

Every time the bucks went clattering
Over Oklahoma
A firecat bristled in the way.

The two stanzas that follow describe how the bucks clatter or swerve to the left or the right "because of the firecat." The fourth and fifth stanzas could be taken to portray a single confrontation between bucks and firecat or, alteratively, to sum up the action of a series of encounters. They add to the pattern of movements the "leaping" of the firecat in different directions while stressing again the clattering of the bucks and the firecat's bristling "in the way," and they note by way of conclusion that "the firecat closed his bright eyes / And slept." (*WSCP* 3)

Altieri rightly asks "whether there is a stranger opening poem to a volume of poetry than 'Earthy Anecdote.'" He notes that the "title itself promises that this text seems unexpectedly casual for an introduction to the volume."[30] "An introduction to the volume," and, one might add, to Stevens's whole oeuvre: the title signals the presence of the same self-deflating disposition that characterizes the arrangement of the poems and the portrait of Crispin in "Comedian" and that continues to inform his work throughout his career.

The poem begins with the phrase "Every time," which lends the encounter between the "bucks" and the "firecat" an air of redundancy that is at once infernal and absurd. It stresses arbitrariness in the way it presents the bucks' avoidance of the firecat, which they swerve away from at random, veering left "or" right. Bristling "in the way" even as it leaps from side to side, the firecat is a symbol of obstruction: the variety of readings it has occasioned— from Bloom's suggestion that it is a version of William Blake's "Tyger," to Richard Blessing's that it is "a prairie fire," to Michel Benamou's that it is an oil well, to Mervyn Nicholson's that it is the sun—suggests that the firecat resists the reader in much the same way that it obstructs the bucks.[31] Some time "later," the firecat withdraws into sleep, its "closed" eyes evoking traditional forms of narrative closure—sleep, death—while also underlining the oft-remarked inaccessibility of this quasi-allegory, with its quasi-mythic "firecat," to interpretation. This inaccessibility can be read as a function of Stevens's interest in keeping his poetic vocation a "great secret": in the poem that Stevens would retain in the prime position not only for both editions of his debut but also for *Collected Poems* (1954), the poet seems to suggest that he writes mainly for himself.[32]

The wildly divergent interpretations of the firecat alone suggest the hazards of attempting to decipher the poem, and Altieri makes an interesting case for resisting the urge to find a key to the allegory.[33] In the interest of challenging the old myth of Stevens's solipsistic disengagement from the world, however, and also of illustrating the extent to which twentieth-century first books, and especially leadoff poems, are dominated by a sense of vocational crisis, I want to propose an interpretation in which the poem recasts in characteristically abstract terms an anecdote recorded in a journal entry from the summer of 1899, when Stevens was still in college. He describes a night at a local saloon talking with friends:

"Also spent a number of evenings listening to the Spanish students—a little orchestra at Kline's saloon on Penn Street. One of them—Bistolfi—kept us there until after two in the morning with his fine talk. He said that a man met Life like a roaring lion in a desert—a figure of tremendous force" (*SP* 58). That Stevens felt the simile embodied such "force" is borne out in the frequency with which lions recur throughout his work.[34] In fact, the image of the lion twice appears in precisely this scenario—"roaring . . . in a desert"—in a 1942 letter to Hi Simons (regarding Stevens's "On an Old Horn") and in "Notes toward a Supreme Fiction":

> The lion roars at the enraging desert,
> Reddens the sand with his red-colored noise,
> Defies red emptiness to evolve his match,
>
> Master by foot and jaws and by the mane,
> Most supple challenger.

Like the lion from the journal, the one in "Notes" symbolizes a stance connected with uninhibited strength, a stance contrasted with that of the adolescent poet:

> But you, ephebe, look from your attic window,
> Your mansard with a rented piano. You lie
>
> In silence upon your bed. You clutch the corner
> Of the pillow in your hand . . .
>
> > You look
> Across the roofs as sigil and as ward
> And in your centre mark them and are cowed. . . .
> (*WSCP* 332)

"Earthy Anecdote" likewise dramatizes a conflict in which youth and maturity, weakness and strength, are contrasted with one another. The dry, open, Oklahoman landscape of the poem may be seen to derive from the "desert" setting of the image in the journal. The "firecat" appears to be a stylized reproduction of the "lion": its "roaring" not only helps to explain the "fire" in "firecat," but also links the image to poetic inspiration by way of its connection to the poem addressed "To the Roaring Wind"—the "misplaced epic opening" that closes the debut that "Earthy Anecdote" opens (and which, reinforcing the symmetry still further, also concerns

withdrawal into the privacy of "sleep"). "Life," with its capital *L* in the journal entry, seems to mean something like the "life in the abstract" that
Stevens brooded upon while he tried to make up his mind about whether
or not literature was a profession, something he could pursue as a career
(*SP* 90). The "bucks" that go "clattering" fit the anecdote in the journal in
that they image "the table-full of us young fellows" as "bucks," used in the
colloquial sense to mean young men, and their table-talk as a kind of
"chatter," which is one of the meanings of "clatter."[35]

On this reading, then, "Earthy Anecdote" captures Stevens's sense of the
indeterminacy of the poetic career—an indeterminacy at once farcical from
the perspective of the rationalized procedures of the modern professional
and also crucial to the poet whose authority depends on autonomy from the
market demand for regular production. The "clattering" of the bucks suggests an inability to control speech; the curvilinear paths inscribed on the
landscape are the unintended product of their interaction with the firecat.
That both the bucks and firecat are explicitly male is in keeping both with
the journal entry—where it is a "man" who meets "Life" in an aggressive
way—and with the prominently gendered terms in which Stevens conceptualizes his notion of vocation. In this regard, it is telling that the entry in
which Stevens recounts the night at Kline's is framed by a later comment:
"What silly, affected school-girl drivel this seems to me now. WS June 14/04"
(*SP* 59). The title of the poem reflects this sense of his college-era journaling
as immature "drivel," since "Anecdote," as Leggett notes, "has traditionally
been associated with biography or informal biography, gossip (from the
Greek *anekdota*, unpublished items)."[36] The irony implicit in framing a published poem as an "unpublished" text reflects the highly charged ambiguity
of the poem's origins in a story about how a "man" meets "Life" that Stevens
would later judge to be "school-girl drivel."

The questioning of the unified, vertically oriented career adumbrated in
the compressed terms of "Earthy Anecdote" is elaborated at more length in
"Comedian," though in the final section of the poem Stevens invites the
reader to view it, too, as a mere "anecdote." Stevens submitted an early version of "Comedian," entitled "From the Journal of Crispin," for the Blind-
man Prize in 1921. Though Stevens was disappointed to lose, Amy Lowell,
who judged the prize for the Poetry Society of South Carolina, gave Stevens an honorable mention. As Edward Ragg notes, "Comedian" "became
the only poem in Stevens's manuscript to be written specifically for *Harmonium*," a condition that drives the poet's ambivalence about being a poet to
an extreme: the closer to the realization of the poetic "dream identity" (to
borrow Anderson's term) that he comes, the more aggressively he "dis-
claims" it, though the disclaimers, insofar as they take the form of verses,

must themselves be disclaimed in turn. So, for example, the directive to "score this anecdote" in the final full stanza of the poem encourages the reader to evaluate the poem's merits and so commemorates the contest it was specifically written for (as does the title of section III, "Approaching Carolina"). The statement reduces the poem to an easily assessable effort, made while "writing furiously against time" for a $1,000 prize as the deadline for submissions approached.[37] But this command to rate the poem coincides with another, still more energetically self-minimizing one, implied through the pun on "score," to cross it out altogether.

The same logic of redoubling self-derogation can be seen on the broader level of structure in the transformation of "From the Journal of Crispin" to "The Comedian as the Letter C." The sections Stevens added to "Comedian" changed Crispin from a poet seeking to shape the "book / That will contain him" to the denizen of "A Nice Shady Home" who is father to four "Daughters with Curls." His "quotidian" life at the end of "Comedian," as Siobhan Phillips observes, represents a "denial of self, and thus a denial of verse," having chosen "facts over 'flights,'" as Crispin is denied the capability Stevens would later develop of seeing "flights" and "facts" as commensurable.[38] Crispin's poet's progress in "Journal of Crispin" is already substantially indeterminate, as his "apprenticeship to chance event" defines not only the present but also the future in which his book is projected. But as Cook points out, in revising "Journal of Crispin" for "Comedian" Stevens "made the poem much more difficult, as he tried to evade expected plot lines, troping, closure, and much else."[39]

Throughout "Comedian" Stevens distinguishes one kind of career, embodied in a relatively orderly pattern and linked both to poetic tradition and the rationalized work life of the professional, from another kind that is less easy to describe precisely because it is still more indeterminate. In the second section of "Comedian," "Concerning the Thunderstorms of Yucatan," the "Maya sonneteers" still make their "plea" to "the night-bird," in the manner, as Bloom remarks, of "such Harvard poets as Trumbull Stickney, George Cabot Lodge, and even [George] Santayana," who follow Keats and Milton despite the opportunity for a new conceptualization of career offered by "the exotic American reality." Crispin, however, is "too destitute to find / In any commonplace the sought-for aid."[40] This destitution is the result of the blotching of the "mythology of self," and it serves him by enlarging his capacity for observation:

How greatly had he grown in his demesne,
This auditor of insects! He that saw

The stride of vanishing autumn in a park
By way of decorous melancholy; he
That wrote his couplet yearly to the spring,
As dissertation of profound delight,
Stopping, on voyage, in a land of snakes,
Found his vicissitudes had much enlarged
His apprehension, made him intricate
In moody rucks, and difficult and strange
In all desires, his destitution's mark.
(*WSCP* 25)

Crispin's development is figured not as a linear advancement, but rather as the abandonment of one path for another, less orderly one. Stevens scorns the career paradigm from which Crispin departs as a form of artificial order, a trait he emphasizes by setting the scene within the tended confines of a "park": the poet's "melancholy" is merely "decorous," just as it is duty to form, rather than genuine feeling, that prompts him to write "his couplet yearly to the spring," a routine Stevens plainly mocks in his hyperbolic description of that perfunctory couplet as a "dissertation of profound delight." Giving these routines up, he becomes "intricate / In moody rucks," where the "rucks," or folds, image the irregular shape of his new path, which makes his goals "difficult and strange." And yet, as Elisa New suggests, this portrait of successful self-shedding—the impossible goal of the "secular pilgrimage" described in the "Comedian"—already shows signs of its own failure, since it places Crispin back in the "land of snakes": "His paradise is an Eden, not discovered but recollected" from the same traditions he sought to escape by undertaking his voyage from Bourdeaux in the first place.[41]

By section IV, "The Idea of a Colony," the visionary potential—however doomed—liberated in Crispin by his "luminous traversing" is already on the wane, and his plans to ritualize life in his colony prompt the recognition that plans of precisely this kind were what "first drove Crispin to his wandering":

He could not be content with counterfeit,
With masquerade of thought, with hapless words
That must belie the racking masquerade,
With fictive flourishes that preordained
His passion's permit, hang of coat, degree
Of buttons, measure of his salt. Such trash

> Might help the blind, not him, serenely sly.
> It irked beyond his patience. Hence it was,
> Preferring text to gloss, he humbly served
> Grotesque apprenticeship to chance event,
> A clown perhaps, but an aspiring clown.
> (*WSCP* 31–32)

Here Crispin increases his efforts to prevent the collapse of his "oracular rockings" into systematic procedure. The career trajectory comes off as intrusive, ordaining in advance not only his emotions, but also such particularities as his "hang of coat" and "degree of buttons"—metonymic figures that call up the restrictions that professionalism tends to place on self-definition. A rationalized career would also dictate the "measure of his salt," a phrase that puns on the Latin verb *saltare*, "to leap," so that the graded sequence of advancements, far from lending him momentum, would work instead to limit his progress. The traditional career stands in the same relation to experience as a "gloss" to the original "text," and Crispin prefers experience in its unreduced, unruly plenitude. His "apprenticeship" is "grotesque" in that it is deformed, really no proper apprenticeship at all, since it will never result in mastery. Such an apprenticeship makes him a "clown" both because it distances him from the ethos of respectable, professional work and because it assumes an impossibly tall order—"To make a new intelligence prevail" without going "stale." His plans, "bland excursions into time to come," are tellingly "Related in romance to backward flights"; so it is that they contain "in their afflatus the reproach / That first drove Crispin to his wandering."[42] And yet, as I have been suggesting, Crispin's willingness to play the clown enables him to preserve his aspirations, and thus to project a book whose disorderly strangeness is a measure of its "accuracy with respect to the structure of reality," as Stevens puts it in "Three Academic Pieces." He will not produce a "Trinket pasticcio, flaunting skyey sheets," and make himself a "tiptoe cozener": "No, no: veracious page on page, exact" (*WSCP* 686).

The particular value of Stevens's "apprenticeship to chance event" is recapitulated in the sonnet-length "Nomad Exquisite," the antepenultimate poem in the collection, whose imagery is anticipated in the second section of the "Comedian," where nature is represented in its overwhelming abundance, with its "savagery of palms" and its "sides and jagged lops of green" (*WSCP* 25). As Cook suggests, it is a "forceful Florida poem, with no reservations," and it confidently employs "biblical diction" to produce an "exuberant flaming-forth." The enabling self-mockery has been toned down, but it is still present: the title presents a "Stevens persona who both roams ('nomad') and quests ('exquisite') in search of pasture, while aware of appearing slightly precious."[43] The poem presents a situation antithetical to the one sketched in "The Snow Man": tropical warmth substitutes for New England cold, palm trees for evergreens, the traveling "Nomad" for the stationary "Snow Man," a colorful repletion for a white emptiness, and so on. Both poems unfold as a single sentence, and both place special stress on the act of "beholding," a verb that not only means to gaze upon but also to possess, as Bloom suggests in his reading of "The Snow Man." This verb sets up the reciprocity between self and landscape that emerges at the end of both poems just as the snow man "beholds" nothing and so recognizes that he is "nothing himself," so the nomad learns by "beholding" the Floridean fecundity to recognize it as his own.[44] Stevens's "grotesque apprenticeship to chance event" comes to fruition in "Nomad Exquisite," where nature exhibits "a harmony not rarefied / Nor fined for the inhibited instruments / Of over-civil stops," and the poet, like the grotesque "young alligator," is at home amid the unruly elements and energies by which he is surrounded (*WSCP* 28). The poem reaffirms Stevens's flagrant disavowal of the orderly career path by presenting his poems, brilliantly and cryptically rendered as "Forms, flames, and the flakes of flames," as the works of a Paterian "Exquisite" whose fidelity to the unpatterned harmonies of reality dictates for him not a steady, calculated progress, but the wandering path of the "Nomad" (*WSCP* 77).

Marianne Moore recognized Stevens's resistance to professionalism and praised it in a 1937 review of *Owl's Clover* and *Ideas of Order*: "America has in Wallace Stevens at least one artist whom professionalism will not demolish." The antagonism between art and professionalism registers in the grim prospect of demolition to which she alludes, just as the pervasiveness of literary professionalism comes across in the implicit difficulty of counting more than "one artist" who has not succumbed to it. As her letters reveal, the tension between writing and professionalism was something she saw early on and felt compelled to sort out. Like Stevens's early letters and journal entries, Moore's letters during her Bryn Mawr years attest both to a desire to conceive of literature as a profession and an uncomfortable awareness that it does not fit the mold: "Writing is all I care for, or for what I care most, and writing is such a puling profession, if it is not a great one, that I occasionally give up. You ought I think to be *didactic* like Ibsen, or poetic like 'Sheats,' or pathetic like Barrie or witty like Meredith to justify your embarking as self-confidently as the concentrated young egoist who is a writer, must. Writing is moreover a selfish profession and a wear-ing (on the investigator himself)" (*MML* 46–47).

That Moore did not find it easy to think of literature as a profession is signaled in the several ways in which the logic of this passage seems to be at odds with itself. "Writing" may be a "puling profession," or it may be "a great one." It is her highest priority, yet in spite of (or perhaps because of) that elevated status, she has given it up more than once. She makes a case for her maturity of judgment and proto-professional sense of self-discipline by naming specific standards one may use to "justify" a life in writing, and yet the list ends up being so inclusive—one may be "*didactic*," "pathetic," "witty," or even just "poetic"—that it becomes difficult to imagine how Moore could fail to do so. The professional writer is portrayed as an "in-vestigator," and the word conveys the idea that the work of writing is ex-ploratory, but on another level it encodes a sense of Moore's indecision as she continues to investigate whether or not writing really is a profession. Her misgivings about literary professionalism come across most plainly in the way she views it as "puling" and "selfish."

One notes that all of the examples of authors that Moore considers as models for her own practice as a writer are male—Henrik Ibsen, Percy Shelley, John Keats, James Matthew Barrie, and George Meredith—just as the "the concentrated young egoist" of the nineteenth century designated a predominantly masculine role: it comes as no surprise that the title of Mer-edith's *The Egoist*, to name an example that Moore may well have had in mind, refers to the shallow and self-interested Sir Willoughby Patterne. A woman considering entry into the modern workforce, Moore comes by her conceptualization of career differently than do Stevens or Crane. The pres-sure to make "literature" a viable "profession," sponsored in part by Garrett Stevens, is reflected in Wallace's short-lived attempt to make his way as a journalist before he enrolled in law school, whereupon he separated his eco-nomic and literary activities. Crane, likewise under pressure from his father to make money, went further than Stevens: as Langdon Hammer suggests, Crane tried to make poetry "*be* money," with the result that the separation between economic and literary endeavors to which Stevens accommodated himself was relentlessly driven home to Crane through his own life experi-ence. "His life," Hammer remarks, "recurrently illustrated the truth (for him) that one cannot make *both* money and poetry at the same time."[45] By contrast, Moore is under less pressure to professionalize from the begin-ning, so the "literary life" is neither dramatically abandoned, as it is by Ste-vens, nor dramatically embraced, as it is by Crane, but instead pursued on and off during the years between her graduation from Bryn Mawr in 1909 and the publication of her debut in 1923. If Stevens, "having a rather sad time with [his] thoughts," sat in his room wondering if literature was "really a profession," Moore, likewise just a month out of college, wrote from Lake Placid of "spending a wild life, wild and glorious," and to declare that her "aim in life at present" was "to become 'beautiful' and sagacious" (*MML* 80, 86). If Moore at one point planned "to have [her] poems published as an appendix" to a collection of prose pieces rather than publish a first book composed entirely of poetry (*MML* 133), Crane was convinced early on that it was only a matter of time before he would be known nationally: "I shall really without a doubt," he told his father in April 1917, "be one of the foremost poets of America if I am enabled to devote enough time to my art" (*HCL* 12). But if these contrasts in self-presentation reflect the role gender played in the different ways these poets' imagined their careers, they also call attention to remarkable similarities between them.

Moore shares with Stevens and Crane a vexed reliance on the romantic myth of poetic production centered on a privileged moment of experience: "'Ecstasy / affords / the occasion and expediency determines the form,'" she claims in "The Past Is the Present," a work ethic precisely at odds with the calculated progress embodied in the professional career (*BMM* 74). Moore's ability to claim the authorizing potential in that myth as her own is complicated by the threats to poetry that I sketched, drawing on Newcomb, earlier in this chapter. For Moore these threats are not alleviated by her status as a woman: the putative effeminacy of poetry in the culture at large does not translate into female dominance within the subfield of poetic production, as a glance at the table of contents of virtually any anthology of modern American poetry will demonstrate. Moore deploys restraint as a "means of purifying her femininity of its disturbing aspects," as Ellen Levy puts it in her invaluable discussion of Moore as modernism's "token woman." She occupies an "impossible position" in a field requiring that she "distance herself from all of the negative connotations that femininity carries with it."[46] As for Stevens, Moore's adoption of a poetic practice in which "ecstasy" serves as the primary "occasion" is bound to run against the grain of the dominant "capitalist-realist managerial ideology." And yet to eschew "ecstasy" in favor of some more rational principle would be to undermine the poet's still-crucial claim to disinterestedness.

This short quotation in "The Past is the Present"—itself a quotation, according to Robin G. Shulze, from A. R. Gordon's *Poets of the Old Testament*, which the Reverend Edwin H. Kellogg quoted to Moore in a Bible class she took with him in 1914—provides an illustration of Moore's way of negotiating these challenges (*BMM* 209). The highly and explicitly mediated style of presentation, for instance, enhanced by Moore's Eliotic notes in her debut, advertises her knowledge of the myth's ancient provenance, its nineteenth-century vogue, and its solidification into textbook orthodoxy. The style of the quotation likewise complicates Moore's relation to the myth it embodies. The staunch summing up seems out of place in a comment on "ecstasy," and Moore's intricate verse forms are difficult to reconcile with the idea of "expediency," which connotes both a sense of fitness and a (less appropriate) sense of haste. These claims make her full endorsement of the statement difficult to imagine. At the same time, closing the poem with such an authoritative pronouncement makes categorizing it as pure mockery equally difficult. Much like Stevens in *Harmonium*, Moore in *Observations* finds ways to invoke this myth of poetic labor, and the radically indeterminate path to which it corresponds, while also holding it at a distance.

Letters Moore wrote prior to the publication of *Observations* frequently recur to the difficulty of writing on command. The irregularity of her inspiration testifies to its legitimacy, because it claims for them, as Menand puts it, "an origin in the unpremeditated impulses responsible for true art."[47] So it is that her sense of her poetic vocation grows more confident as her sense that poetry is not a proper profession grows more assured. She relates in a 1907 letter to her mother, for instance, a conversation she had with Lucy Martin Donnelly, one of her English professors at Bryn Mawr, "about college work in general and the sonnet we are to write. She said, 'you won't have any trouble about that. You write sonnets do you not?' I smiled, I trust not too diffusely and said I had tried versification of various sorts but found it difficult to produce things at definite times and with a serious end in view" (*MML* 27). Professionalism inheres precisely in the "ability to produce things at definite times and with a serious end in view," and it is therefore noteworthy that Moore emphasizes these challenges, rather than others that recommend themselves more readily—those embodied in meeting the formal requirements of the sonnet, for example. In time she came to view the unpredictability of inspiration and the absence of a "serious" purpose to guide her efforts in a more positive light, less as obstacles and more as the concomitants of artistic value itself. In 1921, while working part-time at the Hudson Park Branch of the New York Public Library, the independently wealthy Bryher (Winifred Ellerman) offered to pay for Moore's travels abroad if, as Moore explained to her brother, she would be a "'good pterodactyl that [would] come out of its rock' and write a novel." Though grateful, Moore turned the offer down, explaining that the "annoyances" she encountered in her work at the library, far from hindering any progress she might make in her literary labors, actually served as their most potent impetus: "moreover, the work I am doing and the annoyances to which I am subjected, are to some extent the goose that lays the golden egg and are I am sure, responsible just now for any gain that I make toward writing" (*MML* 142). Moore's refusal of Bryher's offer suggests an interest in courting the very randomness, and even the pathos, of experience itself. When Moore writes in her correspondence of her "sporadic poems," or claims that her "work jerks and rears," she describes an element of her aesthetic that betokens its legitimacy, much though she may seem at times to lament it (*MML* 63, 123).

Moore's reservations about pursuing a poetic career were intense enough to prompt, on occasion, a sense of frustration in her friends. In June 1921, Yvor Winters wrote to Moore, urging her to collect her poems in a first book:

> I know many people who want your poems, and want them badly, and it is very difficult to gather them up from magazines, especially if one lives in the desert as I do. Why won't you? I hope you don't have Mr. Stevens' unwashed aversion to book-publication. It is untidy, you know. People who leave poems littered around in the magazines are so very much like people who leave papers around in the parks.[48]

The presence among Winters's motives of a specific concern about keeping up professional standards registers in the shift in argument. First there is the practical rationale that Moore ought to collect her poems to save admiring readers the trouble of tracking them down in magazines, and one would have thought that that rationale would suffice. But Winters is not just paying Moore a compliment. He goes on to make a case for first-book publication on a more exalted, quasi-ethical basis. The second part of this passage relies on what Menand calls the "rhetoric of hygiene," which emphasizes the professional worker's "ability to keep his researches from adulteration by the corrupting forces of the ideological marketplace."[49] To "leave poems littered around in the magazines," like leaving papers in a park, is to abandon one's responsibility to other members of a society, who, like members of a professional association, depend on one another to maintain standards of conduct so as to enhance the prestige, figured here as tidiness, of the group. "Mr. Stevens" had also refused so far to comply with the code of professional ethics that Winters seeks to instill in Moore, and he is therefore presented in connection with the "unwashed" masses of workers from whom professionals would distinguish themselves.

Winters was not the only writer who wished to see Moore initiate her career properly by publishing a first book. Ezra Pound and T. S. Eliot also encouraged her to do so, and she politely but firmly refused both. She went so far as to inform Pound in 1919 that she had grown "less and less desirous of being published" and that she had "a strong feeling for letting alone what I do produce." And she explained to Eliot in 1921 that she had "certain knowledge that I have nothing to say that ought to appear in book form" (*MML* 123, 152). Much to Moore's dismay, however, the poet H. D., Bryher, and Bryher's husband-to-be, Robert McAlmon, published a collection of Moore's verse entitled *Poems* without her consent in 1921. Moore's consternation makes it clear that she was not so careless of the importance of career as to be insensible to the value of making a strong debut. In particular, her disappointment that "several poems could have been put in that aren't in," that "many should be left out that are in," and that she would have made "changes in half the poems that are in," bespeaks an interest in making a particular kind of beginning, and thus of pursuing a particular kind of career path (*MML* 170). And yet, as her letters to Bryher, McAlmon, her brother John Warner Moore, and Eliot reveal, her concerns derive largely from the fact that the appearance of *Poems* would lead Eliot, Pound, and others who had encouraged her to publish a book to see her as a plotting careerist who was not above compromising the integrity of her friendships if the right "expediency" presented itself.

This kind of integrity was at least as important to Moore as self-advancement, if not more so. In fact, her concerns about premature exposure—the publication of *Poems* was not to her "literary advantage," as she puts it in several letters—appear only in conjunction with her concerns about responsibility to a standard of forthright personal conduct. It may be that Moore speaks of her "literary advantage" primarily out of her sense that it is what her allies, who often seem more interested in launching her career than Moore herself does, want to hear. "I hope T. S. Eliot and the others whose advice I repudiated will not think I have been working up a surprise all by myself," she wrote to her brother. Unwilling to trust that Eliot would sort the matter out for himself, Moore wrote to him to explain: "Since you were so kind as to propose the collecting and publishing of work of mine, I wish to send you a copy of the book which Miss Bryher has brought out. Its publication was a tremendous surprise to me" (*MML* 170, 171). That Moore was able to acknowledge the publication of *Poems* as an act of friendship, and even to express gratitude for the "unstinted care and other outlay bestowed on the book" (*MML* 164), has been misread by some critics as evidence of her quiet complicity with Bryher, H. D., and McAlmon.[50] I would suggest instead that the exceedingly good-natured understanding with which Moore received the book reflects an underlying recognition that her trajectory was beyond her control anyway and a matter of concern in this case mainly insofar as it put her sincerity in question.

Moore claims in "Critics and Connoisseurs" to have seen "ambition without understanding in a variety of forms," and her poems frequently seek to expose the motive of self-interest that underlies several varieties of careerism—including the crypto-careerist variety that makes a show of repudiating personal advancement. In this regard, Moore appears to outdo even her Puritan forebears in their skepticism: if, as Edmund Morgan reports, "William Perkins went so far as to say that 'To see and feele in our selves the want of any grace pertaining to salvation, and to be grieved therefore, is the grace it selfe,'" Moore's poems repeatedly attest to the idea that neither "grace" *nor* the "want" of it can guarantee the authenticity of a calling.[51] Her particular concern with exposing the kind of self-interest that hides in a posture of disinterestedness has been remarked by her critics: "Moore's irony," Bonnie Costello writes, "penetrates layers of masks to discover egocentric motives in apparent unselfconsciousness."[52] Just as Moore defines her sense of vocation against professionalism, she cultivates a mode of irony that is uniquely attuned to revealing a contradiction of professional ideology that crucially concerns career. On the one hand, the well-defined professional path symbolizes an ostensibly disinterested life of service; advancements are predicated upon gains in experience and expertise rather than profit, and they advertise an ethos of fairness by guaranteeing that consumers will get what they pay for. On the other hand, career figures the ambitions of the individual who pursues it, so that it represents a program of increasing payoffs in wealth, power, and prestige. Moore's fascination with exposing defensiveness as a mode of domination and self-effacement as a strategy of attack is bound up with her response to the normative professional career, whose contradictions enfold motives of self-interest and vanity that are at odds with Moore's ideal of the genuine, and which she accordingly seeks to unmask and contain. Her opposition to the normative career registers above all in her refusal to underestimate its power and complexity: like marriage—which symbolizes, among other things, the expected path for a woman of her time and place—the rationalized career requires "all one's criminal ingenuity / to avoid!" (*BMM* 115).

As the first sentence of "Picking and Choosing" suggests, fashioning a writing life without yielding in some measure to the career and its poses is almost impossible, and yet refusing to yield is of the highest importance:

"Literature is a phase of life: if / one is afraid of it, the situation is irremediable; if / one approaches it familiarly, / what one says of it is worthless." "Phase" is used in a sense derived from chemistry, in which matter can exist in one or another state or "phase"—solid, liquid, gas, or plasma. "Literature" *is* "life" in this formulation, "life" in a more rarefied or abstract state. Life, like literature, would seem to be all but impossible according to Moore, who evokes here a sense of impasse in order to emphasize that almost every stance toward "life" represents a pose that compromises an author's ability to write in a way that is "true": "Words are constructive," she goes on, "when they are true; the opaque allusion—the simulated / flight / upward—accomplishes nothing" (*BMM* 97).[53] But Moore is not so inflexible in her championing of sincerity as to fail to distinguish the more blatant forms of careerism from the subtler ones. So it is that she reserves her most scathing satire for those most wrapped up in a careerist mentality, as for example in "Novices," while someone who affects an "inconsequence of manner," like "George Moore"—whose name in the title raises the possibility that Moore is diagnosing her own attraction to this strategy—is exposed as untrue to his best impulses and subjected to raillery rather than ridicule. Creating "true" poems for Moore depends on eluding career altogether and writing, as she puts it in "Black Earth," "Openly, yes, / with the naturalness / of the hippopotamus or the alligator / when it climbs out on the bank to experience the / sun," doing "these / things which I do, / which please / no one but myself" (*BMM* 87).

Just as the indeterminacy of the poetic career in *Harmonium* reflects Stevens's interest in fending off the reasonable (and therefore threatening) conformity his father urged him to submit to, so in *Observations* it reflects Moore's interest in protecting her vocation from influence by the wrong models, conformists she calls "scarecrows / Of aesthetic procedure," one of whom, as John M. Slatin avers, "was her mother."[54] In 1915, on the heels of publishing some of her first poems in *The Egoist*, *Poetry*, and *Others*, Moore remarked to her mother that she could "publish a book anytime." Her mother advised against it until Moore had "changed" her "style," and she told her daughter that her poems were "ephemeral" (*MML* 100). As Linda Leavell suggests, Mary's criticism may not have carried as much force in the full context of the exchange as it seems to when quoted by itself.[55] Nevertheless, that the criticism touched a nerve is evidenced not only in the exasperated tone with which she reported the exchange to her brother, but in the response to it she expressed in "Diligence Is to Magic As Progress Is to Flight," which appeared along with "To a Steam Roller" in *The Egoist* in 1915. In it, she pictures herself traveling on one "of those / Tough-grained animals" that "have outstripped man's whim to suppose / them ephemera":

> With an elephant to ride upon—"with rings on her fingers and bells
>   on her toes,"
>   she shall outdistance calamity anywhere she goes.
> Speed is not in her mind inseparable from carpets. Locomotion arose
>   in the shape of an elephant; she clambered up and chose
> to travel laboriously. So far as magic carpets are concerned, she knows
>   that although the semblance of speed may attach to scarecrows
> of aesthetic procedure, the substance of it is embodied in such of those
>   tough-grained animals as have outstripped man's whim to suppose
> them ephemera, and have earned that fruit of their ability to endure
>   blows,
>   which dubs them prosaic necessities—not curios.
> (*BMM* 64)

Moore defends herself by imagining a mode of travel that, in its emphatically idiosyncratic character, stands opposed to the orderly progress of the professional career. She trades in the "white horse" of the nursery rhyme "Ride a Cockhorse" for an "elephant," an alteration that signifies her resistance to the proprieties that govern the way that a "fine lady" ought to make her way in the world. She revises the fourth line of the nursery rhyme, which says that the "fine lady" will "have music wherever she goes," to read "she shall outdistance calamity anywhere she goes." A "calamity" is for Moore a failure of nerve, a capitulation to convention. The word appears in the title "To Be Liked by You Would Be a Calamity," a poem in which, as Sandra Gilbert and Susan Gubar argue, the "spinster-poet" bows "herself out of the 'plot' of erotic liking" and so avoids "calamity."[56] Similarly, in "Diligence," Moore is bowing herself out of a conventional plot, a rationalizing career-script that calls for "music wherever she goes." Her suppression of this part of the script provides an index to her sense of poetic integrity: her career is impelled not by the conventional desire for a continuous "music," but by a wish to "outdistance calamity," where a "calamity" figures a capitulation to the standardized "aesthetic procedure" practiced by "scarecrows."

Bowing out of any "plot," Moore's poems show, is a tricky business: having abandoned one plot, one inevitably finds oneself caught up in another which must be abandoned in turn. It is in her dedication to representing this predicament in its full complexity that her romanticism manifests itself, as the affinity between her thinking about career and Emerson's bears out. "Conformity," George Kateb writes, "is the main antithesis to self-reliance," the practice of which creates the imperative for individuals "to cut their own channels."[57] And yet to talk of cutting one's own channel, though it is in keeping with the spirit of independence that Emerson celebrates in general, is what he would call a "poor, external way of speaking," for it does not adequately express the more radical and dynamic freedom from all "channels" that he promotes: "The way of life is wonderful," he states in "Circles," "it is by abandonment."[58] This "way of life" is a continuous shuffling off of ways of life, a process of repeated abandonment necessitated by the "truth," as he puts it earlier in that essay, "that around every circle another can be drawn," where "every circle" designates a path from which one must diverge or else suffer the consequences of a new conformity that takes the same shape as the old. The fixed structure of the professional career conflicts with this profoundly unsettled conception of the self-reliant "way of life," and for this reason Emerson frames "life" not as a progress toward mastery, but as a perpetual "apprenticeship."[59]

The difficult poem to which Moore gave the self-consciously ungainly title "In This Age of Hard Trying, Nonchalance Is Good and" provides an example of the way her commitment to a self-reliant course of abandonments is often present in both the theme and the style of a poem. The title pays a compliment to the attitude of nonconformity. "This Age" is one of strained self-exertion and thus of a kind of "Hard Trying" precisely at odds with the wise passiveness Moore cultivated as a way of courting the fortuities that inspire her work. Her advocacy of "Nonchalance" in such an age positions her in opposition to it: to nurture an attitude of unconcern is "Good," because it allows one to bow out of the routine of determined striving. And yet, upon re-reading, the adjective "Good" comes to seem glaringly plain, partly because of the elevated register of the rest of the title, with its ambitious diagnosis of the "Age." The mixing of registers imbues the word with a pair of opposed meanings. Insofar as one must resist conforming to the age-wide trend of "Hard Trying," "Nonchalance" is "Good"—but like "Hard Trying," it represents a way of life that must be abandoned in turn: it is "Good," but it is also *only* "Good." The title's unconventional end-word, "and," emphasizes the idea that the process of self-recovery through abandonment Moore elaborates, like Emerson's, must be ongoing.

The first sentence of the poem exemplifies Moore's flair for whimsical transitions. In the version of the poem that appeared in *The Chimaera* in 1916, the coordinating conjunction "and" is preceded by a comma: by leaving the punctuation out of the *Observations* version, Moore rushes the sentence toward the turn it takes at the beginning of the first stanza (*BMM* 198). The conjunction ironically points up the radical disjunctiveness of the sentence as a whole. Without the line-breaks and capitals in the title, it reads like this: "In this age of hard trying, nonchalance is good and 'Really, it is not the business of the gods to bake clay pots.'" Beneath the disorienting shift of perspective and allusion to Ivan Turgenev's *Fathers and Sons* (not, as Moore mistakenly wrote in her "Notes," to "Dostoievsky"), the sentence addresses the question of how to conduct a life in art in an age of increasingly routinized forms of work, when artists feel pressured, like "gods" who take to the "business" of baking "clay pots," to adapt their activities to the more practical and orderly procedures of artisanship (*BMM* 201). By moving so dramatically from one perspective to another, Moore embeds within the motion of the poem a suggestion that her way of life is predicated upon a refusal to encumber herself with an allegiance to "foolish consistency."

In the lines that follow, Moore sketches a scenario in which the "gods," in "this instance" anyway, have not abdicated their traditionally high offices to "bake clay pots."

> "Really, it is not the
> > business of the gods to bake clay pots." They did not
> > > do it in this instance. A few
> > > > revolved upon the axes of their worth
> > > > as if excessive popularity might be a pot;
>
> they did not venture the
> > profession of humility.
> (*BMM* 28)

The poem does not make clear just who the "gods" are. In *Fathers and Sons*, the sentence is spoken by Bazarov, the main character, to rationalize his penchant for taking advantage of people he considers beneath him. One reason for interpreting it, in the context of Moore's poem, as a kind of indirect self-reference—as a poet, she is one of the gods whose business is something other than baking clay pots—is that, as Bazarov's friend Arkady divines, Bazarov uses it to refer to himself: "'Oho!' thought Arkady, and only then in a flash did all the fathomless depths of Bazarov's conceit dawn upon him. 'So you and I are gods, are we?'" (*BMM* 201).[60] In addition, the scenario reflects and comments on the salient tendency in modernism—the historical moment Moore emphasizes by specifying "*This* Age" and "*this* instance"—for artists to privilege difficulty so as to maintain a distance from mass culture. So it is in this case that the gods' "worth" is something they maintain by avoiding "excessive popularity," as if it were one of the clay "pot[s]" that, given their high station, they ought to avoid handling.

The poem begins by suggesting that in an "Age of Hard Trying" it is important to distinguish art from the kind of labor that requires only training and effort to perform. But having thus separated the work of art from the hard trying of the craftsman, its integrity is in turn threatened by the hard trying of the professional, whose self-authorizing autonomy and pose of disinterestedness are present in the image of the "few" who "revolved upon the axes of their worth / as if excessive popularity might be a pot." Moore allows her dissatisfaction with both of these codes of conduct to bleed through her description of them. So it is that Bazarov's "conceit" tallies with the attitude of self-absorption called up by the image of the gods "revolving upon the axes of their worth": if they do not "venture the / profession of humility," they fall into the "depths" of "conceit." Moore's misgivings about viewing art as a kind of craft—a model of production in which not "ecstasy" but market demand "affords the occasion"—are encoded in the phrase "profession of humility." "Humility" is a virtue Moore values, and as Costello suggests, it signifies a "motive of natural reticence."[61] To "venture the profession of humility," then, is implicitly to betray a want of it. What emerges from Moore's evaluation of these alternatives is her resistance to the conformity implicit in the "profession" of any vocational paradigm. The profession of the sort of romantic egotism Bazarov exemplifies, like the profession of "humility," shares in what Moore denigrates later in the poem as the "haggish, uncompanionable drawl / of certitude."

Moore's self-reliance, at once romantic, pragmatic, and Puritanical, privileges a logic of incessant divagation: in each new "course of procedure," as Moore puts it in "Critics and Connoisseurs," lies a new conformity that must be abandoned in turn, along with its attendant discourse and characteristic stance (*BMM* 36). The rapid juxtapositions and coiling ironies that animate "In This Age of Hard Trying" are in play throughout *Observations*, and they bespeak the strength of her kinship with Emerson, who claims in "Self-Reliance" that "power ceases in the instant of repose; it resides in the moment of transition from a past to a new state, in the shooting of the gulf, in the darting to an aim."[62] The turnings by which she bows herself out of the career story are inscribed in her style itself, which serves her critique of conformity by enabling a serial exposure of the discreditable motives that inform it.

Moore foregrounds this logic of divagation by placing "To an Intra-Mural Rat" at the beginning of *Observations*. Leavell explains that Moore claimed for herself "the persona of the self-reliant and savvy Mr. Rat" after discovering Kenneth Grahame's *The Wind in the Willows* in 1914.[63] That the rat is "Intra-Mural" evokes the idea of fortuitous entrapment that Moore saw as central to her poetic practice, a notion that works against the prospect of an orderly execution of the poetic career, as does the labyrinthine path the title calls up.[64] "To An Intra-Mural Rat" is, as Charles Molesworth suggests, a "coded poem, probably about herself," given that "Rat" became one of her family nicknames during the time between the earliest draft of the poem (titled "Intra Mural Rat") and its first publication in *Others* the next year.[65] The poem ironically makes the process of introduction a means of concealing, rather than revealing, identity:

> You make me think of many men
> Once met, to be forgot again
>   Or merely resurrected
> In a parenthesis of wit
> That found them hastening through it
>   Too brisk to be inspected.
> (*BMM* 51)

The path Moore projects for herself in the poem is, in conventional terms, a failed one. She envisions herself as one of "many" forgettable poets who, if they are not forgotten entirely, are "resurrected" only momentarily, in a quotation or "parenthesis of wit." Even trapped within the confines of the "parenthesis" (whose upright lines image the walls that enclose the "Intra-Mural Rat"), she is nevertheless "Too brisk to be inspected." If inspection works as a metaphor for reading, then the implication is that Moore pursues the stylistic virtue of briskness to an extreme that may preclude ready comprehension. At thirty-one words long, the poem itself is notably brisk, and the differences between the version of the poem published in *Poetry* in 1915 and the version published in *Observations* suggest that Moore took pains to quicken its pace still more: she took out a semi-colon (after "again") and a comma (after "wit") that slow the poem in the first version by bringing it to a full stop in the second line and by accentuating a pause in the fourth. Evoking the frantic hastening of a rat through the walls of a maze, secreting her identity behind a family nickname, projecting a future in which she is all but forgotten, and prioritizing briskness even at the cost of being misunderstood, "To an Intra-Mural Rat" projects a path that registers at once the uncertainty of vocation as well as the radical indeterminacy required to purify her practice of both rational self-interest and the "interest in disinterestedness," as Bourdieu puts it, that characterizes the artist in the field of cultural production (*FCP* 40). In the poem Moore swears never to mind that "these things" she does may "please / no one" but herself.

Hart Crane planned to "take [T. S.] Eliot as a point of departure toward an almost complete reverse of direction," as he wrote to Gorham Munson in the winter of 1923 (*HCL* 117). To reverse what he saw as the unnecessarily pessimistic "direction" of modernism, which he identifies here with Eliot, Crane reversed its characteristic skepticism of the normative career, a skepticism readily legible in Eliot's repeated question—"And how should I begin?"—in "The Love Song of J. Alfred Prufrock," the first poem in his debut.[66] Like Eliot, Stevens and Moore put career in question from the beginning, but Crane, aiming "toward a more positive, or (if [I] must put it so in a sceptical age) ecstatic goal," seeks to affirm it. Thus Crane's title diverges from those of Stevens and Moore, which suppress the normative career by replacing its inauguration with an image of an already complete and forbiddingly compendious whole, in the case of *Harmonium*, and by flattening its traditional angle of ascent into an uncontoured series of perceptions, in the case of *Observations*. By contrast, the whiteness of Crane's buildings figures purity and hope, and his buildings themselves evoke both his lofty ambitions and a notion of ongoing progress in that they are buildings "toward" something greater. There is still a measure of indeterminacy here—evident in the open-endedness of the progressive sense of "Buildings"—but the explicitly developmental logic being invoked clearly contrasts with the more idiosyncratic representations of vocational trajectory we have seen in *Harmonium* and *Observations*.

This sense of Crane's project as one that marks a departure from the general modernist tendency to react against nineteenth-century poetry is in keeping with the portrait that emerges from Brian Reed's invaluable study, *Hart Crane: After His Lights*. "Crane," Reed stresses at the outset, "chose a contrary path," a path that ran counter to those of Stevens and Moore and that was shaped by his "queer-inflected response to the writings of his straight, more strait-laced friends and rivals" as well as his attempt to "extend fin de siècle strategies for articulating queer content."[67] As I have suggested, Stevens adopts in *Harmonium* a poetically enabling "strategic modesty," to borrow Guillory's phrase again, while, similarly, Moore obsessively and productively investigates the posture of "strategic modesty" in *Observations* (knowing that her investigation itself exemplifies the same quality). Crane, however, exhibits very little in the way of interest in either modesty or its potential for strategic application in *White Buildings*, which, set alongside Stevens's and Moore's respective debuts, produces the impression of untrammeled poetic ambition. Such is Crane's faith in his calling that the fantasy of perpetual fluency often hovers close by in his work, just barely out of reach: as Reed remarks, it is possible to "claim that Crane shares the industrial capitalist's dream of production by rote, ad infinitum."[68]

As we will see, however, the representation of career in *White Buildings*, though it aspires to precisely the imagery of regular production that is rigorously eschewed in *Harmonium* and *Observations*, is nevertheless beset throughout by an agonizing sense of indirection. Crane's "contrary path" marks a reversal of high modernist practice, but it does not exempt him from the sense of crisis by which the poetic calling is defined in the nineteenth-century poets—Blake, Whitman, Melville, and Swinburne, among others—he unabashedly draws on as models. As New observes, "For perhaps no other American poet is the will to believe more crucial because [it is] more freighted with disbelief, more undermined, more thwarted."[69] The uniquely "ecstatic goal" toward which Crane aims cannot ultimately be separated from the "sceptical" perspective that defined the "age" in which he lived and wrote.

Crane was fully committed to his project of reversal well before the publication of *White Buildings*: on the evidence of his letters, his sense of "direction," to use the term he favored, seems to have been strong from the start. Whereas Stevens went to Harvard and so followed a conventional course of development, Crane avoided that course, and at seventeen he went to New York City to "concentrate" on poetry, as he put it in a letter to his father (*HCL* 9). Stevens went to law school, and Crane went into advertising, but just as Stevens clings to the dream of pursuing poetry full-time only to abandon it for the separation of business and art to which his submission to his father and "reason" led him, so Crane clings at first to a dream of success in the world of advertising that he later gives up, in defiance of his father and his reasoning, to pursue poetry full-time. In other words, Crane "single[d]" poetry "out" in precisely the way Stevens, who puzzled over that possibility early on, did not. In January 1924 Crane wrote to refuse his father's offer of a position in his company, declaring his "enthusiasm about [his] writing and [his] devotion to that career in life," on the grounds that he felt "satisfied and spiritually healthy only when [he is] fulfilling [him]self in that direction" (*HCL* 178).

Crane's headstrong faith in his calling as a poet stands in marked contrast to Moore's self-effacing doubt in hers. As Costello remarks, "the prosaic, conversational tone, the long, meandering, run-on lines and shifts of figurative level, give the impression of nonchalance. She is not, she seems to suggest, writing anything so grand as a poem."[70] Here is how Moore sounds when she speaks of her plans to write: "for the time-being I have some things to say about acacias and sea-weeds and serpents in plane-trees that will have to appear in fragments" (*MML* 138). Here is how Crane sounds when he does so: "Certainly it is the most ambitious thing I have ever attempted and in it I am attempting to evolve a conscious pseudo-symphonic construction toward an abstract beauty that has not been done before in English—at least directly" (*HCL* 93). In this and other letters Crane ventures precisely the "profession" of poetry—his commitment to, aptitude for, and expectation of reward from it—from which Moore distances herself in "In This Age of Hard Trying."

Moore tends to think of her poetic development as an unconscious process—a kind of evolution over which she exerts little control. This tendency comes across clearly when, writing to Bryher after the surprise publication of *Poems* in 1921, Moore compares herself to a "Darwinian gosling": "In *Variations of Animals and Plants under Domestication*, Darwin speaks of a variety of pigeon that is born naked without any down whatever. I feel like that Darwinian gosling" (*MML* 164). The same is true for Stevens, whose *Harmonium* is the record of his "grotesque apprenticeship to chance event." While Stevens and Moore stress accident, Crane stresses control: "There is little to be gained in any art," he writes to Munson in 1921, "except with much <u>conscious</u> effort" (*HCL* 58). Whereas Moore fortified herself against the allure of writing for an audience in "Black Earth—"I do these / things which I do, / which please / no one but myself"—Crane is explicit in his desire for his audience's acknowledgment. That desire is linked, for Crane, with a sense of "hope." In a letter to Waldo Frank about William Sommer, a painter who "hates to let his pictures leave him," Crane remarks, "It's just as well, of course, if he has triumphed over certain kinds of hope. I admit that I haven't, at least not entirely. I still feel the need of some kind of audience" (*HCL* 205).

Crane's powerful sense of vocation, his belief in his ability to superintend his growth through "conscious effort," and his pronounced interest in his "audience" are all reflected in the ideology of professionalism, which stresses choosing a career by recognizing talents and abilities, willing a course of improvements, and the ideal of work as a form of service. The representation of career in his debut emphasizes his interest in adopting a professional stance that Moore and Stevens both tend to play down or approach indirectly. Accordingly, career inscribes the several contrasts between Crane's sense of vocation and that of Moore and Stevens: it is a sign of election of the sort Moore and Stevens were hesitant to avow, just as it projects a desire for recognition from and connection with an audience that Moore and Stevens were disinclined to acknowledge.[71] And it lays out a program of steady development that Moore and Stevens, by contrast, image as labyrinthine or nomadic.

Crane's attraction to the traditionally defined career registers in the precision of the geometrical terms he draws on to describe it. Writing to Allen Tate in June 1922, Crane explains his plan to reverse Eliot's "direction": "while I haven't discovered a weak spot in [Eliot's] armour,—I flatter myself a little lately that I have discovered a safe tangent to strike which, if I can possibly explain the position,—goes through him toward a different goal" (*HCL* 89). The "tangent" he would "strike" puts him on a course whose straightness and continuity contrast with the curvilinear, split, meandering, and blocked paths that appear in *Harmonium* and *Observations*. Similarly, his obsessive references to his "direction" in letters and poems evidence the intensity with which he cherished a belief in his ability to pursue an orderly career. He writes to Munson that "Black Tambourine" has become "a kind of diminutive model of ambition, simply pointing a direction"; he writes to Alfred Stieglitz that he feels their "identities" are very "much alike in spiritual direction"; he writes to Tate that he "chose from Donne" the poem entitled "The Progress of the Soul" as his "direction." Interestingly, the word may also apply to the age, or to the movement of a poem: Crane complains to William H. Wright that the "age" is a "period that is loose at all ends, without apparent direction of any sort," and he tells Jean Toomer that a poem he may call "White Buildings"—probably "Recitative"—may not yet have "any sense, direction or interest to anyone" but himself (*HCL* 73, 155, 183, 112, 169–70). The word exemplifies the lucidity with which Crane imagined his relationship to the "age": its "direction" is negative, his is positive. That lucidity is a sign of Crane's confidence. But at the same time the word puts the extent of his confidence in question. It emphasizes movement *toward* a goal, but leaves open the question of attaining it. In this respect Crane's sense of the direction of his career parallels the characteristic direction of his lyrics, which trace movements toward forms of unity whose realization is deferred, as the endings of "Legend" and "Possessions" respectively show:

> Then, drop by caustic drop, a perfect cry
> Shall string some constant harmony . . .

> The pure possession, the inclusive cloud
> Whose heart is fire shall come,—the white wind rase
> All but bright stones wherein our smiling plays.
> (*HCCP* 3, 14)

These endings illustrate Crane's confidence that by moving in a specific direction he would eventually arrive at a particular destination, and it is in this regard that his difference from Stevens and Moore comes across most strongly. But the fact that neither destination is situated in the present betrays an underlying sense of uncertainty about their realization. Crane's sense of "direction" is curiously self-contradictory, as it evokes a confident progress toward an unreachable goal.

The vectors of achievement through which Crane imagines his career are frequently threatened by disintegration and confusion—his line of progress divided into "decimals," as in "Passage," his "direction" stolen, as in "Possessions." If Crane tends to express confidence in his career in geometrical terms, he tends to express his skepticism of it in terms drawn from basic arithmetic. In a letter to Stieglitz of July 1923, Crane identifies his poetic—which he calls the "logic of metaphor" here, as he will again in his letter to Harriet Monroe about "At Melville's Tomb" and in the brief manifesto he wrote for Eugene O'Neill called "General Aims and Theories"—as distinctly anti-arithmetical: "I have to combat every day those really sincere people, but limited, who deny the superior logic of metaphor in favor of their perfect sums, divisions, and subtractions" (*HCL* 156). Arithmetic, for Crane, represents a logic of separation; by privileging it, the "sincere people" whom Crane views as enemy combatants imply their acceptance of a world broken into the discrete quantities that "sums, divisions, and subtractions" presuppose. By contrast, the "logic of metaphor," as Crane explains in "General Aims" and the letter to Monroe, functions as a "connective agent," for it relies upon the establishment of "metaphorical inter-relationships" among the elements of the poem (*HCL* 281).

Contemptible sums and ominous divisions run all through *White Buildings*: consider, to name a few examples, the "trembling tabulation" and the "blind sum" in "Possessions," the "decimals of time" in "Passage," the "dim inheritance of sand" that "you know and count" in "Wine Menagerie," the "atrocious sums" in "Recitative," and the "counted smile of hours and days" in "Voyages IV" (*HCCP* 13–14, 16, 18, 19, 26). The "integers of life" that appear in the second stanza of "Paraphrase" offer a compact illustration of the problems attendant upon writing a poetry of discrete moments of intensity:

> Above the feet the clever sheets
> Lie guard upon the integers of life:
> For what skims in between uncurls the toe,
> Involves the hands in purposeless repose.

The "integers of life" represent the fingers and toes of a body, but for Crane they are also the privileged moments into which life fractures, and which he strives to record in his poems—encoded in this scenario as the "clever sheets" draped over the body. Poems "guard" or preserve the "integers of life" by representing and thus commemorating them. But Crane wants poems to embody the "integers of life" themselves, not rest "Above" them. For that reason, he is troubled by the distance "between" poems and the body, a distance which exerts the deadening effect registered in the images of the "uncurl[ed]" toe and the "purposeless repose" of the hands. Because of this distance, Crane disparagingly calls them "clever sheets"— texts that throw into relief those ambiguous "feet" that refer, by means of the familiar pun, both to parts of the body and metrical units of verse.[72] Their cleverness puts the integrity of the "record" they form in question, as if their "connective" logic were inadequate to the task of presenting life's "integers" as a kind of continuity. What Crane confronts in the poem is the idea that the separation between "integers" of experience makes a "lie" of any attempt to reproduce them in poems, whose discursive continuities can only yield an unsatisfactory "paraphrase" (*HCCP* 12–13).

In the letter to Munson I quoted earlier, for example, Crane grounds his confidence in his ability to "take Eliot as a point of departure toward an almost complete reverse of direction" in "a kind of rhythm and ecstasy" he experiences "at odd moments, and rare!" The randomness and rarity of such moments mark their legitimacy and power, but these qualities also compromise the unity of the very path on which they propel Crane. The terms in which he tends to formulate this problem are borrowed from Walter Pater, who figured for Crane among "the best things of life" (*HCL* 113). The thought of life's brevity drives Pater's preoccupation with "number" in *The Renaissance*, particularly in the "Conclusion":

A counted number of pulses only is given to us of a variegated, dramatic life. How may we see in them all that is to be seen in them by the finest senses? How shall we pass most swiftly from point to point, and be present always at the focus where the greatest number of vital forces unite in their purest energy? To burn always with this hard, gem-like flame, to maintain this ecstasy, is success in life.[73]

Like Crane, Pater relies on the logic of arithmetic—the wistful reflection that all we have is "a counted number of pulses"—to express the limitations of the human condition. And like Crane, Pater imagines overcoming those limitations in geometrical terms—passing "from point to point" in order to "maintain this ecstasy." Pater argues that since our experiences are "infinitely divisible," we must seek the "multiplied consciousness" available through the love of art, particularly poetry, in order to compensate for it.[74] Crane would also overcome division through multiplication—the lone arithmetical operation absent from his criticism of the people who "deny the superior logic of metaphor in favor of their perfect sums, divisions, and subtractions." Thus for example, in "Legend," winning "the bright logic" depends upon a process of multiplication whereby Crane "Spends out himself" repeatedly, "Twice and twice / (Again the smoking souvenir, / Bleeding eidolon!) and yet again" (*HCCP* 3).

Pater's influence on Crane comes through powerfully in the ending of "Possessions," where Crane imagines the "pure possession" in the coming of an "inclusive cloud / Whose heart is fire" and the razing, by a "white wind," of "All but bright stones wherein our smiling plays" (*HCCP* 14). These lines approximate the metaphor of the "hard, gem-like flame" with which Pater represents the condition of enduring "ecstasy": Crane inverts the emphases of Pater's trope—his "bright stones" are, as it were, hard, flame-like gems. The razing action of the "white wind" also reflects the influence of Pater, whose program for maintaining ecstasy calls for the form of purgation he called "ascesis." Ascesis is prominent in *White Buildings* generally, since it describes the process, at once sexual and poetic, by which the state of purity Crane frequently colors "white" is reached. For Crane, sexual and visionary motives are analogous, and they propel him along paths that mirror one another.[75] This convergence helps to explain why "Possessions," whose imagery is overtly sexual in its first two stanzas, turns midway through to the issues of "speech" and text. Crane's poetic career may be read through the trajectory of his sex life: in his poetry both are plotted serially and summed up (despairingly), after which Crane envisions a future state of permanent fulfillment.

The title of the poem carries both a sexual meaning—"possession" by or of another person—and a specifically imaginative one, as it was Crane's word for the state of mind in which he wrote poems:

> The actual fleshing of a concept is so complex and difficult, however, as to be quite beyond the immediate avail of will or intellect. A fusion with other factors not so easily named is the condition of fulfillment. It is alright to call this "possession", if you will, only it should not be insisted that its operation denies the simultaneous functioning of a strong critical faculty. It is simply a stronger focus than can be arbitrarily willed into operation by the ordinarily-employed perceptions. (*HCL* 240)

In this letter to Munson of April 1926, Crane stresses the point that the phenomenology of "possession"—the state of "focus" that will enable the "actual fleshing of a concept" into a poem—is one of accident, for it cannot "be arbitrarily willed into operation." The convergence of sexual and poetic meanings in "Possessions" is also present in the letter. Crane speaks earlier in it of the "life of perfect virtue" he is forced to lead in Patterson, New York, and his lament that it "doesn't seem in any way to encourage the Muse" is followed, tellingly, by the expression of his desire to come to New York City: the implication is that he might be able to encourage the Muse if, by cruising the city streets (as he does in "Possessions"), he could depart from the conventional "life of perfect virtue." The "condition" of creative "fulfillment" involves a "fusion with other factors not so easily named," and in this it resembles homosexuality, likewise "not so easily named" during an era in which it constituted criminal behavior.

Crane's defense of his "critical faculty" springs from the complex tensions—"charged with homophobia," as Hammer suggests—between Crane and the Tates, Allen and Caroline, with whom he shared a house in Patterson.[76] Tate's turn away from the visionary art he identified with Crane, as Hammer shows, was also a turn away from Crane's homosexuality. Tate thought Crane's romanticism (and his sexual orientation) was enabled by a loosening of the reins of reason: thus when Crane defends his "critical faculty," he defends his abilities against Tate's homophobic reductions. For Tate, Crane "could not possibly see things divorced from the satisfactions of [his] own ego" and thus could not distinguish his poetry from "merely moral situations." Interestingly, Tate thinks "possession" is "quite" the right word for Crane's flights of inspiration, and he therefore pays Crane's Marlovian power a compliment. But at the same time, he disdains the idea of actually feeling such a power as childish: "You have often referred to a 'demonic' possession, something like Marlowe's; that's quite all right; but you shouldn't act upon it in ordinary life, for you can't expect others to take it seriously" (*HCL* 246). Crane wrote "Possessions" before he received the note from Tate quoted above, but the opening of the poem seems to respond to Tate's injunction that he should not act "in ordinary life" on any feeling, such as "possession," if "others" could not be expected to "take it seriously." When Crane tells the reader in the first line of the poem to "Witness now this trust," he is asking his audience to take the intense experience the poem elaborates seriously—as seriously as the imagery of torment and sacrifice indicates that *he* takes it. In exchange for the "trust" he places in the reader, Crane is tacitly asking for the reader to "trust" the account the poem offers of his state of mind. Through the pun on "tryst,"[77] Crane reinforces the link between sexual and artistic aims, for it suggests that the tryst the poem's speaker searches for is related to the trust he hopes the reader will reciprocate.

The first two stanzas of the poem are preoccupied with the issue of "direction" and with the idea of the "moment" as an integer of experience:

> Witness now this trust! the rain
> That steals softly direction
> And the key, ready to hand—sifting
> One moment in sacrifice (the direst)
> Through a thousand nights the flesh
> Assaults outright for bolts that linger
> Hidden,—O undirected as the sky
> That through its black foam has no eyes
> For this fixed stone of lust . . .
>
> Accumulate such moments to an hour:
> Account the total of this trembling tabulation.
> I know the screen, the distant flying taps
> And stabbing medley that sways—
> And the mercy, feminine, that stays
> As though prepared.

As I have previously suggested, "direction" is a key term in Crane's thinking about his path. The desperate tone of these lines shows the importance of career for Crane—to have it stolen, to be "undirected," is a matter of grave importance, for it reflects his confidence in his visionary powers and his hope for recognition. This lack of direction is related to the difficulty of imagining career as a continuous, unified whole. Crane's compulsion to revise the romantic myth of production as it was formulated by Pater may be glimpsed here in his projection of another realm—on the other side of the threshold he stands poised upon with his "key, ready to hand," on the other side of "the screen"—in which such moments resolve into "One moment." As for Pater, the "infinite divisibility" of experience is the heart of the problem, and thus "One moment" fractures into many lightening-like "bolts" as it is "sift[ed]" through the "thousand nights" of a life. Such "bolts" seem to take on duration only in a "hidden" domain. Yet in each bolt is a clue that it constitutes part of a greater whole, for the "mercy" felt in its aftermath "stays / As though prepared."[78]

The certainty that someday the "pure possession" will come, which Crane voices at the end of the poem, is founded on the intimations his impure possessions afford him that such an integral moment exists. But in the meantime he must endure his unfulfilled desires, for his attempt at crossing that threshold lands him not in that realm in which time is made whole, but back in "Bleecker Street":

> And I, entering, take up the stone
> As quiet as you can make a man . . .
> In Bleecker Street, still trenchant in a void,
> Wounded by apprehensions out of speech,
> I hold it up against a disk of light—
> I, turning, turning on smoked forking spires,
> The city's stubborn lives, desires.

Though Crane may have the "key, ready to hand," his attempt at "entering" leaves him "still trenchant in a void." That this result has to do with his inability to transcend time is suggested by the image of the stone held "up against a disk of light," which approximates the face of a clock—a connection his "turning" and "turning" in the next line reinforces.[79]

The correspondence between Crane's poetic career and the trajectory of his sex life—registered here in the apposite relation between "lives" and "desires"—is reinforced in the last stanza of the poem:

> Tossed on these horns, who bleeding dies,
> Lacks all but piteous admissions to be spilt
> Upon the page whose blind sum finally burns
> Record of rage and partial appetites.

> The pure possession, the inclusive cloud
> Whose heart is fire shall come,—the white wind rase
> All but bright stones wherein our smiling plays.

The "page" is a synecdoche for Crane's oeuvre, and the part-for-whole sub-stitution conveys his sense that his work cannot exist as a whole, only as an indeterminate assemblage of parts. This despairing thought about the fragmentation of his career is reflected in the thought about unfulfilled physical desires captured in the phrase "partial appetites." The stanza turns abruptly from these "piteous admissions" to project a future in terms that allude, as I have already suggested, to Pater's "hard, gem-like flame," and thus represent a recuperation of the possibility of unity between the moments of "possession" that structure Crane's vocational and sexual tra-jectories. The very abruptness of this turn is itself noteworthy: it is as if Crane's trust in the coming of "the pure possession" depends upon his confession "of rage and partial appetites," which yield a "blind sum" rather than the "multiplied consciousness" Pater calls for. The transition replays in miniature the movement of reversal that determines Crane's "direction" from the start.

"Legend" resonates with "Possessions" in several ways, but Crane's de-sire to project a unified career is expressed still more explicitly in "Leg-end": the "bright stones" of "Possessions," for example, reappear as the "bright logic" to which Crane looks forward in the later poem (*HCCP* 3). As Alfred Hanley puts it, "'Legend' is the poet's manifesto of his conse-cration to the visionary and a declaration of the course to be taken."[80] The urgency with which Crane plots his "course" comes across in the title—a near-synonym for "career" that imbues the idea of a way of life with a sense of drama and risk—as well as in the placement of the poem: "Leg-end" introduces the idea of the normative career at its very beginning, boldly declaring both his high ambitions and his confidence in his ability to achieve them in the opening poem of his first book.

Alan Trachtenberg points out that the "earliest meanings" of "legend" "included 'the exemplary biography of a saint,'"[81] a meaning which Crane was surely mindful of (especially given his use of the word "Legende" for an uncollected poem of 1919), and which reflects the orderliness of the spiritually inflected career Crane sought to project. It suggests that his path will follow that of an "exemplary" model, a course already marked out, just as, in turn, it will serve as a model to future poets once it is com-plete. That orderliness is reflected in the poem's symmetry. The idea of a "silent" belief in a "mirror" that occurs in the first stanza is itself mirrored in the "Unwhispering" belief in a "mirror" mentioned toward the end of the poem. The "white falling flakes" in the second stanza reappear as the "caustic drop[s]" of the last. And as Trachtenberg notes, "the formality of stanzas one and five frame this poem," and " 'cry' recovers the suspended rhyme 'by' in line two."[82] This symmetry highlights the reversal in the poem by which the "silence" of the first stanza is metamorphosed into the "cry" of the last, a movement that dramatizes both a passage into poetry and the confirmation of poetic calling.

Pater's description of the predicament of solipsism in the "Conclusion" provides a relevant context for the opening of "Legend":

> Experience, already reduced to a group of impressions, is ringed round for each of us by that thick wall of personality through which no real voice has ever pierced on its way to us, or from us to that which we can only conjecture to be without. Every one of those impressions is the impression of the individual in his isolation, each mind keeping as a solitary prisoner its own dream of a world.[83]

The first stanza of "Legend" portrays the very silence and solitude that Pater describes: "As silent as a mirror is believed / Realities plunge in silence by." The plural term "Realities" unsettles the idea that any one reality is absolute, an idea in keeping with Pater's sense that "the individual" only knows a "dream of the world." It is this passive condition, watching "Realities plunge in silence by," which Crane imagines overcoming in the poem; thus he would "step," as if out of Plato's cave, "into the noon." That crucial "step" is contingent upon Crane's ability to break the "silence" by which he is confined in the first stanza, a silence that reflects the internalization of a moral code that required homosexuality to be repented and regretted. Thus Crane announces in the second stanza that he is "not ready for repentance; / Nor to match regrets." Breaking away from the solipsism of the mirror-world evoked in the first stanza, Crane is also breaking away from the "homosexual despair," according to Hammer, that "he associated with Aestheticism":[84] "Legend" inscribes a career narrative in which Crane's self-acceptance as a homosexual and his self-authorization as a poet coincide. The escape from confinement enables the drastic change imaged in the self-immolation of a "moth" in a "flame."

The communion Crane enjoys with the world from which he had previously been separated by a "thick wall of personality" is represented in "kisses" that are also poems: "And tremorous / In the white falling flakes / Kisses are,— / The only worth all granting." The "white falling flakes" bear the kind of excess of meaning one expects from Crane's characteristically dense language. They represent the ashes of the dead moth. They serve as a metaphor for "kisses." And they are the poems through which Crane communes with his audience—"white" like sheets of paper (and, of course, like "white buildings") and "falling" like "drop[s]" (which is one of Crane's words for his poems).[85] "Flakes" also fits a description of Crane's poems, for flaking is an action he associates with dissemination, as Bloom's remarks on "Repose of Rivers" suggest: in that poem Crane hears "wind flaking sapphire," which Bloom interprets as the "breaking up," as well as the distribution, of "the Shelleyan azure of vision."[86]

In the first two stanzas of "Legend" Crane presents pivotal movements from solitude to communion and from silence to speech. In the remaining three stanzas he departs from the present tense, first-person account of that transformation to elaborate the career logic that it initiates. Crane did not like to think of himself as a "professional," as his irritated response to Edmund Wilson's "advice" to poets like Crane not to be "so 'professional'" suggests.[87] But Crane's articulation of the poetic career appears to be steeped in the ideology of professionalism, as the second movement of "Legend" shows, a fact that clarifies the meanings inscribed in the unified path for Crane even as it points up the pervasiveness of professionalist ideology during the time Crane, Moore, and Stevens made their debuts:

> It is to be learned—
> This cleaving and this burning.
> But only by the one who
> Spends out himself again.
>
> Twice and twice
> (Again the smoking souvenir,
> Bleeding eidolon!) and yet again.
> Until the bright logic is won
> Unwhispering as a mirror
> Is believed.
>
> Then, drop by caustic drop, a perfect cry
> Shall string some constant harmony,—
> Relentless caper for all those who step
> The legend of their youth into the noon.

The most salient correspondence between the vision Crane espouses here and the ideology of professionalism has to do with his interest in construing "this cleaving and this burning" as activities that might be converted, through "learn[ing]," into expertise. The main instrument of professional advancement is the ability to perform "a cognitive activity that is esoteric, yet formalized and standardized enough to be, in principle, accessible to all who would undergo prolonged training," as Larson observes.[88] The "training" regimen Crane outlines here is nothing if not "prolonged": he calls for a program of repeated self-expenditure ("Twice and twice," "again" and "again") that parallels that of the professional, who sacrifices immediate gratification so as to invest the self (rather than capital) in the process of winning what Crane calls "the bright logic"—the "esoteric" knowledge on which professional authority is based.[89] The democratic and elitist elements Larson finds characteristic of professionalism are present in "Legend" in the contradictory emphases Crane puts on the accessibility of professional work: the rewards of career are open to "all those who step / The legend of their youth into the noon," and yet Crane stresses that the "bright logic" may be "won" "only by the one" capable of the particular sacrifices he describes.[90] And it is of course in keeping with a specifically professional notion of career that its unity should come into being following a successful period of education, and that it should enable a sense of solidarity with other members of the profession: thus at last he imagines each of his poems, those "caustic drop[s]," as part of a "perfect cry," and that cry, in turn, as part of "some constant harmony" that blends Crane's cry with those of fellow poets.

That Crane's claim about mastery is so counterintuitive—how to learn experiences that would entail the obliteration of the self that would learn them?—signals the urgency of his desire to construe his life as a coherent narrative of development, since the formalization and standardization of "learn[ing]" is a key precondition of the continuity of the professional career. Insofar as career and character are two sides of the same coin, as Bledstein claims, the continuity of the professional career held special significance for Crane, whose homosexuality repeatedly opened him (and his poetry) to the charge of incompleteness.[91] The career he projects in "Legend" symbolizes, then, a counterargument against the view that homosexuality entailed a failure to progress to full maturity, a divided self, and a poetry marred by irrationality and discontinuity. At the same time, career embodies the visionary motive that, as Allen Grossman argues, Crane refused to renounce, in defiance of examples set by poets such as Yeats and Eliot:

At about the time of Crane's birth Yeats, to take the salient case, decisively redefined the idealist poetic enterprise that he had brought to high finish (but not to completion) in *The Wind Among the Reeds* (1899), and in so doing passed judgment on the poetic task that Crane was compelled to labor at in the next generation. Yeats' ironic distancing (as in "Adam's Curse" [1901]) of his own death-bound early ambition . . . made Yeats as a poetic speaker the audience and interpreter, in effect, of his own early motive, and announced that ironization of questioning that Eliot identified for his generation in the allusive poetics of "The Love Song of J. Alfred Prufrock" as the mark of high modern structural innovation in poetry.[92]

Crane's refusal to move forward by passing judgment on his "early ambition," as Yeats had, is implicit in the connection he draws between the "idealist poetic enterprise" represented by the achievement of a "constant harmony" and the willingness of aspiring poets to "step / The legend of their youth into the noon." The realization of high ambitions depends on the transfer of the "legend" of "youth"—the "mythology of self" (to borrow Stevens's phrase) at its most grand, prior to any revisions made in light of obstacles or failures—"into the noon," which is a figure for artistic maturity.

Crane's doubts about achieving such a career are encoded in the poem in a number of ways. The deferral of the unity of the career ("Shall string"), and even of the training necessary for it ("It is to be learned"), are only the most obvious signs of his uncertainty. He emphasizes the difficulties attendant upon a "perfect" mastery of activities that seem to hold meaning only as ongoing processes by linking them through a slant rhyme, "learned" / "burning," that highlights their incompatibility as a difference of verb tense. It seems telling that at the very point of transition where the repetitions end in "bright logic," Crane brings the sentence to a full stop (after "again") that stresses the failure to articulate the logic by which training yields mastery. In the final stanza Crane declares his skepticism almost openly. There he refers to the whole process—by which mastery is attained, the "perfect cry" uttered, and the "constant harmony" strung—as a "Relentless caper," thereby reducing the whole project to a prank that represents the antithesis of the ethos of professionalism.[93] As I have been suggesting, his skepticism proceeds not from a doubt in his own abilities, nor from a sense that Tate or Winters were right to think of his homosexuality as a personal or poetic flaw, but rather from the conflict between the ideal unity of the poetic career and the disparate moments that sponsor it.

Those moments issue in poems that are produced "drop by caustic drop"—
that is, in a broken sequence. True to the visionary motives inscribed in the
"legend" of his "youth," Crane persists in attempting to restore that sequence as a unity projected in the future—a "perfect cry." True also to the
moments that inspire that vision, Crane's poems reflect the dividedness of
his experience, as that ideal future seems never to arrive except "at odd
moments," as he once put it to Munson, "and rare!" The meanings in the
title of the poem reflect Crane's awareness of the double nature of the personal path—its absurdity as well as its value. It is a tall tale, a story about
development from which authority is derived, and therefore prone to exag-
geration. At the same time, it evidences aspirations—growth and unity,
both of the self and of the greater human community—whose nobility, for
Crane, seemed to redeem whatever failures his commitment to them
entailed.

2

"Poets of the First Book, Writers of Promise"

Beginning in the Era of the First-Book Prize

> Many young poets, nowadays, are insured against everything.
> For them poetry is a game like court tennis or squash racquets—
> one they learned at college—and they play it with propriety, as part
> of their social and academic existence; their poems are occasional
> verse for which life itself is only one more occasion.
>
> —Randall Jarrell, "Recent Poetry"

Randall Jarrell's disparaging remarks reflect what was in 1955 a growing consensus among critics that while the teaching of poetry in colleges and universities opened up new opportunities to learn the art and earn a living, it also put the authenticity of the vocation of "many young poets" in question. The post-1945 proliferation of first-book prizes for poetry made launching a career without turning life into "one more occasion" for improving one's "social and academic existence" still more difficult. "When the author is a university man," writes Harvey Shapiro in a 1962 review, "... it may be that his first book can have little organic life because it represents mainly a claim to advancement in the academy."[1] How to hold on to the "organic life" when debuts were often seen as stepping stones to academic "advancement," and the normative career was increasingly likely to be stamped on it from the start in the form of a first-book award?

This impasse can be seen to descend from the impasse confronted by the modernist poets I discussed in the last chapter. The consolidation of the culture of professionalism at the turn of the twentieth century exacerbated the predicament of poets seeking fresh strategies of self-definition in the wake of the enormously popular and critically acclaimed Fireside group.

As a result, representations of career in *Harmonium, Observations,* and *White Buildings,* among other modernist poetic debuts, tended toward complication: making it "new"—not just in first books of poetry, but in modernist literature in general—seemed to necessitate making it "difficult." The challenges of understanding the kind of poetry that often wore its difficulty on its sleeve helped to supply the impetus for the development of the New Criticism and its accession to the post-1945 university. Through close reading, the New Critics promoted a method of arduous explication specially adapted to the conspicuous complexities of modernist poetry. Furthermore, as Gerald Graff explains, the method "seemed systematic and could easily be replicated" in the classroom, thus answering the need "for a simplified pedagogy" at a time when the system of higher education was undergoing rapid expansion.[2] The quasi-scientific objectivity of the New Criticism provided a necessary condition for the growth of literary-prize culture by nurturing the notion that poetry, like "court tennis or squash racquets," could be "learned at college" and rationally evaluated by properly credentialed experts.

Accounts of the period often explore questions of career and careerism by focusing on the evolution of poetic style over a series of books. That evolution is described on the model of the "breakthrough narrative," epitomized by Robert Lowell's career and allegorized in his *Life Studies* (1959): "[T]he volume begins," James Longenbach states, "with formal poems that recall the high-church values of Lowell's earlier work, moving on to the free verse anxieties of poems about his family and mental collapses." As Longenbach goes on to explain, partisans of the breakthrough narrative "agree that a great deal of cultural weight depends on the choice of poetic form": freer verse forms are taken to evoke an anti-establishment stance, while traditional meters and regular rhyme schemes suggest a willingness to give up the organic life for mere (school-taught) virtuosity in order to expedite progress on the tenure track.[3] Longenbach follows Langdon Hammer in developing a critique of the "breakthrough narrative," noting, for instance, that it oversimplifies the shapes of poetic careers by obscuring their continuities, and that the "easy confluence of formal and social vision" it assumes is undermined by "the rhetoricity of all poetic forms, however 'open' or 'closed' we imagine them to be."[4]

The breakthrough narrative is predicated on the division between margin and mainstream, outside and inside, raw and cooked, which has governed critical discussion of post-1945 verse. Woven into studies by a host of critics including not only Longenbach and Hammer but also Christopher Beach, Paul Breslin, Michael Davidson, Alan Golding, and Libbie Rifkin, among many others, this scheme provides a convenient way of mapping the values, norms, and practices that inform American poetry during the 1950s and '60s.[5] If the inside is generally aligned in this discourse with conformity, the school, formalism, *The New Poets of England and America* (1957), and the East Coast, the outside is aligned with revolt; the gallery, café, or bookstore; experimentalism; *The New American Poetry* (1960); and the West Coast. In their different ways critics have shown how these distinctions collapse, so that, for instance, as the title of Golding's book suggests, the cultural outsider is eventually absorbed by the establishment as his or her work passes from "outlaw to classic." The prevailing approach to complicating this binary system of classification has been to expose the establishment ethos of ostensibly anti-establishment groups such as the Black Mountain poets, the Beats, and the Language poets, in an effort to offer a demystified appreciation of them.[6] Legible here is an implicit assumption that, while we need to revise our understanding of countercultural poetry in its myriad forms by calling its claims to disinterestedness into question, the mainstream poetry of the post-1945 period is just as unequivocally accommodating of institutional norms and procedures as it appears to be in the context of the neat opposition between margin and mainstream. I seek to challenge that assumption by illuminating the ways in which the "official verse culture" is at once constituted, interrogated, and resisted by the very poets who appear to comprise it.[7] In this chapter my primary focus is on mainstream first books of the 1950s and '60s, but I conclude with a survey of leadoff poems from various countercultural debuts, together with a glance at first books in general from the 1970s and '80s—the moment when, according to Jed Rasula, "the bifurcation of the poetry world into square versus hip, official versus renegade, metropolitan versus provincial, was rapidly eroding."[8] In doing so I aim to reinforce the idea that many beginning poets on both sides of the divide grapple in interesting, and interestingly similar, ways with the problem of vocational integrity at a moment so dominated by institutional literary practice that opposition to it is often indistinguishable from the central forms it takes.[9]

In this way I follow Mark McGurl in reevaluating the work produced during what he calls the "program era." Arguing that the emergence of creative writing programs "stands as the most important event in postwar American literary history, and that paying attention to the increasingly intimate relation between literary production and the practices of higher education is the key" to understanding the literature of the period, McGurl suggests that the "image of 'system' as a gray plain of deathly regularity" belies the richness and variety of the literary work that has come out of it.[10] Writing against the grain of a half century of bad press for the university-based literary scene, he offers a fresh appreciation of the "aesthetic-institutional totality" that dominates the literary landscape while also laying the foundation for "studies that take the rise and spread of the creative writing program not as an occasion for praise or lamentation but as an established fact in need of historical interpretation."[11] In this chapter I build on McGurl's study, which deals exclusively with post-1945 American fiction, by concentrating instead on poetry. In doing so, and by focusing on debut poets, I analyze a body of work subject to a maximum degree of pressure to "get with the program," as McGurl puts it, since as he notes, the teaching, reading, writing, and publication of poetry, even more than fiction, "has been all but entirely absorbed by institutions of higher education."[12]

In what follows I sketch the emergence of first-book prizes and their impact on poets' sense of vocation as it is reflected not in the stylistic changes that ostensibly characterize the poetic career as it unfolds, but rather in how career is thematized in the poetry itself. Instead of looking again at poetic form as the decisive indicator of a poet's capitulation or resistance to the establishment, I examine representations of career in first books of poetry, since it is through these representations that poets were responding to the increasingly professionalized academic culture of which debut prizes are a characteristic expression. Writ large in the dozen or so titles I quoted in the introduction, the rampant emphasis on beginning in poetic debuts during the era of the first-book prize reflects poets' willingness to contend with— rather than simply submit to—the crisis of vocation brought about by the new conditions under which they were writing. I argue that if poets' willingness to position themselves as beginners signifies a willingness to accommodate a culture of professionalism that demanded regular development from the start, it must also be read as a strategy of defense, for beginners are also amateurs still living the organic life the normative academic career threatened to replace.

Sylvia Plath's letters and journals provide an instructive example of the degree to which writing and winning went hand in hand for poets coming of age in the university-based literary scene during the 1950s and '60s. Plath grew up winning prizes. Her many honors—for academic achievements, art work, and most frequently for writing—marked her progress as a professional, delineating a career path which began, by her own account, in 1941, the year she published a couplet in the *Boston Sunday Herald*. "I wrote my first poem, my first published poem," she told the BBC in 1962, "when I was eight and half years old. It came out in the Boston [*Herald*], and from then on, I suppose, I've been a bit of a professional."[13] While a rising senior at Smith College, she wrote in her journal of her "fear of failing to live up to the fast & furious prize-winning pace of these last years" (*UJSP* 187). Her pace had indeed been "fast & furious." She won two Wellesley Awards for most outstanding student while in middle school, commendations for straight As and perfect attendance, and even a "sixth academic letter, an award never before given, for 'being the only pupil in the history of the school who had earned enough credits for a sixth letter.'"[14] Her high school honors, which included honorable mention and publication in the *Atlantic Monthly*, helped her to gain admission to Smith College, where the trend continued: she twice placed among the winners of the annual *Seventeen* fiction contest, took a $500 first prize in the 1952 *Mademoiselle* fiction competition, and was chosen to serve on the *Mademoiselle* College Board. In the letter I discussed in the introduction, Plath tallies up—so her mother would "remember it all"—"a list of the prizes and writing awards for this year" that included eleven different honors and the money earned from each, ranging from Smith College prizes such as the Marjorie Hope Nicholson Prize for her thesis to intercollegiate awards like the prestigious Glascock Prize for poetry. The list points up the degree to which appearing in print carried a sense of competitive triumph for Plath, since several items on the list—an *"Alumnae Quarterly* article on Alfred Kazin," for instance—do not refer to "prizes" or "writing awards" really, but simply to works she had managed to publish (*LH* 176).

Prizes were so important to Plath's sense of her developing literary career that when the "fast & furious" pace slowed during her first semester of graduate school at Cambridge University, she felt lost, as the path before her trailed off in several different "directions." "Gone is the simple college cycle of winning prizes, and here is the more complex, less clear-cut arena of life," she wrote to Olive Higgins Prouty in December 1955, "where there is no single definite aim, but a complex degree of aims, with no prizes to tell you you've done well." Plath struggled to accustom herself to life in this new "arena." Farther on in the letter to Prouty she describes her "increasing awareness" of the need to face "tragedy and conflict" head-on, a process of maturation for which "one doesn't get prizes" and which is therefore all the more difficult to accomplish. She wrote to her mother the following day of her failure to win a Borestone Mountain Poetry Award: "With the return of my Borestone Mountain manuscript, all my pigeons are home to roost. Gone are the days where I got prizes for everything. This mature-market competition demands constant writing, so instead of waiting for a whole bulk of time, which I come to rusty and paralytic, I am going to do an hour or two every day, like Czerny exercises on the piano" (*LH* 202–3).

The increasingly intense "mature-market competition" is identified here with what critics have begun to call "prize culture"—a term for the values, norms, practices, and various kinds of capital that make up the cultural awards industry, which grew rapidly after World War II.[15] Plath's letter illustrates how prize culture promotes literary professionalism: sensing that her natural talent will not be enough to net prizes in this competitive market, she vows to give up her habit of "waiting" for inspiration to strike and adopts instead the discipline of writing daily. The new level of professionalism that the prize-focused literary market demanded of Plath is nowhere more evident than in her indefatigable efforts to publish her poetic debut. As Peter Davison notes in his review of *The Yale Younger Poets Anthology*, "Sylvia Plath . . . unsuccessfully sent her poems to book publishers no fewer than seven times before she turned twenty-six."[16] Her letters and journals reflect her particular concern with making a debut by winning a first-book contest: as she wrote in June 1959, "my book needs a prize to sell it" (*UJSP* 497).

It was not only an interest in boosting sales of her debut that fueled Plath's interest in first-book prizes, but also an interest in winning access to the prestigious career that so many of the people she knew had begun. When one considers the number of first-book prizewinners in her circle of acquaintance, her obsession with winning one seems less eccentric. Even a list limited to those she mentions in her journal and correspondence gives the impression that she was virtually surrounded by winners of the Yale Series of Younger Poets Award, the Lamont Prize, and other first-book honors. There was Paul Engle, winner of the Yale award in 1932, who was introduced to Plath while she was a guest editor at *Mademoiselle*. There was W. S. Merwin, winner of the Yale award in 1952, whose study both Plath and Ted Hughes used while they lived in England. (Merwin and his wife Dido were the godparents of the Hughes's daughter Frieda Rebecca.) She was married to a first-book prizewinner in Hughes, whose *The Hawk in the Rain* won the award of the Poetry Center at the 92nd Street Y and was published by Harper's in 1956. Philip Booth won the 1956 Lamont Poetry Prize, and Adrienne Rich the 1951 Yale award; Plath met both poets at Hughes's reading at Harvard University in 1958. While auditing Robert Lowell's poetry seminar at Boston University in 1959, she met George Starbuck, who won the Yale award in 1960, much to Plath's chagrin. Also worth noting in this context are W. H. Auden and Davison. Auden visited Smith during his tenure as editor of the Yale Series and sat in on the modern poetry seminar Plath was taking, met with her for an interview, and read some of her poems (he recommended that she work on her verbs).[17] Davison, who went on to win the Yale award in 1964, dated her in 1955 and corresponded with her throughout the later 1950s and early '60s.

Davison states that by 1957, "when Sylvia Plath began sending out *The Colossus*, the Yale Series of Younger Poets (then edited by W. H. Auden) was the destination she coveted. She struck out twice."[18] Actually, Plath "struck out" three times—in 1957, 1959, and 1960. And it is incorrect to say that she sent out *The Colossus* in 1957: Auden rejected a collection called *Two Lovers and a Beachcomber*; Dudley Fitts, Auden's successor, rejected *The Bull of Bendylaw* in 1959 and *The Colossus* in 1960 (*UJSP* 689, 492).[19] The changes in title are important not only as matters of fact, but also because they highlight Plath's willingness to adapt herself to her chosen market by repeatedly revising her first book, rather than striving to publish it in its original form. *The Colossus and Other Poems* was eventually published by Heinemann in England in 1960 (and two years later, reduced by several poems, including "Metaphors," "Black Rook in Rainy Weather," "Maudlin," "Ouija," and sections one, two, three, four, and six of "Poem for a Birthday," by Knopf in the United States). Written in 1959, "The Colossus" captures Plath's sense of chagrin. Like the figure that the speaker has labored long and hard to assemble and maintain, the book named after it went through a process of repeated reconstruction through which Plath tried to resolve a "barnyard" cacophony into an integral music:

> I shall never get you put together entirely,
> Pieced, glued, and properly jointed.
> Mule-bray, pig-grunt and bawdy cackles
> Proceed from your great lips.
> It's worse than a barnyard.[20]

Plath mentions the Yale award in a letter to her mother that resonates with the remarks quoted in my epigraph: "I am turning out five poems a week, and they get better and better. I hope to write a lot this summer and try to get a little book of them into print in about a year: think I'll try out for the Yale Series of Younger Poets. Just for fun" (*LH* 164). Plath's professionalism is evident here in her sense of steady improvement, certainty of publication, and display of disinterestedness. That the Yale Series is something she plans to "try out" for suggests that for Plath (as for Jarrell) the competition is comparable to an extracurricular activity, like crew, which she mentions a plan to "go out for" in the same letter. Even her misgivings about her chances derive from a professional perspective: "Of course, I really don't think I have a chance [for the Yale award], as most [of the poems] are in that limbo between experimental art of the little magazines and the sophisticated wit of *The New Yorker*, too much of the other for either. But I shall try" (*LH* 172). Tellingly, in her assessment, the weakness of her manuscript has less to do with the quality of the poems in it than with its unity, viewed here as a function of its suitability to a particular market.

Plath did not "try out" for "the Yales" (as she commonly referred to the award) until 1957, when Auden, who was one of the three judges to give Hughes the Poetry Center first book prize in 1956, rejected *Two Lovers and a Beachcomber*. Her response to the news that he had won—"I can hardly wait to see the letter of award and learn details of publication. To smell the print off the pages!" (*LH* 270)—is as ecstatic as her response to her own loss is miserable:[21]

> Yesterday, the rejection of my poetry book, after an almost malicious false alarm from mother, and after half a year of hoping and yes, even counting on the damn thing. It was like receiving back the body of a cancerous lover whom you hoped dead, safely, at the morgue, in a wreath of flowers to commemorate the past.
>
> It Came Back. And with the misery of knowing half of the poems, published ones, weren't any longer, or in two years would definitely not be, passable in myself because of their bland ladylike archness or slightness. And I become linked to the damned book again, weeding it out like an overgrown garden. . . . And if A. C. Rich wasn't so dull, and Donald Hall so dull, and they putting in a hundred pages of dull published poems, I wouldn't feel so lousy. It would have backed me up at Smith in my work, given me that toehold on my adult work instead of making me go on from a five year gap, and only 16 poems published in the last year. (*UJSP* 294–95)

Plath's professionalism manifests itself again as an assurance of success, and it exacerbates the rejection: that she was "counting on the damn thing" makes the news a bigger, more upsetting surprise. The passage elucidates her concern with making progress in her career, which is why the fact that "It Came Back," that she is "linked to the damned book again," and that she must begin "weeding it out like an overgrown garden" (which anticipates the image of "weedy acres" that need tending in "The Colossus"), is especially distressing. The strategy of categorizing some poems as "second book poem[s]" even though her first book had not yet been published, which she practiced on Hughes's recommendation in 1959, illustrates a related interest in the solace available even through hypothetical career advancement (*UJSP* 526). What comes across most strongly here is Plath's high level of competitiveness, evident not only in the gothic description of her rejected manuscript, but also in her negative appraisals of Rich and Hall, previous winners of the Yale and the Lamont awards, respectively.

That prize culture encourages professionalism should not be a surprise, given the extent of the homology between them: both privilege merit and autonomy in conjunction with the idea of a developing career. Plath's repeated submissions to the Yale prize, for example, reflect her confidence that her superior merit—embodied in and verified by her previous honors—must one day be recognized: "Last night I mentally composed a letter to Dudley Fitts about sending my book to the Yales again. Sure I'd win, of course" (*UJSP* 510). Part of the reason she could place such a ready trust in Fitts to recognize her was that he was also a poet (and translator of poetry). Prize culture serves to reinforce the idea that poetry is an autonomous field of cultural activity whose standards can only be upheld by a credentialed expert—the contest judge. As James English observes, a prize "can be a nodal point for communitarian identification and pride, a means of positing an 'us' and an 'our' around which to rally some group of individuals, as well as a means of raising the status of that self-avowed community within the symbolic economy of all such groups."[22] This is particularly true of first-book honors, which typically give special prominence to the role of the poet-judge and invoke the "communitarian identity" English speaks of by offering membership in a "series." In the case of a first-book prize like the Yale award, the judge is required to write an introduction to the winning volume, thereby dramatizing the assumption that a poet's initial effort is mysterious enough for the lay reader to require expert mediation.

Prize culture, like professionalism, privileges the notion of career, which, as the award-studded summary of almost any post-1945 poet's writing life will show, is conventionally construed as a sequence of honors. The first-book prize evokes career directly, formalizing the moment of entry into a public writing life. It also raises the prospect of subsequent publications, and so evokes by a kind of synecdoche the prestige, drama, and security of the career as a whole, which it projects as a course of systematic progress. Judging by the success of the Yale winners, attaining that reward appeared to be virtually assured by winning a first-book prize. Remarkably, there was not a single winner of the Yale contest between 1950 and 1970 who did not go on to publish a second book; except for Helen Chase, the winner in 1968, all of the winning poets went on to multiple post-Yale publications, and, in most cases, long stays on university faculties. As Louis Simpson's remarks in a 1957 review suggest, the first-book prizewinner resembles nothing so much as a professional who has just passed the examination that assures her of a career: "We have many poets of the First Book, writers of promise" who, having "passed" the "first barrier" with favorable reviews, pass "beyond criticism, and also, unfortunately, beyond editing."[23] Whether we view the extraordinary success of the winners as a result of the tendency of "symbolic riches to beget symbolic riches," as English observes, or as a result of the judges' editorial genius, the important element in this scenario is that the prize appeared to Plath and other poets of her generation to virtually guarantee a highly sought-after writing life.

But it was not just the Yale award, newly prestigious during the Auden years, that prompted Plath and many poets of her generation to pursue a first-book prize with such doggedness and discipline. First-book prizes proliferated during the middle decades of the century and took on a prominent role in the literary culture as a whole. The Yale Younger Poets Series was founded in 1919. The reputation of the series grew substantially under the editorship of Stephen Vincent Benét, who took over in 1933 and went on to make some of the first notable selections in the series—James Agee's *Permit Me Voyage*, Muriel Rukeyser's *Theory of Flight*, and Margaret Walker's *For My People*, which was published in 1942 and has never been out of print. Archibald MacLeish succeeded Benét and edited the series for three years, from 1944 to 1946, after which W. H. Auden became editor and made the selections—Adrienne Rich, Merwin, John Ashbery, James Wright, and John Hollander, among others—on which the current prestige of the series still depends.

It was during Auden's tenure that the series spawned its first notable imitator—Alan Swallow's New Poetry Series, based in Denver, Colorado, which was started in 1949. Swallow brought out one to four first books each year, many of which were reviewed side by side in major publications with winners of the Yale award; Edgar Bowers and Harvey Shapiro were among the notable poets to make their debuts as part of the New Poetry Series. Twayne Publishers initiated its Modern Poetry Series in conjunction with a first-book contest in 1949, the same year the company was launched.[24] The contest was successful enough that by its second year it drew three hundred entries. The series featured introductions by such figures as F. O. Matthiessen and MacLeish; Theodore Weiss debuted as a Twayne poet with *The Catch*, published in 1951. The Lamont Poetry Prize, sponsored by the Academy of American Poets, was instituted in 1954. The all-star panel of judges for the first annual contest, which included Louise Bogan, May Sarton, Mark Van Doren, Rolfe Humphries, and Jarrell, helped boost the prize's publicity. When the Academy initiated the Walt Whitman Award for a first book of poetry in 1975, the Lamont became a second-book award (recently it was renamed the James McLaughlin Award), but by then it had already launched the careers of Donald Hall, Donald Justice, X. J. Kennedy, and Marvin Bell. The Poets of Today Series was also initiated in 1954. Published annually by Scribner in omnibus volumes, the series introduced May Swenson, Louis Simpson, Robert Pack, and James Dickey, among others.[25] In addition, there was the First Publication Award of the Poetry Center of the 92nd Street Y, which launched the careers of Hughes and, in 1963 (as the Helen Burlin Memorial Award of the Poetry Center at the Y), of Frederick Seidel.

The Yale Series also prompted a number of university presses to follow suit by developing poetry series of their own. Just as poets began to move into the university during the middle decades of the century, so, to a large extent, did the publication of poetry. Indiana University Press announced plans to publish its poetry series, to be edited by poet-professor Samuel Yellen, in April 1953.[26] Wesleyan University, the University of Massachusetts, Louisiana State University, and the University of Pittsburgh initiated similar series in 1958, 1962, 1964, and 1968, respectively. Of these, only the University of Pittsburgh series provided—through its United States Award—a vehicle designed solely for poetic debuts, but as George Bradley remarks, while the other series "have not confined themselves to printing first books . . . neither have they avoided them."[27] In fact, these series had reputations for being particularly receptive to manuscripts from previously unpublished poets. The original plan for the Indiana series, for instance, called for the publication of sixteen books over the course of four years; of these, four were debuts, and they came out, much like contest winners, at the rate of one per year from 1953–56.[28] Early titles in the Wesleyan series included such major first books as Donald Justice's Lamont Prize-winning *Summer Anniversaries* (1960) and Richard Howard's *Quantities* (1962). More than half of the volumes of poetry brought out by the University of Massachusetts Press during the 1960s were debut collections. (As Bruce Wilcox, who recently retired after thirty-two years as editorial director, explained, the early interest of the University of Massachusetts Press in bringing new poets to light eventually crystallized in the creation of the prestigious Juniper Prize, a first-book award, in 1976.)[29] Similarly, three quarters of the poetry list of the Louisiana State University Press during the 1960s consisted of first books, including notable poetic debuts by Miller Williams (1964), Joyce Carol Oates (1969), and Stanley Plumly (1970).

Even before they had acquired much standing on the basis of the quality of the selections themselves, first-book prizes and series enjoyed significant media attention. In part, this was a result of the idea that they performed a service noble enough to warrant special praise. The critical attention that a debut received was in this way compounded: the need to applaud the cultural goodwill of the prize sponsor or the series could supply an occasion for a review even if the poetic merit of the volume did not. The institutions that sponsored first-book prizes and poetry series were routinely commended for prioritizing art over profits, since larger publishing houses seemed less and less inclined to do so. "The young poet's real difficulties begin when he feels himself ready for book publication," wrote J. Donald Adams in the *New York Times* in 1953. "Every publisher worthy of his profession would like to publish some good poetry, but only the sale of prose makes that possible. . . . And so most young poets, good or bad, must either turn to the vanity firms and pay at least part of the costs, or else surrender the dream." Adams portrays the Yale Series as the heroic exception to the rule—"We need, and badly, more projects like the Yale Series of Younger Poets"—and goes on to sketch the history of the series, including its original mission, its distinguished winners, and its judges.[30]

Adams set the tone for later commentators. Reviews in *Poetry*, the *New York Times*, and the *Chicago Daily Tribune* during the 1950s show virtually all of the series and prizes being commended both singly and en masse. Eda Lou Walton, for example, wrote in a similar vein in *Poetry*: "In these days when the established publishers reject poetry because of the high cost of printing, smaller presses like the Hand and Flower in England, the Indiana University Press, Alan Swallow of Denver, and the Yale press are the only sources from which we obtain the work of the lesser known poets."[31] Yale prize winner Merwin ended his review in the *Times* of Ted Hughes's *The Hawk in the Rain* with a paragraph-long commendation of the Poetry Center prize for making the publication of his friend's book possible.[32] Paul Engle wrote in the *Tribune* in praise of the Indiana University Press, since "the problem of [poetry's] continuing appearance is greater each year as fewer publishers dare take the certain loss on it," in praise of the Poets of Today Series from Scribner, which he declared "one of the country's most valuable enterprises in keeping poetry alive," and also in praise of the Lamont, another important "aid to poetry."[33]

It was not only the publishing ethics of the sponsors of first-book prizes and series that generated the high level of publicity that poetic debuts commanded during the 1950s and '60s. High-profile editors and judges also helped attract attention, even as they augmented their own standing by appearing in roles of authority. Bourdieu's notion of the art world as a "world of belief" in which "the consecrated writer is the one who has the power to consecrate and to win assent when he or she consecrates an author or a work—with a preface, a favorable review" or a "prize"—sheds light on how prize culture enables editors and judges to intervene on their own behalves: they reconsecrate themselves by naming as a prizewinner a debut they then introduce with a preface that serves in effect as a first "favorable review" (*FCP* 42). Auden's editorship of the Yale Series stands as a particularly important instance. A well-known poet when he came to the United States in 1939, his introductions to the volumes in the series sometimes garnered attention in their own right and could even upstage the poetry they were supposed to publicize. An essay on the broad topic of "nature poetry" in the *New York Times*, for instance, takes its occasion from Auden's introduction to Daniel G. Hoffman's *An Armada of Thirty Whales* and mentions Hoffman's poems only once, parenthetically.[34]

The prestige of the "new," founded on the connotation of opposition to the status quo, also helps to explain why first-book honors generated so much publicity. As William Meredith, himself a Yale prize winner, wrote in a review of Hoffman's book, "To acclaim a new poet as remarkable as Mr. Hoffman is a reviewer's most pleasant function."[35] The reviewer of a debut has the opportunity to set the tone for the reception of a poet's entire oeuvre, and so stands to gain authority if she can rise to the challenge of recognizing a new talent. The titles of many first-book reviews reflect what Thomas Lask described as "the instant appreciation of the new, indeed a hysterical surge to greet it."[36] Headlines in the *New York Times* consistently allude to the debut poet's youth, while they rarely point to the maturity of a more established poet: "Princeton Man Wins Yale Poetry Contest," "A Quartet of Younger Singers," "Young Poet Wins Lamont Award," "Tactics of Shock, Discoveries of Innocence," "Three First Books of Poetry," "The Yale Younger Poets," "Firsts."[37]

In addition to inciting the ambitions of young poets such as Plath, the publicity attendant upon the proliferation of first-book prizes helped to produce the poetic debut as something of a defined type of literary production, fitted out with its own lore. No critic elaborated the complete generic code for the first book, but many wrote as if the tradition and conventions of the poetic debut were common knowledge. Writing in the *Partisan Review* in the fall of 1958, Alfred Alvarez praised Thom Gunn's debut, *Fighting Terms*, by locating it within a tradition of remarkable first books: "It is, for my money, the most impressive first book of poems since Robert Lowell's" and "as little the conventional first volume of poems as *Harmonium*."[38] The notion that there is such a thing as a "conventional first volume of poems" is sponsored in part by just this kind of tradition-making claim, which resounds throughout debut reviews of the period, as in Frank O'Hara's assertion that *Some Trees* is "the most beautiful first book of poems to appear in America since *Harmonium*," or Hayden Carruth's claim that John Hollander's *A Crackling of Thorns* "is in point of technique the best first book of poems I have read in a good many years."[39]

The tradition of the debut, explicitly evoked in the concept of the first-book series, could seem so powerful as to threaten the beginning poet's hopes for originality. Considering the subject of the decline of poetry, John Simon introduces the following quotation, asking which of the passages "strikes you as better poetry":

(A) The tempering, forgotten shrines: four gardens.
    Spires and poplars—the white god—where Lilith dances
    Wild geese. Horizons.

    Wampum and old gold? The golden darkness?
    White April dreams, and a sword hidden.
    Waters. Attitudes.

(B) And I am as greedy of her, that the black
    Horse of the literal world might come
    Directly on me. Perspective. A place

    To stand. To receive. A place to go
    Into from. The earthy by language.

    Who can imagine antelope silent
    Under the night rain, the Gulf
    At Biloxi at night else?

"Let me tell you," he continues, "that (A) is a list, in chronological order, of the first fourteen titles in the Yale Series of Younger poets," while "(B) is the middle part of the second poem in *Views of Jeopardy* by Jack Gilbert, the fifty-eighth and current Yale Laureate, the punctuation—and everything else—exactly as Mr. Gilbert wrote it, alas."[40] For Simon, the first-book prize series has formalized the debut to such a degree that the voice of the beginning poet is indistinguishable from the collective voice of the debut-tradition as a whole. Simon's procedure may seem idiosyncratic, but the assumption that poetic debuts of the 1950s and '60s were of a piece both with their precursors and their coevals was not uncommon. John Thompson, in a review of ten first books, manages to put a positive spin on their homogeneity: "They sound intelligent, they are very aware of their craft in diction and meter, they are most of them, as young people seem to be these days, traveled, cultured, knowing, and unperturbed. Poems could wander from one of these books to another without feeling lost."[41] But the notion that debuts increasingly seemed to resemble one another typically goes hand-in-hand with a lament for their inferiority. Even James Dickey, who debuted in the Poets of Today Series and went on to serve on the Lamont Prize committee in the mid-1960s, takes a dim view of first-book prize-winners: "Robert Mezey is right in there with the rest of the poets of his generation, having studied 'with John Crowe Ransom at Kenyon College and Paul Engle at the University of Iowa,' and with this book has won the Lamont Poetry Prize, surely the most infallible badge of accepted-and-forgotten mediocrity our culture can bestow. Between the Yale Series of Younger Poets . . . and the Lamont Prize, given the likes of Ned O'Gorman and Donald Justice, I don't believe we could choose, and I'm glad we don't have to; both show the dismal state of our verse, and both go on awarding and publishing as though it mattered."[42]

The most commonly noted characteristic of the "conventional first book of poems" in reviews of the period is the privileging of technique at the expense of feeling. The suspicion that first-book prizewinners and debut-series honorees were out to show off their technical accomplishment is bound up with the prevailing sense that first-book poets were more interested in the advancement of the careers that first-book prizes evoke than their own emotion, thought, and experience. As Matthiessen writes in his introduction to Marshall Schacht's *Fingerboard*, "American literature, in our time especially, has known far too many first books of showily forced growth for the quick return, whose promise was all in the store window."[43] In the article I quoted earlier, Shapiro begins by observing that "a first book is a 'trying on of styles.'" Like Matthiessen's, Shapiro's statement reflects not only the widespread tendency to generalize about first books, but also the idea that first-book style is not integrally related to first-book subject matter. Instead style is something the young poet is only "trying on," according to Shapiro, primarily with the goal of progressing along a career path: "When the author is a university man (teacher, fellowship holder) as are four of the five young poets here (the fifth is an ex-teacher), it may be that his first book can have little organic life because it represents mainly a claim to advancement in the academy and comes about after the poet thinks he has piled up enough publication credits in the quarterlies to make that claim."[44] Michael Goldman, reviewing a pair of debuts, strikes a similar note: "Too many poems today return us not to life but to a kind of Green Room of poetry, where the actors endlessly discuss their parts and their performances. It's only natural that first books should be especially prey to this difficulty; happily each of the two considered here reveals, in its own way, an energy that may in time direct itself fully and richly to life."[45] The implication is that first books of poetry are the "natural" home for overwrought, self-concerned verse (a style he calls "Dormitory Mandarin," which evokes the academic career that Shapiro links to the debut). The over-reliance on style is a function of the poets' concern with an abstract life of scripted "parts and performances" rather than the "full[ness]" and "rich[ness]" of "life" itself.

The technical mastery of a poetic debut was not solely a target for derision. It could also serve as evidence of "promise"—the characteristic critical term for the particular form of merit that the "conventional first book of poetry" displayed. To attain a certain degree of technical accomplishment is, after all, preferable to failing to attain it. In addition, technical accomplishment lends itself to the evocation of "promise" in that it leaves the work of accumulating experience to a future for which the young poet is specially prepared. Such is the logic of many of the more favorable debut reviews of the period. William Arrowsmith's review of "Nine New Poets," in which the word "promise" is repeated ten times in eight pages, is just one of the innumerable reviews in which the brightness of a poet's future serves as the standard of merit for his or her present achievement.[46]

Technique could serve as a basis for critical approval or disapproval, or, paradoxically, for both at the same time, a fact that helps to reveal the presence of a central contradiction of professionalism in the poetry and criticism of the 1950s, '60s, and beyond. In a review of Adrienne Rich's first two volumes, Donald Hall praises her for "the variety of tones and styles which she can assume," an "easy competence" that "is the most promising of her characteristics."[47] However, Hall goes on to suggest that mastery poses a problem in itself: "By definition, perfection is not promising," he claims, and so he calls on Rich to "extend the range of her performances still further." Her technical accomplishment serves as both the basis for her achievement and its limitation. Hall places the poet in a curious bind. Rich must "extend the range of her performances" but be careful not to master style completely, for as she approaches "perfection" she ("by definition")

forfeits "promise"—a quality ironically more appealing than the fulfillment it anticipates.

The conflicting imperatives evident here combine to produce the special emphasis on beginning that typifies the poetic debut during the era of
the first-book prize. These imperatives reflect the increasingly professional
cast of the poetic vocation in the context of the university-based poetry
scene I have been discussing, for they correspond to the complementary
elements of the sociological definition of professionalism I discussed in my
introduction—technicality and indetermination. The first-book prize promotes a developmental career narrative—a story of advancement predicated upon the idea of steady progress toward technical mastery. Drawn as
she may be to the disinterested stance of poets like Stevens and Moore and
the occulted or meandering paths they projected to evidence that stance,
the poet starting out during the era of the first-book prize had difficulty
playing down the regular progress of the career, since that progress was
likely to inform the writing life from the beginning through awards and
other forms of official recognition. But the developmental narrative (and
the "technicality" imperative that it dramatizes) is checked by the imperative of "indetermination," which manifests itself in debut reviews and debuts alike as the virtue of "promise." Because it is not solely a function of
the cultivation of technique, it offers itself uniquely to the judgment of the
professional through the logic that it takes one to know one. As I have
suggested, that the poets of the era presented themselves as beginners,
"writers of promise," signifies, on the one hand, their capitulation to the
developmental imperative encouraged by the rise of first-book prizes in
conjunction with the emergence of the university-centered post-1945 poetry scene. On the other hand, the special emphasis on beginning in debuts of the 1950s, '60s, and beyond functions as a deferral of the normative
career and thus allows poets to avoid being isolated as specialized practitioners of an art form traditionally supposed to engage common experience and feeling.

As the titles I listed earlier show, the debuts of the period are saturated
with the theme of beginning. Critics' emphasis on new poets' promise may
be heard as an echo of the potential that poets themselves sought to evoke
by accentuating their status as beginners. The titles quoted earlier provide
some idea of the variety of ways poets have chosen to represent the career,
which is figured metaphorically (*Birth of a Shark*), metonymically (*Primer
of Kinetics*), and synecdochally (*First Poems*). Such titles disguise the career
by presenting it in terms borrowed from other plots of growth; these three
titles, for example, suggest schemes of maturation, education, and addi-

tion, respectively. At the same time they unmistakably evoke the poetic career by putting the debut collection into close proximity to the conspicuously appropriate theme of beginning. This tendency to underscore the moment of starting out is also apparent in the titles of some of the poems with which debuts themselves begin. To cite only those that mark the beginning of the career as a "first" moment in a rising sum, there are Galway Kinnell's "First Song" in *What A Kingdom It Was* (1960), X. J. Kennedy's "First Confession" in *Nude Descending a Staircase* (1961), and Jean Valentine's "First Love" in *Dream Barker* (1965).

For all their ambivalence, titles such as these illustrate in miniature how much more explicit the inscription of career is in post-1945 debuts than in those of their modernist forebears. The question of how to begin is certainly at stake in Eliot's first book, *Prufrock and Other Observations* (1917), but it is important that it remains a question, and a peculiarly agonizing one at that. By and large, first-book titles from the first half of the century— Ezra Pound's *A Lume Spento* (1908), William Carlos Williams's *Poems* (1909), Wallace Stevens's *Harmonium* (1923), Marianne Moore's *Observations* (1923), Langston Hughes's *The Weary Blues* (1926)—exhibit little of the self-assurance reflected in the relatively forthright ground-breakings, firsts, dawns, and arrivals announced in later titles. Similarly, modernist debuts often begin, as we saw in the last chapter, with elusive poems in heavily coded language; think of Eliot's "The Love Song of J. Alfred Prufrock," Moore's "To an Intra-Mural Rat," or Stevens's "Earthy Anecdote," whose oblique evocation of career couldn't be farther from the straightforward procedures of so many leadoff poems in post-1945 first books, as the following readings will make clear. Of course modern American poetry is not all of a piece in this regard. But if Hart Crane's *White Buildings* (1925), which opens with the explicitly career-oriented poem "Legend," displays a focus on beginning commensurate with post-1945 practice, it is important to remember that it is more than simply the exception that proves the rule, for it reflects Crane's deliberate opposition to what he saw as the typical modernist practice of self-authorization via self-effacement in the first book.

Post-1945 debut poets make use of a variety of beginning ideas. In addition to the class of "First" poems listed above, there are poems about finding a voice, making a name, the onset of spring, the moment of waking, daybreak, establishing a homestead, and climbing to a prospect, among others, but none is more common than birth: "Great Leo roared at my birth" writes Donald Justice in "Anniversaries" from his Lamont-prize winning first book, *The Summer Anniversaries*, and "Beside my bed / The tall aunts prophesied, / And cousins from afar, / Predicting a great career."[48]

Well-suited to the representation of career, this theme projects a course of orderly development while at the same time grounding the poet's authority in the "organic life," which the academic career threatened to supplant. Plath's "The Manor Garden," the leadoff poem of *The Colossus and Other Poems*, is suffused with precisely the tension between life and career that drives the thematization of beginning pervading post-1945 debuts. The title highlights both organic productivity, emblematized by the "Garden," and artificiality—evoked through the pun on "manner"—which Plath always felt to be a prominent threat to her work.[49] This opposition is reflected in the way the poem juxtaposes birth and death, the maternal and the poetic, as it begins: "The fountains are dry and the roses over. / Incense of death. Your day approaches." The first line ironically extends the period of poetic inspiration, represented by the fountains, by pronouncing its end, and the second line replicates that ironic effect, but in the context of motherhood rather than poetry, for the "day" on the horizon ambiguously marks both the end of life and the birth of a new one. Not surprisingly for a poem in which beginning and ending are so compulsively yoked together, its closing lines recapitulate the tension embodied in its opening: "The small birds converge, converge / With their gifts to a difficult borning." With their "gifts" and their capacity for song, these "small birds" present a ready image of Plath and her colleagues at Yaddo, the artists' community on which she and Ted Hughes "converge[d]" in 1959, and a symbol of the institutional support by which young poets felt themselves to be both liberated and confined. The word "borning" captures the ambivalence with which career is characteristically viewed during the era of the first-book prize, though it must be added that Plath's ambivalence is unique in its severity. The word draws attention to the professional trajectory by marking its inception as a kind of "difficult" birth. But the choice of the word "borning," rather than "birth," recalls the term "borning room," which, as Jo Gill observes, was "a room, familiar in seventeenth-century architecture, built solely for giving birth and—crucially in the context of the persistent ambivalence of the poem—for caring for the dying."[50]

Plath's poem reflects concerns that would continue to inform her work for years to come, but in the manifesto poem, a close relative of the birth poem so prominent in post-1945 debuts, the poet's aesthetic credo and characteristic procedure are set forth in terms that are still more drastically explicit, as if the very straightforwardness with which a poet proclaimed her intentions might itself be taken as an earnest of her professional competence. Like the birth poem, the manifesto poem focuses on beginning, but it emphasizes prescription over narration: "The only complete language is suspended in the life of the blood"; "Brother, / Nothing is real that has happened / Only once; and nothing can happen / Again and still be true"; "Would you lay well? Don't watch."[51] Take, for example, Howard's "Advice from the Cocoon," the first poem in *Quantities*. Longenbach notes that the poem's "final lines seem—too perfectly—to prefigure the entire shape of his later career" in that they express Howard's "preference for the dramatic guise."[52] Its title neatly balances the imperatives of technicality and indetermination that inform professionalism. That the speaker presumes to give "advice" reflects an authority founded upon mastery of a form of knowledge susceptible to transmission. But the "advice" issues "from the cocoon," which calls up the idea of immaturity and evokes a foreground too short to have allowed for the mastery of such knowledge. Thus the title presents a notion of poetic authority that seems grounded in an acquirable competence and at the same time "organic," mystical. As I have suggested, these contradictory imperatives combine to produce an emphasis on beginning—a theme evoked here in the figure of the "grub / Of summer," which represents the poet.

> Here is a grub
> Of summer, modest in its public state
> But growing by a private appetite
> To prouder life. If property is theft
> As Proudhon claimed, the proof is in his jaws—
>
> A larceny of leaves. What grub can own
> Grub eats, and eats away the rest to weave
> A serviceable shroud against the cold.
> The larva, not quite wool, but not yet will,
> Is wrapped up well between his other lives.
>
> Would you, like him, survive at any cost?
> Then seal yourself in layers of yourself,
> Warm as a worm, until there is enough
> To eat your heart away and still have left
> Enough for the hungriest winter beyond.[53]

The importance of maintaining the precarious balance between maturity and immaturity established in the title is reflected in the equivocal constructions through which Howard defines the moment of beginning: the grub is "modest," but will soon grow "To prouder life"; it is "not quite wool, but not yet will."[54] The poem defers the narrative of development by lingering over the process of preparation: just as the grub eats leaves in order "to weave / A serviceable shroud against the cold," so the would-be poet must "seal" himself "in layers" of himself, so as to be able to "eat" his "heart away and still have left / Enough for the hungriest winter and beyond." The poetic career is imagined here as a process of gradual self-consumption, such that its duration depends entirely upon the patience with which stores for the future are laid up at the start. The poem's last stanza illustrates the gravity with which the theme of career is typically treated in the debut: much like Plath, for whom the inception of the career is inseparable from its conclusion, Howard directs the reader to the importance of the beginning, if he would "survive at any cost."

This sense of gravity is captured from a different angle in debut poems about mentors. The respect for the poetic vocation evident in the seriousness with which the manifesto poem articulates the proper method for conducting the career is channeled, in the mentor poem, into respect for the mentor's exemplary life. "A great spirit is dead," Charles Bell proclaims in "To Dick Wendell, Teacher and Man" from his debut *Songs for a New America*, which appeared in the Indiana University Press Poetry Series in 1953: "Our age also is wasting, struck to the bone / With want of what he was, truth's champion."[55] This teacher elegy, like most debut mentor poems, embodies what Edward Said describes as "the creation of authority for a beginning" through "the act of achieving discontinuity and transfer: while in this act a clear break with the past is discernible, it must also connect the new direction not so much with a wholly unique venture but with the established authority of a parallel venture."[56] Robert Pack's "On Waking from a Late Afternoon Dream in Which My Teacher Died," the leadoff poem of his debut collection, *The Irony of Joy: Poems*, offers a succinct example of the logic of "discontinuity and transfer" that Said describes:

> I am afraid now I have seen who dies,
> Afraid that I may come to fill the space
> Of your authority, and find myself
> Unchanged: no taller in the sun, my face
> Without new lines or deepness in my eyes.
>
> For I had ever been content to strive—
> Imagining the skies' still blue around

Your head, a statue moving always through
Its history. Secure on my own ground,
My working toward you made me most alive.

But now, as a wind, the sky swoops down the West;
I feel the beating weaken in my heart,
And I am changed: the long day's sun has pressed
Its shadows in these eyes—I speak your part.
O wake me now, nor let me dream the rest.[57]

The elegy does not spend much time elaborating the trauma of the (antic-ipated) loss; instead, it is primarily concerned with determining the speak-er's suitability as a successor to "the space / Of" the teacher's "authority." In Said's terms, the poem moves straight past the matter of "discontinuity"—spelled out in the title—and on to the matter of "transfer." Having "ever been content" to follow in his teacher's footsteps, the speaker is at first "Afraid" of finding himself inadequate to the task of assuming his teach-er's role. But the teacher's death itself turns out to be the experience that gives the speaker the maturity and wisdom—imaged here as "new lines" on his face and "deepness" in his eyes—to speak with his teacher's author-ity: "I am changed: the long day's sun has pressed / Its shadows in these eyes—I speak your part." But tellingly, the poem does not end with this idea of a successful promotion, for in the final line the speaker moves to check this development by waking out of the dream, so as not to have to "dream the rest." What the poem accomplishes, much like Plath's and Howard's poems, is to establish the poet's authority while at the same time preserving his status as a beginner precisely by deferring his progress down the career path.[58]

"I greet you at the beginning of a great career, which yet must have had a long foreground somewhere, for such a start," wrote Ralph Waldo Em-erson to Walt Whitman to commend him on the first edition of *Leaves of Grass*.[59] Debut poets of the era of the first-book prize turn the assumption that great careers "must" be rooted in some kind of preliminary develop-ment to their advantage in the many debut poems that deal with "Arriving at the Point of Departure," to borrow a title from Stanley Plumly's 1970 debut, *In the Outer Dark*. Just as "a great career" presupposes "a long fore-ground" in Emerson's formulation, so "a long foreground" may be used to project "a great career."[60] Such poems put in perspective the care that American poets of the post-1945 period took to position themselves at the starting point of the career path—at the starting point and no further, as if even the smallest progress could be construed as a forfeiture of promise and a capitulation to the careerism that was often suspected to be the driving purpose behind first-book publication. This sort of poem works by elaborating developments that would seem to dramatize career advancement, then consigning those developments to the preparatory space of the "foreground" by designating a true beginning that comes *after* them.

Donald Hall's "Apology," from his Lamont Prize-winning debut *Exiles and Marriages*, begins by taking stock of the failed poet he once was. In the first of the poem's two numbered segments, Hall portrays himself much like the poet "Finesse," whom he mocks in "Six Poets in Search of a Lawyer" as one "Whose cleverness in writing verse is just / Exceeded by his lack of taste and lust," and "Who writes his verse in order to amaze, / To win the Pulitzer, or *Time*'s sweet praise."[61] It goes some way toward showing how appealing the anti-careerist pose of the promising beginner could be that Hall in fact won "*Time*'s sweet praise" for *Exiles and Marriages*, thus launching him on precisely the trajectory from which he attempts to distance himself, both in "Six Poets" and in "Apology":[62]

> These mirrors give my face its truest frame.
> Look at my pose: I mimic for the crowd
> Sequent like couplets to my glittered name—
> My horde of eyes that mirrors shout aloud.
>
> My poems posture less, but primp and stand
> Like manikins I made in my despite
> And hate their maker—not to understand
> What fire it was that gave me working light.[63]

Like "Finesse," the poet Hall used to be is vain, as his many "mirrors" suggest: even his "couplets" are represented here as pairs of "eyes" he apparently has only for himself. (The word "eyes" also puns on "ayes," which the mirrors "shout aloud," thus reinforcing the sense of self-absorption here.) His "poems," though they may "posture less," are nevertheless fake as well—"manikins . . . made in my despite," rather than to fulfill the nobler purpose of "understand[ing] / What fire it was that gave me working light." By the end of the first section, Hall has arrived at an "end" that will serve as the starting point of the career projected in the second half of the poem: "I have come to where those poems end. / I stand alone and weaponless to say / That my small mouth is broken. I must mend."

Because of this elaboration of his "foreground," the career the poet stands poised to begin in the second half of the poem has been purged of careerism, for the poet brings to it knowledge of the harm that self-interest can do to the integrity both of the poet and his work. Even so, Hall is careful to set himself up as a beginner by locating the decisive "achieve[ment]" of "virtue" in the indefinite future:

> There is a virtue which I must achieve
> Whose struggle will decide this heavy change,
> A singleness, whose excellence must leave
> This personal mountain for a greater range.

The "virtue" of "singleness" that Hall hopes to "achieve" stands in opposition to the multiple selves represented in the first stanza. Interestingly, Hall preempts the criticism he leveled at Adrienne Rich—that she must "extend the range of her performances still further": by avowing his intention to "leave / This personal mountain for a greater range," he makes the "promise" to grow that her "perfection" threatened to stifle. In the penultimate stanza, Hall pauses once more in the moment between his "long foreground" and the "great career" that takes shape in its wake, bidding farewell to "irony," which has grown "weary on [his] tongue," and "bury[ing] the cheap magic" of his old poetic style, before announcing his arrival:

> Now with my single voice I speak to you.
> I do not hear an echo to my voice.
> I walk the single path that heroes do
> And climb the mountain which is my own choice.

The poet lays claim to the integrity or "singleness" of self that he lacked in the first part of the poem. The echo chamber of the first stanza, with its hall of shouting mirrors, has been replaced by a space in which the poet may "speak to" the reader without "hear[ing] an echo." The deliberate "climb" with which the poem ends (and which harks back to the idea of the *gradus ad Parnassum*) fittingly evokes the poet's rising powers and thus the promise of his future. The unabashed sense of heroic purpose reflects the effectiveness of the logic of arrival: lessons learned in the "foreground" augment the authority with which the poet will begin.[64]

I conclude my discussion of mainstream debut poetry with an interpretation of another poem that elaborates the logic of arrival at the point of departure, for more even than the birth poems, lyric manifestoes, and teacher elegies discussed above, it is this sort of poem, with its multiple beginnings, that best illustrates the particular authority of the beginner in the context of a university-based poetry scene in which independence is valued so much. The arrival that Hall portrays as a journey to the foot of a mountain, Richard Howard portrays as a journey, by train, from his native Ohio to New York in "Sandusky—New York," the poem with which he concludes *Quantities*. The poem traces a progress from one beginning—the Ohio of Howard's birth and childhood—to another—the New York in which he would launch his career as a poet and translator in the later 1950s. The opening of the poem emphasizes Howard's sense of alienation: "Ohio from a train / Looked always other; half his way across / The unimportant chain / Of Alleghenies that intended east."[65] "Landscape and weather were his enemies," he goes on to declare, and the poem traces a progress toward both personal integration and harmony with the elements:

> his purpose grew
> Within him like an East.
>
> Such travelling was true
> In parallel. Along the simple tracks
> Which accurately flew
> Beneath, he followed himself away, away
> From weather came into
> That unconditional country of his blood
> Where even landscape grew
> Dim as he had never dared to hope
> And when he breathed he knew
> The air as sick men breathe and know the spring:
> Cold still, but coming to.
>
> Now, the train running on,
> He clambered up the enterprising bones
> His body reached him down
> So carefully for the ascent, he climbed
> The scaffold skeleton
> Up shoulders to the summit of his skull
> (Past marshes overgrown
> And hollows filled by sudden rubbishes)

Until he stared upon
The shore of all his history, as it
Would look when it was done.

His progress allows him to escape both the "weather" and the "landscape" of his youth, and so to enter a new environment, the "unconditional country of his blood." Coming into that "unconditional country," Howard comes into his own, a process of maturation represented here in the gradual way he takes possession both of his "body" and his "history." The poem serves to emphasize Howard's poetic authority, which is rooted in the characteristically romantic sense of reciprocity between self and nature: "the landscape lived in him / As he might live in it." Like Hall, though, Howard is careful to portray the achievement of an integral selfhood as a step preliminary to the initiation of the career proper. Throughout the poem, he stresses the idea that although he knows where he is going, he is still, at this point, on his way—"Cold still," as he puts it here, "but coming to." So it is that by the end of the poem, Howard's journey remains incomplete: from the shores of Lake Erie he has come to a point within sight of the shores of the Atlantic: "The mountains fell, and far / Ahead he thought he saw the sea." Like so many other "poets of the First Book" during the post-1945 period, Howard portrays himself as a beginner, poised between the self-assurance of the professional and the uncertainty of the amateur, at the moment of arrival: "What if / It was, if it was there? / Then that was where, tonight / He wanted to arrive."

In the next chapter, I explore the ways in which John Ashbery's *Some Trees* adopts strategies of self-presentation similar to those that run through the more markedly mainstream post-1945 debuts surveyed so far. Turning beforehand to a survey of first books from oppositional poetry movements other than Ashbery's New York School, I aim to show that countercultural poetry is energetically responsive to the same crisis of autonomy that animates the work of the university-based mainstream. The poems of beginning that frequently open post-1945 debuts—including those by Beat, Black Arts, and Language poets, among other groups positioned on the cultural margins—reflect the inexorability of vocational crisis in an era in which autonomy counts for so much, but is increasingly hard to come by, given the entanglement of even the most staunchly anti-establishment poets in a culture of "administrative environments," as Rasula puts it.[66] Tellingly, as he goes on to show, the stock in trade of poets on both sides of the divide is the repudiation of mainstream poetry. By the mid-1950s, "the

academy was so saturated with poets that it was possible for the most reac-
tionary metrical technicians to point the accusing finger at someone even
more narrow-minded and say 'now *there's* the problem: academic verse.' "[67]
What McGurl calls the "vertiginously dialectical mobilization of the distinction between 'inside' and 'outside' " during the period produces a situation in which insiders and outsiders alike define themselves against the
mid-century mainstream, which may be seen as the "threatening Other"
that "must be discovered or invented in order to be attacked and de-
stroyed," according to Stephen Greenblatt's classic formulation of the process of self-fashioning.[68] The presence, then, of the rhetoric of beginning
in first books—and particularly in first poems in first books—by both
establishment and anti-establishment poets marks their shared dissent
from the imperatives of the mid-century culture of "administrative environments." But it also signals an awareness of the limits of dissent at a
moment in which it was so much a defining characteristic of an increasingly institutionalized culture that even to oppose that culture was to
begin to feel a part of it.[69] I conclude the chapter by glancing briefly at a
varied selection of opening poems from debuts of the 1970s and '80s in
order to suggest the continuity of the era of the first-book prize and to illustrate the variety of ways in which poets from a wide range of sites on the
map of contemporary poetry have introduced themselves.

Few poetic careers bear witness more explicitly to the enormous pressure to invent and reinvent oneself during the era of the first-book prize
than that of Amiri Baraka. (In chapter 4, I discuss this imperative at more
length in the context of the poetry of Louise Glück.)[70] Born Everett LeRoi
Jones, Baraka changed his name to LeRoi Jones before publishing his first
book, *Preface to a Twenty Volume Suicide Note*, in 1961, and later changed
it to Imamu Ameer Baraka, and then to Amiri Baraka, as he moved from
Greenwich Village to Harlem to Newark in the process of identifying
himself first with the Beats (but also with the New York School and Black
Mountain poets), then the Black Arts Movement, and later, Marxism.
Dedications and references to his friends Jack Kerouac, Gary Snyder,
Allen Ginsberg, and Michael McClure mark *Preface* as a first book arising
from the Beat coterie. An advertisement for Corinth Books published "in
association with Totem Press / LeRoi Jones," printed on the reverse of
"Notes for a Speech," the last poem in the collection, places the debut in a
context encompassing not only the Beats, but a range of countercultural
poetry milieux by listing *Preface* together with books by Edward Dorn,
Frank O'Hara, Gary Snyder, Philip Whalen, and others, plus an anthol-

ogy co-edited by Baraka (the patronizingly titled *Four Young Lady Poets*, which included early work by Diane Wakoski). "A Note on the Poems" on the copyright page takes a different tack, however, linking *Preface* to the work of "other young (?) poets" in general, a more diffuse but apparently scrupulous group who will presumably understand—the explanation is elided—why Baraka has endeavored to organize the collection chronologically: "For the most part, these poems cover a period from 1957 until 1960, with the last few poems having been written this year (1961). I have arranged the book in as strict a chronological order as I could manage . . . for reasons best known to other young (?) poets." Baraka positions himself both outside the mainstream and inside it, where he appears as a member of a class of "young (?) poets" whose definition, articulated and accentuated in the media coverage of debut prizes I discussed earlier, is teasingly put in question. These multiple identifications—Beat poet, New York poet, Black Mountain poet, young poet, middle-aged poet, poetry publisher, anthologist—suggest simmering conflicts that point to the often-remarked metamorphoses to come.

The dynamic relation between self-invention and self-denial evident in the transformations that define Baraka's career is also evident in the title poem of his debut, which opens the volume. The poem describes what Houston A. Baker calls the "jaded world" littered with "bare glimmerings of hope" that serves as the setting of the book in general. The speaker is "accustomed to the way / The ground opens up and envelopes me / Each time I go out to walk the dog," and he notes with disappointment that "Nobody sings anymore." The burial suggested in the image of opening ground, combined with the use of "envelope" as a verb, casts the speaker as a kind of dead letter, a text headed toward oblivion rather than sympathetic reception. He is not unlike Eliot's Prufrock, with his troubled resignation to quotidian routine in an environment devoid of heroic possibilities. His imaginary daughter (Kellie Jones, to whom the poem is dedicated, was not yet born at the time of the poem's composition), like Eliot's "women" talking among themselves and his mermaids "singing, each to each," is a feminine presence set in a world apart, which the speaker approaches with care, but nevertheless cannot fully enter. The ending of the poem evokes both hope for transcendence and a renewed sense of defeat:

And then last night, I tiptoed up
To my daughter's room and heard her
Talking to someone, and when I opened

The door, there was no one there . . .
Only she on her knees, peeking into
Her own clasped hands.[71]

As Baker notes, "The 'room' appears time and again in Baraka's poetry," and it tends to figure the price in alienation the poet pays to gain the distance necessary for an "understanding of his own and society's plight."[72] The girl's conversation holds up the prospect of communication and thus relief from the isolation of the earlier stanzas, but upon opening the door the speaker sees "no one there." On one level this statement means she is alone, but on another level it captures the sense that she, too, is "no one," a fantasy figure or muse who must be conjured up again in the indeterminate moment opened by the ellipsis. In "The Turncoat," from later on in *Preface*, Baraka likewise appears "alone and brooding" before visiting his home and "peering in at the pitiful shadow of [him]self" in the house. The similar situations portrayed in the two poems reinforce the impression that he is in a sense "peering in" at his own "pitiful shadow" in "Preface" as well. "On her knees," she has evidently given up on prayer, for her "peeking into / Her own clasped hands" suggests a nascent skepticism of the efficacy of poetry, which is implicitly invoked here through the conventional notion of lyric as the overheard eloquence of a solitary speaker. As a "Preface," the poem serves to introduce the literary career imaged—with notable ambition—as a "Twenty Volume" sequence in the title. That the projected work is a "Suicide Note," however, means that the career is also being conceptualized from the start as an account of its own discontinuation.

The Black Arts Movement that Baraka played a key role in founding when he abandoned Greenwich Village for Harlem in 1965 figures as both a supportive community and an impediment to individual freedom in the leadoff poem of Nikki Giovanni's 1968 debut, *Black Feeling Black Talk*, "Detroit Conference of Unity and Art (for HRB)." A mentor poem as well as a love poem, "Detroit Conference" is dedicated to H. Rap Brown (who later changed his name to Jamil Abdullah Al-Amin), the prominent civil rights activist who was chairman of the Student Nonviolent Coordinating Committee at the time of the conference. Beginning with the word "We" and ending with the word "me," "Detroit Conference" explores the tension between the revolutionary values that are articulated and confirmed at the meeting and the personal priorities with which those values seem to be at odds.[73] In "Letter to a Bourgeois Friend Whom Once I Loved (And Maybe Still Do If Love Is Valid)," which also appears in *Black Feeling Black Talk*, Giovanni questions whether "Love" is "Valid" in a society so riddled with inequality that political action becomes not only the foremost but the only concern: revolution must be dealt with first "if we are to get back to love and hate and anxiety and all those foolish emotions."[74] In "Detroit Conference of Unity and Art" Giovanni is, by contrast, startlingly clear on the point that, for her, the personal—a category that includes both her sense of poetic vocation and her relationship with Brown—takes precedence over the broad social issues addressed at the conference, including "the possibility of / Blackness / And the inevitability of / Revolution," "Black leaders / And / Black Love," and "Women / And Black men." As in "Letter to a Bourgeois Friend," Giovanni takes the measure of competing claims on her time and attention in terms of how "Valid" they are:

No doubt many important
Resolutions
Were passed
As we climbed Malcolm's ladder

But the most
Valid of them
All was that
Rap chose me

Henry Louis Gates explains that Brown "earned his byname [Rap] because he was a master of black vernacular rhetorical games and their attendant well-defined rhetorical strategies."[75] The last line of the poem suggests not only that Brown "chose" Giovanni, but also that poetry itself "chose" her; in this way the conference marks the beginning of both her personal relationship with Brown and her calling as a poet. Though the passiveness evident in the last line runs against the grain of the occasion of revolutionary activism, it is, of course, very much in keeping with the traditional notion of the poetic vocation as something that cannot be "single[d] out," as Stevens put it in the journal entry I discussed in the last chapter, but must "decide in you for itself." At the same time, though, Giovanni frames the experience of being chosen by "Rap" not only as a privileged moment of epiphany, but also as "the most / Valid" of the "Resolutions" passed at the conference. Evoking tensions between collectivity and individuality, passivity and agency, "Detroit Conference" reflects the difficulty of defining vocation during the post-1945 period in terms of organic experience and institutional protocol at the same time.

The explicitly avant-garde impulse of Language poetry tends to privilege discontinuity over transfer, to borrow Said's terms once more, in debuts by poets affiliated with the movement: mentor poems like Giovanni's "Detroit Conference" and poems of thwarted self-renewal like Baraka's "Preface" run against the grain of a project guided by the goal of "debunking the figure of the poet as a solo egoist," as Lyn Hejinian puts it.[76] Perhaps not surprisingly, given the inevitable predisposition to self-critique implicit in a group defined by such a goal, the rhetoric of beginning through which debut poets so often attempt to negotiate the contradictions of career in the post-1945 era is particularly prominent among the Language poets, whose work exhibits a stress on that rhetoric comparable to that of their mainstream counterparts. Hejinian's remarks on the structure of her poetic career shed light on this trend as it appears both within the Language group and beyond it: "to the extent that I've attempted to undertake a completely new project with each book I've written, I find myself over and over in the position of a 'beginner'—with all of a beginner's quandaries and clumsinesses, trying to figure out where I am and how things are done there."[77] Or as she puts it in the title of the final section of *My Life in the Nineties*: "*Now long past / beginning, as a / long-term beginner, / I begin.*"[78]

This emphasis is also evident in the untitled leadoff poem from Michael Davidson's first book, *The Mutabilities*, which begins by describing the arrival and initial reception of the "vanguard":

I am watching the vanguard move in,
it speaks from the everywhere it has left
and it takes everyone by surprise
even though they have waited for spring
for a thousand years.[79]

Similarly, the opening poem from Bob Perelman's debut, *Braille*, offers a critique of a generation stuck in its habits—we are "too sensitive to the cut of our diaries to bask in the blank pages"—that clearly resonates with the anti-confessionalist orientation of Language poetry.[80] The image of "blank pages" (as an alternative to "our diaries") looks forward to Hejinian's notion of the "open text," which is "open to the world and particularly to the reader" and which "rejects the authority of the writer over the reader."[81] In evoking the idea of the material beginnings of a text in "blank pages," the image re-emphasizes the importance of origins suggested in the word

"Protoplasm" (from the Latin *protoplasma*, "first created thing"), which is the poem's title.

Hejinian's stress on multiple beginnings is still more clearly illustrated by "Its Form," the opening poem in *Blake's Newton*, Michael Palmer's first book. Such guiding principles of the Language movement as the critique of narrative, conventional syntax, reference, and lyric subjectivity are in evidence from the start:

> Its form, at tables by fours
> leap . . . relieved of their weight.
> She turns green
> to begin. The Natural History
> peregrine, Peale's hawk
> is forgetting to talk
> like those coast homes
> lost in the deeper part.
>
> But to begin a procession
> or a succession of lines
> replacing the elms whose warps
> and curves are called contradictions.
>
> To begin, 'the stamp'
> of autumn . . . these parades
> whose curved names
> folded in as pilgrims.
> You start to swim
> through a little darkness
> and see some trees.
>
> In the New Spring this
> snow is the cold
> water running off
> what it was. The moth
> loves the rose but who
> does the rose love. It
> goes and
> around her
> dusting some lady's clothes
> from an edge like

> trees, turning pages, around or
> else about her, the wings marked
> by eyes, and seeing twice.[82]

In the epistolary poem "To Thomas Butts," William Blake identifies Isaac Newton with the "single vision" characteristic of the degraded, scientific perspective against which Blake contrasted his own ideal of the "fourfold vision" enabled by the artistic imagination.[83] Palmer's volume title sheds light on the mysterious opening of its opening poem, which presents a subject that is at once singular and plural—a "form" that multiplies (perhaps "by fours") under the poet's manifold, Blakean perspective into a quantity demanding the plural verb "leap." This transformation coincides with an act that is identified with the transcendence of gravity ("relieved of their weight") and linked with the traditional metaphor for inspiration as a bird in flight, which reappears in the closing lines. These concerns cast the poem as a manifesto geared toward enacting, by way of illustration, the aesthetic principles being elaborated.

As such, it underlines Palmer's affinities to the Language movement, whose "animating principle," according to Perloff, is that "poetic language is not a window, a transparent glass to be *seen through*," but rather a material presence that distorts or even occludes the messages it is conventionally supposed to transmit.[84] This principle haunts the poem in the form of a special consciousness of the interpenetration of language and the world that it only seems to represent transparently: so it is that "names" are "curved" just like "elms" are, and "trees" can be seen as so many "turning pages." The rhetoric of beginning so prominently featured in the poem— "to begin" is thrice repeated, "You start to swim," "the New Spring"— serves both to initiate and disrupt its progress. That progress is, in turn, represented in a sequence of increasingly stylized figurations: first it is a "procession / or a succession of lines," then "parades" with "curved names," and last, more obliquely, it is imagined as "running" water, an image that literalizes the ideal of discursive fluency. Resisting closure even as it proceeds inevitably toward its ending, "Its Form" evokes a notion of the poetic career defined, on the one hand, by the discipline with which its progress is called into question and, on the other, by the progressive pattern of repeated beginnings that that discipline ironically engenders.

Additional evidence of the pervasiveness of the logic of beginning on exhibit in "Its Form" might be drawn from a range of first books written both inside and outside of the various institutions and communities that constituted American poetry culture in the 1970s and '80s. Of course many first books either evoke beginning more indirectly than the ones I have focused on here, or ignore it altogether in favor of alternative strategies of self-presentation, but its persistence reflects the endurance of anxieties both deeply rooted in poetic tradition and shaped by the continuing professionalization of poetry. As I hope the following notes on debut leadoff poems will demonstrate, such anxieties cross ethnic boundaries, bridge the division between East Coast and West Coast poetry cultures, and connect the various groups and trends that define the field of poetic production during the era of the first-book prize.

Take Ai's debut, *Cruelty* (1973), published the same year as Palmer's *Blake's Newton*, as a first example. The book opens with "Twenty-Year Marriage," which presents an arrival at the point of departure in the manner of the poems by Hall and Howard discussed earlier, but frames the speaker's progress as dependent upon her husband's haste: "waiting in a truck" for him, the speaker proposes "roll[ing] out of here, / leaving the past stacked up behind us; / old newspapers nobody's ever got to read again."[85] Alfred Corn's *All Roads at Once* (1976) begins with "Promised Land Valley, June '73," which similarly situates the speaker on the verge of a voyage that can also be seen as a flight, insofar as the darkening lake in the poem reflects the sky. His trajectory appears as an indeterminate "golden scribble" cast by a "lantern" in the water, but it assumes intelligibility when it reappears, lifted into the air under the sign of imagination, and sanctioned by a more secure sense of vocation, at the end: "And still, we can imagine some clear call, / a spoken brilliance blazing the trail . . . / ourselves moving out across the sky." (The book's closing poem returns to this scene, positioning the speaker "On the Beach," "Enduring a world of water," and "waiting / for the stars to wheel in place / as image   story   future.")[86] The title of John Yau's first collection, *Crossing Canal Street* (1976), evokes a similarly ambiguous movement "across" space. In Yau's case, the boundary to be crossed is the street that lies between New York's Chinatown and SoHo (or between SoHo and Chinatown, since the direction is left unspecified). The initiation of the poetic career is imagined as a contradictory progress both toward and away from Chinese-American culture, and toward and away from the bohemian art world, both of which function as constitutive " 'sites' of Yau's identity (white / downtown / artsy and Chinese / Chinese American)," according to Dorothy Wang.[87] Yusef Komunayakaa's *Dedications & Other Darkhorses* (1977) opens with "Returning the Borrowed Road," a mentor poem dedicated to Richard Hugo in which Komunyakaa records his teacher's advice and then describes its impact in a surrealistic idiom that proves he has taken it to heart: "You said, *Get away / from the poem. You're too close.* / Now, I let each stone / seek its new mouth."[88]

Leadoff poems that foreground the topic of career initiation continue to pervade first books of the 1980s. In J. D. McClatchy's "Fetish" from *Scenes from Another Life* (1981), the speaker calls on the magical powers of "an azurite eagle" pendant to "release" his "breath" and inspire him with the "power to answer outcry with insight."[89] Wyatt Prunty's "The Kite," which opens *The Times Between* (1982), could serve as a manifesto for the New Formalist movement with which he and McClatchy are often associated: its pentameter lines, organized into quatrains, embody the tension between freedom and restraint that the poet cultivates in his writing, which is implicitly compared to "the private craft of kites," a "craft of putting fragile things aloft, / Of letting go and holding on at once."[90] "In the Beginning," the leadoff poem in Alice Fulton's first book, *Dance Script with Electric Ballerina* (1983), compares her career to a voyage and herself to a ship holding "unknowable / cargo, headed for a speck / on the sea's rim in the hope / it can contain a shore."[91] In Thylias Moss's "Alternatives for a Celibate Daughter" from her first book, *Hosiery Seams on a Bow-legged Woman* (1983), the speaker's dying father bequeaths to her a new name in a recurrent dream: "his name for me is a flower: Hyacinth, / a final pink breath."[92] Rachel Hadas's debut, *Slow Transparency* (1984), begins with "Journey Out," whose speaker tells herself to "Shut / your eyes and let a pin-pricked map direct / your journey. The arrival is what's hard."[93] Mark Halliday's "Get It Again," the opening poem from *Little Star* (1987), yokes writing and reading together as parallel versions of "the adventure of starting over."[94] Titles such as Olga Broumas's *Beginning with O* (1977), John Bensko's *Green Soldiers* (1981), Eric Pankey's *For the New Year* (1984), B. H. Fairchild's *The Arrival of the Future* (1985), Jed Rasula's *Tabula Rasula* (1986), and Cole Swenson's *New Math* (1989) evidence the continuation of the emphasis on beginning exemplified in the titles from earlier debuts that I quoted in the introduction.

To proceed in this way from close readings of mainstream and counter-cultural poems from the 1950s and '60s to a series of sound bites from leadoff poems from the 1970s and '80s is to give a great many debuts, particularly from later in the post-1945 period, short shrift. Examining just one poem each by Plath, Baraka, and Palmer scarcely does justice to their first books, while collections such as Ai's *Cruelty,* Corn's *All Roads at Once,* and Moss's *Hosiery Seams on a Bowlegged Woman*—to single out a few that I admire in particular from the group touched upon above—invite much more extensive discussion. A comprehensive survey of representations of poets' paths in post-1945 debuts lies beyond the scope of this book, not least because the representation of such paths is apt to be considerably varied and, in many cases, dauntingly—and intriguingly—oblique. In addition, the rising volume of poetic production in general, and debut publication in particular—the latter driven with special intensity by the proliferation of creative writing programs and first-book prizes over the last half century—helps to ensure that combining detailed interpretation and broad representation will prove difficult. Bearing such challenges in mind, I have tried to capture a sense of the remarkable pervasiveness of fairly explicit evocations of career along with a sense of the continuity of earlier and later moments in the era of the first-book prize. Having brought my survey of post-1945 first books up to the end of the 1980s, I turn in the next two chapters to more thoroughgoing readings of contemporary poets, first revisiting the beginning of the era of the first-book prize in the 1950s for a discussion of Ashbery's *Some Trees* and then moving to the '60s for a discussion of Glück's poetic career, starting with her debut, *Firstborn*.

3

"Everything Has a Schedule"

John Ashbery's Some Trees

"From the start," Edward Brunner writes, "the very existence of the book had been problematic."[1] W. H. Auden, editor of the Yale Series of Younger Poets, had not declared a winner in 1954, which meant he was under extra pressure to name one in 1955, when Ashbery and Frank O'Hara entered their manuscripts in the contest. That spring Auden read the twelve manuscripts that the readers at the Yale University Press had forwarded to him at Ischia, an island off the coast of Italy where he stayed part of every year, and came up empty. He came up empty again after having Anthony Hecht, who had met Auden by chance while traveling, read through the manuscripts to provide a second opinion. Auden then wrote to Eugene Davidson at the Press to say that he was disappointed by all of the finalists. The fact that Ashbery, whom Auden knew personally, was not among them, aroused his suspicion that the preliminary screening process, in which hundreds of entries were whittled down to just a dozen, was unreliable:

> I am very worried because, for the second year in succession, I do not find among the mss. submitted to me one that I feel merits publication. It so happens that there is another poet staying here, and I have asked him to read them also as a check on my own judgment. He came, however, to the same conclusion.
>
> What bothers me particularly is that a young poet (John Ashbery) whom I know personally told me he was submitting a manuscript this year. I have reservations about such of his poems as I have seen, but they are certainly better than any of the manuscripts which have reached me. I don't know how or by whom the preliminary sieving is

done at the press, but I cannot help wondering whether I am receiving the best.[2]

Rather than refuse again to name a winner, which would result in bad press for the prize, Auden asked Ashbery and O'Hara to resubmit their manuscripts directly to him through Chester Kallman, who was a mutual friend. After that, his choice came quickly: "He received the manuscripts in little more than a week and made up his mind within days. The winner was Ashbery, salvaged from the slush pile to become in time one of the best-known poets the Yale Series has ever published."[3]

That Auden had slighted the judgment of in-house editors at the press by choosing a manuscript they had already weeded out did little to sweeten their reaction, which ranged, as Bradley remarks, "from confusion to outrage." One editor wrote an angry memorandum in response to Auden's choice that ended with a declaration of withdrawal from all future involvement with the series. Others were similarly "unenthusiastic, and a couple of staff members refused their complimentary copies when [*Some Trees*] appeared the following year." Bradley observes that, to its first readers, the surpassingly difficult book that emerged from this strange selection process "must have seemed sheer gobbledygook."[4] But perhaps the most curious element in the aftermath of Auden's choice was that Auden himself seemed to dissent from it. Auden links Ashbery to Rimbaud in the foreword to *Some Trees*, largely in order to diagnose them both with the same "problem": if the danger for neoclassical poets is to "neglect" the particulars of experience, "the danger for a poet working with the subjective life is the reverse," that is, "he is tempted to manufacture calculated oddities as if the subjectively sacred were necessarily on all occasions odd."[5] He wrote to O'Hara in a similar vein: "I think you (and John too, for that matter) must watch what is always the great danger with any 'surrealistic' style, namely of confusing authentic non-logical relations which arouse wonder with accidental ones which arouse mere surprise and in the end fatigue."[6] Ashbery himself has expressed skepticism, on the basis of the foreword, in the idea that Auden "liked" his poetry at all: "I never had felt that he particularly liked my poetry, and his introduction to the book is rather curious, since it doesn't really talk about the poetry. He mentions me as being a kind of successor to Rimbaud, which is very flattering, but at the same time I've always had the feeling that Auden probably never read Rimbaud. He was very outspokenly anti-French."[7]

The "outrage" and "confusion" with which the press awkwardly greeted the winner of the contest they themselves sponsored prefigures the response of Ashbery's reviewers, who were often glad to take their cues from Auden. "I could make very little headway in understanding Mr. John Ashbery's *Some Trees*," William Arrowsmith writes, "and I take some comfort in what I take to be Auden's similar difficulties in the Introduction." Arrowsmith finds in the volume only "two or three poems in the customary idiom of English poetic communication" and confesses to having "no idea most of time what Mr. Ashbery is talking about."[8] Similarly, Donald Hall is more interested in sorting out Ashbery's "faults" than he is celebrating his virtues, and he uses Auden's words to anchor his criticism: "W. H. Auden, speaking in his introduction of the class of poets to which Ashbery belongs, says of the hypothetical representative, 'He is tempted to manufacture calculated oddities.' Ashbery is sometimes such a factory. If writing a poem *about* anything seems impossibly difficult (because of the condition of the world and word) the poet may write only to give his verbs an airing. Ultimately the result will be stale and repetitious." Even Hall's title alludes to Auden: "Oddities and Sestinas."[9]

If the early response to Ashbery portrays both the poet and his first book as "problematic," then it is this same sense of Ashbery's unconventional poetic that more sympathetic critics have seized upon in his defense. For critics such as Marjorie Perloff, Vernon Shetley, David Lehman, and David Herd, recovering *Some Trees* as the promising first installment in the career of one of America's most influential poets means turning the fairly negative early assessment of the book on its head. Having no idea "what Mr. Ashbery is talking about" signals in this context a daring opposition to an institutionalized literary culture that seemed to demand conformity on every front. This reading, in other words, leaves much of the first impression elaborated by the likes of Auden, Arrowsmith, and Hall intact, but ascribes value to the "oddity" that had formerly served as grounds for complaint. In this way, what for Auden was a risky experimentation with the subjective mode of Rimbaud figures in Lehman's account as the admirable abandon of an avant-garde poet bent on revitalizing "the American poetry of the time," which had grown "crusty with convention."[10] In order to "mount an avant-garde assault on the proprieties of literary America, [Ashbery and the other poets of the New York School] conceived of themselves as outsiders and consciously looked to foreign climes for alternative models to try on for size." Similarly, in Herd's account, the value of Ashbery's poetry derives in part from the energy with which "the poets of the New York School felt impelled to write against what became thought of—owing to the poets' university affiliations, their friendship with the New Critics, and their preoccupation with matters of form—as the academic style of the Lowell-dominated middle generation."[11] Shetley goes the farthest to substantiate the opposition between Ashbery and the New Criticism, which consists, in his account, in Ashbery's disruption of the New Critical notion of "speaker" by using ambiguous pronouns and his defiance of the New Critical taste for emotional detachment by allowing feelings into his verse.[12] Like Lehman and Herd, Shetley's claims seem to take their impetus from Ashbery's own claims to feeling alienated from the climate of 1950s conformity, when, "with the rise of Robert Lowell," as Ashbery explains in an interview, "everything became much more codified and academicized."[13] "Without the contribution of poets" dedicated to opposing the New Critics, Ashbery claims in his introduction to the *Collected Poems of Frank O'Hara*, "there probably wouldn't be a generation of young poets committed to poetry as something living rather than an academic parlor game."[14]

The opposition of *Some Trees* to the established poetic practice of the 1950s is a matter of critical consensus from Auden, Arrowsmith, and Hall to Shetley, Lehman, and Herd. I want to put that consensus in question here. If the Ashbery of *Some Trees* is committed to poetry as something other than "an academic parlor game," why, once we have put aside the negative connotation it carries in the context of Ashbery's observation, does his poetry often seem to fit that description so well? (The title of Ashbery's 2003 collection, *Chinese Whispers*, connects poetry to a "parlor game" directly, and it recalls a New York School atmosphere that favored all kinds of artistic competition and collaboration.) That both his detractors and his defenders share an emphasis on the unconventional aspects of Ashbery's poetic—those "oddities" that seem out of keeping with the "customary idiom of English poetic communication" used in the "academic parlor"—reflects the impoverishment of a reception hobbled by the division between establishment and countercultural poetries that has often structured discussions of post-1945 American poetry.

As I noted in the preceding chapter, recent critical work has complicated this division by showing how, for example, a poet may undergo a metamorphosis from "outlaw to classic," as Alan Golding puts it in the title of his study, or how this binary system of classification fractures upon closer inspection into multiple versions of both the mainstream and the margin so that the line between them becomes more difficult to isolate, as Michael Davidson has demonstrated.[15] More recently, in a valuable discussion of Ashbery as a "Janus-faced personage" aligned both with tradition and the avant-garde, Ellen Levy rightly observes that most commentators "have been concerned not so much with considering what it might mean that Ashbery's poetic persona is so relentlessly divided from within, as with establishing which of Ashbery's faces is the true one."[16] Planting *Some Trees* on a margin that traffics almost not at all with the mainstream, critics tend to stress the ways in which Ashbery resists the intelligence at the expense of the ways in which he courts it. As I will argue here, *Some Trees* is very much in keeping with the conventions of an increasingly professionalized, university-centered, and prize-focused post-1945 literary mainstream in which the award-winning first book occupies a uniquely contradictory position, one that ensures that the newcomer's challenge to establishment norms and public consecration in the name of those norms coincide with one another. Ashbery's sensitivity to the ironies of this position suffuses the volume, which demands to be read as a hybrid work, one that brings the discourses of tradition and the avant-garde into dynamic relationship with one another.

Crucial to the account of *Some Trees* that I seek to articulate here is the notion of career. In his first book and throughout his work, Ashbery's crossing of registers is enabled by his paradoxical representation of his path. On the one hand, career enacts a break from establishment norms, for it reflects a "drive for self-distinction and self-assertion."[17] On the other hand, career also entails a return to the mainstream from the margins: it is a "pattern of organization of the self," as Larson puts it, one whose defined course of development bespeaks a unitary selfhood and a disciplined work ethic that figure as prominent establishment values.[18] So it is that career in Ashbery's poems goes hand in hand with the theme of beginning, and his exploration of heroic progress in *Some Trees* anticipates a central strain of ambivalence in his subsequent work that involves "always coming back / To the mooring of starting out," as he puts it in a passage I quoted earlier.

Lehman's claim that Ashbery made his "assault on the proprieties of literary America" as an "outsider" to the mainstream poetry scene of the 1950s becomes more difficult to allow in light of the facts of Ashbery's coming of age. The story of his emergence runs parallel, to a surprising extent, to that of Sylvia Plath, whose dedication to the inside track to success is documented in her journals. Like Plath, Ashbery was precocious. He won "school prizes and spelling bees" just like she did; he "went on a national radio show as a 'quiz kid'" just as she won a national competition to serve as guest editor at *Mademoiselle*.[19] While still in high school, he published poems in *Poetry*, just as she published work in the *Atlantic Monthly* and other national magazines before college. Each received an undergraduate education at an elite Northeastern school—Plath at Smith

College, Ashbery at Harvard University: he served as an editor of the *Harvard Advocate*, she served as editor of the *Smith Review*. Ashbery won departmental honors upon graduation for his thesis on W. H. Auden; Plath, who interviewed Auden when he visited Smith (and who wrote in her copy of his *Collected Poems*, "I found my god in W. H. Auden"),[20] graduated *summa cum laude*. Ashbery earned a master's degree from Columbia University and soon after moved to France to stay; Plath went to England directly after graduating from Smith to earn a master's degree at Cambridge University. (That both went to graduate school, but neither earned a Ph.D., reflects the difficulty of writing poetry while fulfilling the professional obligations of the academic, on the one hand, and the difficulty of writing it without the support of the academy, on the other.) Both poets submitted their work to Auden in the mid-1950s in hopes of winning the Yale Younger Poets award. That Ashbery won the award straightaway thanks in part to his connection with the judge, while Plath tried and failed several times, casts Ashbery as more of an insider than critics have generally been inclined to allow.

Even the unusual circumstances surrounding Auden's selection of Ashbery were not out of keeping with his typical procedures. Auden already had a well-established reputation for eccentric editorial practices. His first selection for the series was *Poems* by Joan Murray, whose manuscript had been edited and submitted to the contest by another poet, Grant Code, since Murray herself had been dead for five years. As Bradley remarks, "It seemed a bit odd to print a posthumous Younger Poet—it could hardly be said to provide fair promise for the future—but the press let Auden have his way."[21] Auden's second selection for the series, Robert Horan's *A Beginning*, was never submitted to the competition in the first place. Auden had heard of Horan, Bradley speculates, "through his opera connections," and was an admirer of the Activists—a poetry group that counted Horan as a member. Disappointed by the manuscripts the press had sent him, Auden took it upon himself to recruit Horan for the series. Murray's book, Horan's, and that of Rosalie Moore, who won the next year, were so "flagrantly inaccessible," according to Bradley's account, that Eugene Davidson had half a mind to replace Auden just a few years into his tenure as judge.

In 1949 Auden declined to choose a winner, claiming that none of the finalists were up to his standards, and he would do so again in 1954. Auden's refusals to choose winners, his openness to "inaccessible" work, and his reliance on insiders like Horan and Ashbery to fill the ranks of the series work to privilege what James English calls "an aesthetic paradigm in terms of which only a handful of people (genuine artists) are actually capable of producing authentic works of poetry, and the failed attempts of others cannot be said to hold any artistic value whatsoever."[22] Thus the strange circumstances that led to Auden's selection of Ashbery set the stage not so much for a "problematic" debut, but, from a broader historical perspective, a fairly typical one. Auden's scandalous editorial procedures represent an affirmation of the autonomy of the aesthetic: his decision to ignore the imperative for the Yale Press to publish a winning manuscript, for example, reflects his sense that a work of art must be evaluated solely on its own terms, without reference to external interests. In this way his procedures serve to frame *Some Trees* as the embodiment of a central principle of the very New Critical orthodoxy to which Ashbery is often thought to be opposed.

The context in which *Some Trees* first appeared is reflected in the text of the book itself, which, for all its antic energy, can seem to put New Critical prescription into practice with an almost programmatic comprehensiveness. I wish to build here on Andrew DuBois's useful account of the affinities between the volume's title poem and the norms of mid-century modernism by showing how those norms permeate the whole collection.[23] If the New Critics laid a particular stress on form, for instance, it makes little sense to present as the leading voice of the resistance a poet who included in his debut three sestinas, two sonnets, an eclogue, a pantoum, and a canzone, without some qualifications. With the exception of the sestinas, he used the terms for these forms as the titles of the poems, so that just a "glance at the table of contents tells us, first of all, how thoroughly aware Ashbery is of his conventions—more than aware, elated to have them at hand," as Richard Howard remarks.[24] The resemblance of the table of contents of *Some Trees* to that of a poetry handbook or "instruction manual," as Ashbery might put it, is reinforced by the many additional poems that take their titles from other literary forms: "Two Scenes," "Popular Songs," "The Instruction Manual," "Illustration," "A Long Novel," and "A Pastoral." Ashbery promotes the importance of form much in the manner of the New Criticism, according to which—to quote here from its "instruction manual," *Understanding Poetry*—form is not a "kind of container, a kind of box, in which the stuff of poetry has been packed. Form is much more than that. The form does more than 'contain' the poetic stuff: it organizes it; it shapes it; it defines its meaning."[25] While the conspicuousness of Ashbery's privileging of form is exceptional, he is not alone among beginning poets of the time in bringing form to the fore: *Some Trees* represents an extreme enactment, in this regard, of a common tendency among post-1945 American poetic debuts. As Brunner's discussion of the pervasiveness of the sestina during the 1950s suggests, Ashbery's overt formalism does not set him at odds with a decade dominated by the New Criticism; rather, it reflects a striking accord with it: "two sestinas to a book was hardly exceptional. John Ashbery went for three in *Some Trees* (1956), and Donald Justice followed his two standard sestinas with two variant examples in *The Summer Anniversaries* (1959). Sestinas were commonplace in first books of poetry, especially award-winning books. . . . Prize-winning or not, a book of poems in the 1950s must have seemed unfurnished without a sestina."[26] If Ashbery's handling of traditional forms is sometimes satirical or irreverent, the fact remains that such experimentation unmistakably signals virtuosity in a category of aesthetic competence that the New Critics valued highly.

Ashbery is often characterized as an anti-autobiographical poet. If "Ashbery's poetry tells 'anybody's story' in general," as Shoptaw remarks, "it sounds like nobody's story in particular: 'This is / No one's story!' "[27] This effect is achieved in part through a willingness to allow anything and everything to serve as the raw materials for a poem, with the result that the materials themselves—though one senses that Ashbery glories in their variety—yield their priority to form in the scheme of his aesthetic. This notion is adumbrated in "Syringa," which portrays the "subject" of a poem as if it were "helplessly" remote from a poem's "meaning": "Its subject / Matters too much, and not enough, standing there helplessly / While the poem streaked by, its tail afire, a bad / Comet screaming hate and disaster, but so turned inward / That the meaning, good or other, can never / Become known" (*JACP* 536). For Ashbery as for the New Critics, emphasis on the formal aspect of poetry goes hand in hand with a tendency to assign the subject—and subject matter generally—a position of secondary importance in the evaluation of "poetic effect." Repeatedly in *Understanding Poetry*, Brooks and Warren demonstrate the significance of poetic form at the expense of *materia poetica* by quoting passages that take as their subject something "that in real life would be disagreeable or mean" and transform it through adroit formal management into "great poetry," because "the poetic effect depends not on the things themselves but on the kind of use the poet makes of them."[28] *What* the poet intends to say and *what* materials the poem addresses, tend, according to New Critical doctrine—insofar as it is embodied in such key principles as the "intentional fallacy" and the "heresy of paraphrase"—to take a back seat to the questions of *how* the poem communicates its effect and *how* its materials are arranged and presented. In *Some Trees* we find poems so resistant to attempts to infer

Ashbery's intention, so impervious to paraphrase, that they enforce by example the reading practices that the New Criticism promoted.

With Ashbery's early career trajectory and his alignment with some of
the central tenets of the New Criticism in view, it is easier to see some of
the ways in which he fits the mold of the post-1945 "academic" poet. Claude
Rawson has commented on Ashbery's "academicized literary idiom." Like
the ostensibly more conventional poets to whom Ashbery is often contrasted, "he is," as Rawson explains, "in many ways a critics' poet," "the
product of a culture whose reading is shaped in the seminar-room and
which accepts 'explication' (even defeated explication, which is a permanent
invitation to more explication) as an essential constituent of the reading experience."[29] Rawson captures the way in which Ashbery's extreme difficulty—the capacity of his poetry to "defeat[] explication"—is not so much
a sign of what Lehman calls his "anti-establishment, anti-academic" stance,
as it is a clue to the radical intensity with which he practices the sort of
writing that the academic establishment endorsed. Even Frank O'Hara's
1957 review of *Some Trees* in *Poetry*, which attempts to position Ashbery
"outside the Academic-suburban-communications area," cannot help but
praise the book for qualities that tend to play well in the academy: its "considerable technical achievement," its "dry wit," and its rampant allusiveness
(he lists Blaise Cendrars, A. E. Housman, W. H. Auden, and Walt Whitman, though one might add Wallace Stevens, Andrew Marvell, Ovid,
Shakespeare, and Daniel Defoe).[30] There is no question that *Some Trees*
does in many ways run counter to the conventions that defined mainstream
poetry of the period: think of the difference between Ashbery and Lowell,
whose clenched style and high seriousness represent the antithesis of Ashbery's light touch with verse forms and mischievous sense of humor.[31] But
riddled as it is with irony, paradox, and ambiguity, laced with learned allusions, virtually devoid of autobiographical reference, filled with intricate
verse forms, stamped with Auden's *imprimatur*, and published in the Yale
Series, *Some Trees* may also fairly be said to epitomize the prize-winning
post-1945 poetic debut.

While Shetley and Herd both emphasize Ashbery's ostensible resistance
to convention, they are nevertheless both alert to the paradoxical situation
in which Ashbery found himself, wherein alignment with the avant-garde
was virtually indistinguishable from submission to traditional authority.
"Ashbery's reaction to the academic poetic and critical establishment of the
1950s and 1960s is complicated by that establishment's identification with
an experimentalist aesthetic," Shetley observes.[32] Like Shetley, Herd suggests that for Ashbery and the poets of his generation, the problem was that

the prestige of the new had itself become old, "or as O'Hara ... put it, 'New is an old word let's get a new one.' "[33] For both Shetley and Herd, Ashbery successfully responds to this dilemma by evading the stance of the (modernist) poet as the hero of the new, who would forge ahead by breaking with tradition. He accomplishes this evasion, according to Shetley, by pursuing a course *"between"* the alternative "dogmatisms of both the vanguard and the establishment."[34] Both critics' accounts illuminate the double bind of post-1945 literary professionalism, but the idea that Ashbery is able to avoid the poetic career by striking a path "between" the alternatives is problematic. After all, to "question the ongoing viability of the distinction between vanguard and tradition," as Shetley claims for Ashbery, is to critique the assumptions that dominate the literary discourse of the period in a way that fits the very model of heroic progress that Ashbery is supposed to elude. In other words, Ashbery's antiheroic questioning of progress in the arts can be seen as a kind of heroism in itself. Something of that heroism comes through even in Shetley's own account, in which Ashbery figures as a covert operative, "undermin[ing]" the "authority" of "traditional forms" from within, or else as the leader of a "two-pronged attack on the New Critical notion of the speaker."[35] Likewise, for Herd, Ashbery is supposed to be writing in opposition to the "heroic individual being" exemplified by Lowell, and yet what could be more heroic—in the field of poetry anyway—than "inaugurat[ing] a new poetic" and thereby "saving American poetry from the parlor"?[36]

Ashbery, for his part, nowhere conceives of himself as free of the constraints of the "heroic" career. Quite the opposite: his poems tend to portray career as a tragic necessity, an inevitable course of progress toward an empty mastery. In "What Is Poetry" from *Houseboat Days*, for example, it appears as a "thin vertical path," that "might give us—what?—some flowers soon?" (*JACP* 520). As much as Ashbery would prefer to escape it, the career notion persists, as its frequent appearances in his work suggest. "The System" offers Ashbery's most explicit theorization of the idea:

> But still the "career" notion intervenes. It is impossible for us at the present time not to think of these people as separate entities, each with his development and aim to be achieved, careers which will "peak" after a while and then go back to being ordinary lives that fade quite naturally into air as they are used up, and are as though they never were, except for the "lesson" which has added an iota to the sum of all human understanding. And this way of speaking has trapped each one of us. (*JACP* 292)

Ashbery critiques the career "notion" here. It is a "way of speaking" that makes it "impossible for us . . . not to think" of others as "separate entities." Not only does it enforce a kind of isolation, but it offers little in the way of significance—the "aim" is to add "an iota to the sum of all human understanding"—and still less in the way permanence, for although careers will "peak," they eventually "fade" away until they "are as though they never were." Ashbery elaborates the pathos of career, but he cannot offer a saving alternative—a discourse other than this one that has "trapped each one of us." Not only does career come between the individual and other people, it also distances the individual from her own experience. As David Bromwich puts it, "Ashbery writes about life with the guarded pleasure of one who cannot possess it."[37] This comes through clearly in "Some Words" from *The Double Dream of Spring*:

> Whether you pass through fields, towns or across the sea
> You will always retain your melancholy
> And look after it; you will have to think of your career
> Not live it . . .
> (*JACP* 218)

The deeply problematic nature of the poetic career as it is represented in Ashbery's poetry reflects not an evasion of the vocational trajectory, but a profound engagement with it. Rather than pursuing a course "between" the vanguard and the traditional, the unconventional and the conventional, I would suggest that he embraces the two in *Some Trees*. The tension between mainstream and margin registers not only in the book's style, which reflects both an interest in traditional forms and an interest in innovation, but also, as I have suggested, in the way that it represents career, which Ashbery, like many of his peers, evokes through the rhetoric of beginning. By elaborating in *Some Trees* such beginning ideas as youth, precocity, and aspiration, among others, Ashbery presents a conventional career narrative that projects a regular course of progress, and yet he also emphasizes the indeterminacy of a path that always tends to lead back to its starting point.

Examining *Some Trees* with an eye to Ashbery's paradoxical formulation of career helps to clarify his notoriously elusive subject matter.[38] The leadoff poem of the volume, "Two Scenes," has baffled some of Ashbery's finest close readers: for John Shoptaw, the poem "deliver[s] little more than the ring of truth," while Marjorie Perloff, in the fashion of those critics who are inclined to emphasize Ashbery's "oddity," suggests that the poem's "signification is purposely left blurred and open," for the "particulars refuse to add up."[39] But Nicholas Jenkins, who views *Some Trees* as "a book of the 1950s" whose "subject matter seems almost deliberately conventional," recognizes in "Two Scenes" the thematization of beginning so typical of leadoff poems in post-1945 debuts: "The starting point, for [Ashbery], is a moment of pure potentiality, a state of unsullied, dewy freshness of perception and inspiration, a time when, as the first lines of Ashbery's first book put it, 'We see us as we truly behave: / From every corner comes a distinctive offering. / The train comes bearing joy.'"[40]

That these lines have to do specifically with beginning a career is reflected not only in the way that they evoke the conspicuously appropriate sense of "pure potentiality" precisely at the beginning of Ashbery's first book, but also in the way they resonate with other moments in which he broods on the career notion. The idea of the "offering," for instance, which figures here as a sign of artistic election, comes up again later in *Some Trees* in "Illustration," where we meet the very type of the beginner—a "novice"—who is "offered . . . some nylons," "little offerings of fruit and candy," and, as the novice herself proclaims, "every good thing" (*JACP* 24). In addition, the presence of the "train" and the "water-pilot" in "Two Scenes" calls up one of the characteristic contexts in which Ashbery reflects on career in his later work. Consider the passage from "Some Words" quoted above, in which the "career" must govern life, "whether you pass through fields, towns or across the sea." Or consider the passage from "A Wave" quoted in the introduction: "So all the slightly more than young / Get moved up whether they like it or not, and only / The very old or the very young have any say in the matter, / Whether they are a train or a boat or just a road leading / across a plain, from nowhere to nowhere" (*JACP* 799). The various modes of travel alluded to here suggest that the career notion intervenes regardless of the terms on which the journey is conceived.

The key to the poem is in the way the second of the poem's two "scenes" misrepresents the first and thus serves to introduce—by way of a particularly clear example—what Shoptaw calls Ashbery's "misrepresentative" poetics:[41]

I

We see us as we truly behave:
From every corner comes a distinctive offering.
The train comes bearing joy;
The sparks it strikes illuminate the table.

Destiny guides the water-pilot, and it is destiny.
For long we hadn't heard so much news, such noise.
The day was warm and pleasant.
"We see you in your hair,
Air resting on the tips of mountains."

II

A fine rain anoints the canal machinery.
This is perhaps a day of general honesty
Without example in the world's history
Though the fumes are not of a singular authority
And indeed are dry as poverty.
Terrific units are on an old man
In the blue shadow of some paint cans
As laughing cadets say, "In the evening
Everything has a schedule, if you can find out what it is."
(*JACP* 3)

Shoptaw observes that "several of the poems in *Some Trees* separate into two parts, which function most often as a narrative and its reflective aftermath," though in his account, "Two Scenes" represents an exception to this tendency: "There is no definite relation (such as there and here, then and now) between the numbered scenes. Each nine-line scene with its closing quotation reflects the other; in fact, 'Two Scenes' could be read with the stanzas reversed."[42] That the scenes are numbered and so placed within a specific sequential relation to one another suggests, on the contrary, that the poem may be more in keeping with the narrative function Shoptaw sees in Ashbery's two-part poems than Shoptaw himself allows. I would suggest that the two-part structure so common in *Some Trees* frequently delineates a logic of development. A more comprehensive enumeration than Shoptaw provides of the correspondences between part I and part II of "Two Scenes" may clarify that logic: the two parts do mirror each other, as Shoptaw suggests, but the second part rings changes upon the ingredients of the first part, and those changes mark a particular sort of advance.

The stylistic signature of part I is a sort of stuttering repetition or nearrepetition: "Destiny . . . is destiny," "so much news, such noise," "hair, / Air." This unsystematic form of order yields in part II to the strict formality of its prominent scheme of end rhyme: "machinery," "honesty," "history," "authority," "poverty." There is the suggestion of a temporal change in the passage from "day" to "evening" that is underlined by the change in the weather, which starts off "warm and pleasant" but turns in the second part into the drizzle of the "fine rain." The aura of promise and plenty that pervades the first stanza, with its "joy," its "news," and its unique "offer-ing[s]," seems to have been used up by the second, with its "fumes" that are "dry as poverty." The sense of confidence in the truthfulness of vision in the first stanza—"We see us as we truly behave"—fades to a more modest, skeptical mode of observation in the second, in which a "general honesty" may only "perhaps" hold sway. Both stanzas grapple with the question of how time is ordered. The "table" that is "illuminate[d]" by "sparks" in the first section calls up the notion of a time-table by way of its connection with the "train," its proximity to its fellow end-word "destiny" in the next line, and its resonance with the "schedule" in part II, which also stands in need of illumination.

How should we interpret these changes? What sort of action is drama-tized by the differences between scene one and scene two, each of which, as if the poem were a sort of abbreviated play, ends in lines of speech? Considering the poem's obsession with time—"table," "destiny," "history," "day," "evening," "schedule"—I would suggest that the effect of these sub-stitutions is to evoke a kind of maturation: the idealized scene of begin-ning darkens, yielding to a more realistic, "evening" perspective. This com-ing of age is reflected in the shift in the poem's form. The confused sonic play of the first scene yields to a more conventional kind of formal rhyme in the second: like the "cadets" who appear at the end of the poem, it is as if the speaker of "Two Scenes" has gone to school and learned to march. Interestingly, however, the result of this growth is that, while the poem has progressed beyond the beginning, it has nevertheless arrived at another beginning, as the cadets' uncertainty about the "schedule" of things to come in the poem's final lines suggests. Career is most assuredly in effect, though its course, only just begun, remains to be seen.

In the "old man" and "cadets," "Two Scenes" presents the first instance of the filial relationship that reappears throughout the volume. That rela-tionship serves as the primary context for Ashbery's exploration of the mo-ment of beginning, and it invests that moment with special significance, for it allows a coming-of-age story to unfold against a story of generational succession, and thus casts the poet's beginning as the inauguration of a new moment in literary history. "The Mythological Poet," another poem in two numbered sections, offers a variation on the "cadets" and the "old

man" of "Two Scenes" in the figures of the "child" and the "pervert," who
are likewise introduced at the end of the poem (*JACP* 17). Just as the "old
man" is framed by a "blue shadow," so the "child" and "pervert" are pic-
tured "in the shadow / Of a million boats." These resonances take on additional interest in light of the fact that Ashbery opened debut collections
with both poems: "The Mythological Poet," as Shoptaw explains, "opened
Ashbery's privately printed first collection, *Turandot and Other Poems* (1953).
In *Some Trees*, however, it gives way to the more finished 'Two Scenes.'"[43]
The main difference between the two, as Shoptaw's adjective "finished"
seems to suggest, is that "The Mythological Poet" connects the coming-of-
age theme to poetry with an explicitness that Ashbery later transcended,
as he found more effectively subtle ways of handling this material. "The
Mythological Poet" is nevertheless powerful in its own right, and its affinities with "Two Scenes" help to illuminate the hybrid character of *Some Trees*.

The first segment of "The Mythological Poet" describes the replacement of "the toothless murmuring / Of ancient willows, who kept their
trouble / In a stage of music," with a "new / Music, innocent and monstrous / As the ocean's bright display of teeth." Significantly, that historical
development coincides with the birth of the "Mythological Poet":

> The music brought us what it seemed
> We had long desired, but in a form
> So rarefied there was no emptiness
> Of sensation, as if pleasure
> Might persist, like a dear friend
> Walking toward one in a dream.
> It was the toothless murmuring
> Of ancient willows, who kept their trouble
> In a stage of music. Without tumult
> Snow-capped mountains and heart-shaped
> Cathedral windows were contained
> There, until only infinity
> Remained of beauty. Then lighter than the air
> We rose and packed the picnic basket.
>
> But there is beside us, they said,
> Whom we do not sustain, the world
> Of things, that rages like a virgin
> Next to our silken thoughts. It can
> Be touched, they said. It cannot harm.

But suddenly their green sides
Foundered, as if the virgin beat
Their airy trellis from within.
Over her furious sighs, a new
Music, innocent and monstrous
As the ocean's bright display of teeth
Fell on the jousting willows.
(*JACP* 16–17)

The willows, as Bloom remarks, are "sacred images of outworn seers," and so the "new music" represents Ashbery's new poetry.[44] If the "new music" is aligned with Ashbery's poetry, then the old music, as Shoptaw suggests, is aligned with "aestheticism," which comes through in the "rarefied" form of the willows' murmuring.[45] The poem thus replays precisely the sort of break with aestheticism attempted by such modernist poets as T. S. Eliot and Ezra Pound. Ashbery's opposition between "toothless" music and a new music that is likened to "the ocean's bright display of teeth" alludes to the particular imagery through which Pound and Eliot imagined the tradition they rebelled against, which figures as "an old bitch gone in the teeth" in "Hugh Selwyn Mauberly" and as a "Dead mountain mouth of carious teeth that cannot spit" in *The Waste Land*.[46] On this reading, "The Mythological Poet" is difficult to square with Shetley's claim that Ashbery does not attempt yet another break "with the past designed to repeat the avant-garde's initial transgressive success."[47] The poem not only explicitly describes such a break, but does so in a way that recalls the terms in which the modernist avant-garde announced its rebellion. That rupture is contingent, in the poem's account, upon the poetic birth encoded in the third stanza, which describes the emergence of the "new / Music" as a consequence of the "founder[ing]" of the womb-like enclosure constituted by the "green sides" of the willows' "airy trellis." Ashbery positions himself, albeit ambivalently, as the inaugural figure of a new poetic generation, as the presence of "founder" in "Foundered" suggests.

The second part of the poem, much like that of "Two Scenes," focuses on the moment of "arrival": "The heavenly / Moment in the heaviness of arrival / Deplores him." Ashbery pursues the poetic career with an ambivalence discernible not only in the way he stresses beginning, a theme which simultaneously lays claim to and defers achievement, but also in the way the beginning itself is portrayed. So it is that the moment of arrival figures here both as a pleasure and a burden: its "heaven[liness]" is inseparable from its "heaviness." The "new music" ushered in by the poet's "arrival" is antithetical to the old music in that it embraces precisely the virginal "world of things" ignored by the seers of part I in their absorption with their own "silken thoughts." That Ashbery's poetry draws on an enormous range of subject matter reinforces the idea that he aligns his work with the "new music" with which the "world of things" is identified. That "world of things" reappears in part II in the image of the "zoo," where the poet "acquiesce[s] / To dust, candy, perverts," for "He has eloped with all music / And does not care." The poem ends with a prophecy of union: "Might not child and pervert / Join hands, in the instant / Of their interest, in the shadow / Of a million boats . . . ?"

"The somewhat sinister 'pervert' appears elsewhere in *Some Trees*," as Shoptaw observes, in "The Pied Piper" and in "He," which presents "a shady character, who 'has had his eye on you from the beginning.'"[48] I would suggest, building on Shoptaw's claim, that these "shady" old men are types of the father-figure we find throughout *Some Trees*: the parallel between the "old man" of "Two Scenes," literally shady in that he appears "in the blue shadow," and the "pervert" from "The Mythological Poet," likewise framed in shadow, may serve as a first piece of supporting evidence. But consider, in addition, the sexual overtones in the father-son conversation in "Eclogue," in which "Colin," the son, exclaims: "Father, I have long dreamed your whitened / Face and sides to accost me in dull play. / If you in your bush indeed know her / Where shall my heart's vagrant tides place her?" (*JACP* 4). These lines evoke a dream of incestuous "play" and then go on to pose an overtly Oedipal question about how Colin should relate to his mother if his father has already "know[n]" her." Or consider another "old man" from *Some Trees*—the "Dad" from "A Boy," whose every word seems saturated with an inappropriate eros: "'My child, I love any vast electrical disturbance.' / Disturbance! Could the old man, face in the rainweed, / Ask more smuttily?" (*JACP* 9).

With this context before us, I think we can recognize in these representations of a heavily fraught intergenerational relationship the outline of what Bloom calls "the primal scene of instruction," a fantasized return to origins driven by "the ambivalent love that a newcomer poet feels for his precursor" and riddled with the same tensions that animate the Family Romance.[49] If the relationship in "The Mythological Poet" is a variation on the filial relationship we see throughout the book, then the union with which the poem closes can be seen as a return to the story of succession elaborated in the first part of the poem, in which the "toothless murmuring / Of ancient willows" gives birth to a "new music." In Bloom's account, the "primal scene of instruction" enacts a "scheme of transumption or meta-leptic reversal" in an attempt to "recover the prestige of origins."[50] And that is precisely what is accomplished in the closing image of the poem, which presents a prophecy of desired union that is also a return to—and reversal of—the traumatic break with tradition out of which Ashbery's "new music" is born. Bloom's model helps to reveal Ashbery's paradoxical imagining of career in "The Mythological Poet" and points up his ambivalence about the establishment to which his path leads back despite being directed toward escape. In the contrast between the "heavenl[iness] and "heaviness of arrival," in the tension embodied within the "new music" that is at once "monstrous and innocent," and on a deeper level, in the redress of a violent poetic birth by means of a closing image of unity, Ashbery upsets the simplistic distinction between breaking new ground and respecting the old—between experiment and convention, margin and mainstream—and instead articulates a dynamic vision of their dialectical relation to one another.

It is worth noting that this ambivalence about career animates not only those poems in *Some Trees*, such as "The Mythological Poet," whose larger ambitions make them apt candidates for analysis on the model of the Bloomian "crisis poem," but also the book's slighter poems. For example, "Glazunoviana" takes an interest in the representation of life as a disorderly array of odds and ends. The poem appears to collect items that are linked to one another only because they have something to do with the nineteenth-century Russian composer Alexander Glazunov. The first of its two stanzas consists of a series of unanswered questions regarding what's "here" in the assemblage, which the speaker wants or expects to encompass such things as a polar bear, a "window giving on shade," "my initials in the sky," and the "hay of an arctic summer night," among others. The second recycles some of these details, including the bear, the window, the arctic, and the night sky, which are set in motion through a series of end-stopped declarative sentences that recall the progress of "Two Scenes" from the chaos of part I to the deliberately forced end rhymes of part II:

> The bear
> Drops dead in sight of the window.
> Lovely tribes have just moved to the north.
> In the flickering evening the martins grow denser.
> Rivers of wings surround us and vast tribulation.
> (*JACP* 10)

The variety of images in the first stanza points to the impossibility of narrating a life as a coherent story of development. And yet the poem also takes up the career notion in ways that suggest it intervenes even amid life's seeming randomness, like a "schedule," as "Two Scenes" portrays it, that is in effect, though it is difficult to "find out what it is." A telling concern with precocity is present here in the figure of Glazunov, who was, like Ashbery, a child prodigy. (That Glazunov's teacher, Nikolai Rimsky-Korsakov, appears in "The Instruction Manual" suggests that Ashbery may again be exploring the theme of generational succession here.) The image of his "initials in the sky," which figures as one of "the little helps," is consistent with the poem's concern with precocity in that it evokes the idea of promise; moreover, the image attests to the persistence of the stable sense of subjectivity that underpins career despite the chaos of memory fragments and inexplicable experiences that engulf the speaker, much as it does in that other poem about precocity from *Some Trees* in which it figures prominently, "The Picture of Little J. A. in a Prospect of Flowers" (*JACP* 13–14). Like "Two Scenes" and "The Mythological Poet," "Glazunoviana" is divided into two parts, and the movement from the first to the second seems to mark a movement forward in time. That the bear "drops dead in sight of the window" suggests a new awareness of mortality, and the concern with the presence of such ordinary things as "the man with the red hat" is replaced in the second stanza by a more serious, even sublime, "evening" vision. The nature of the "vast tribulation" remains undisclosed (though it is linked through a subtle echo to the "lovely tribes" that have "just moved" in). That uncertainty, along with the idea of sudden "grow[th]" encoded here, helps to accentuate the affinity of the poem's developmental logic to that of "Two Scenes," which also ends poised on the brink of a momentous future.

"The Hero," which follows "Glazunoviana" in *Some Trees*, revisits this idea of development. It begins with an unanswered question about the identity of the titular hero, whose "face" is "Lifted to the future / Because there is no end." But the high ambitions encoded in this image, "Like flowers" and the "first days // Of good conduct," have not survived the passage of time, which helps to explain why the speaker of the poem knows why the face is "Lifted to the future," but nevertheless fails to recognize it, at least at first. The poem then turns to the prospect of a confrontation with the figure of the "strong man": "Pinch him," the speaker commands, before ominously adding, in lines that suggest Ashbery's recurrent interest in self-critique, that "There is no end to his / Dislike, the accurate one" (*JACP* 10–11).

Shoptaw notes that one of the earlier titles of the poem was "Doctor Gradus ad Parnassum."[51] That title is taken from a piano composition by Claude Debussy that satirized Muzio Clementi's "Gradus ad Parnassum"—a collection of piano pieces meant for educational purposes in the typical manner of the "Gradus," a term which has historically been used to refer to textbooks in music or language that are intended to lead the student up the "steps to Parnassus." By titling his poem after Debussy's satirical work, Ashbery would have been aligning himself with Debussy in his ridicule of the idea that anyone could reach the heights of Parnassus by following the steps laid out in a primer. In an earlier ending, Shoptaw explains, "the heroic figure with his 'high resolve' was labeled 'a mere // Gigolo.'"[52] In the final version of the poem, Ashbery renders his critique of the "hero" with a softer touch: the heroic posture of the figure whose face is "Lifted to the future" is not so much subjected to ridicule as he is consigned to the past, just like "the first days / Of good conduct."

But although Ashbery regards the *gradus* with a degree of contempt, he does not escape it. Like other poems in *Some Trees*, "The Hero" unfolds in two movements, the first of which presents an idealized vision of the beginning, and the second of which marks a progress away from the beginning even as it returns to it, in a way that evokes the moment of arrival attendant upon coming of age. So it is that the heroic image at the beginning of the poem is replaced in the end by the heroic task of confronting "the strong man," a figure borrowed from Wallace Stevens. In Stevens's "The Latest Freed Man" from *Parts of a World*, "the strong man" is a figure for the "sun," who "bathes in the mist / Like a man without a doctrine" (*WSCP* 187). The freedom of the "freed man" is gained, in the poem's account, when he changes from "a doctor to an ox" through a "strength that is the strength of the sun." Much as Ashbery would like to be "freed" in "The Hero" from the trappings of his own heroism and so, like the "strong man" in Stevens's poem, enable himself "to be without a description of to be," the very fact that he must still "Visit / the strong man" suggests that he remains for the moment a "doctor" living according to a "doctrine." The earlier title of the poem points to the idea that the speaker is himself Doctor Gradus ad Parnassum: the imperatives to "Visit" and "Pinch" the strong man, along with the warning about the accuracy of the strong man's "Dislike," offer a sort of cryptic guidance, then, to the hero about how to make his way. On this reading, the poem acknowledges the authority of the heroic *gradus*, even as it claims that the heroic ideal has "faded." That "There is no end" to the strong man's "Dislike" also returns us to the beginning of the poem, which presents the hero's face "lifted to the future / Because there is no end." This repetition implies the idea that although the hero's "face" may have "faded," he is nevertheless compelled— because "there is no end" even at the end of the poem—to lift it "to the future," just as he does from the start.

The conflicted embrace of the career articulated in "The Hero"—in which the fading of the heroic ideal is ironically combined with instructions on how to achieve it—is articulated in similar terms in "The Instruction Manual," in which Ashbery introduces his poetry as a "new metal" that is also a new "mettle," a form of courage that betokens the heroic stance Ashbery is repeatedly compelled to take up (*JACP* 5). Here again Ashbery makes as if to transcend the career, which is represented, as in "Two Scenes," in the notion of the "schedule." But as in "The Hero," the peculiar resilience of the career notion makes escape impossible, for in Ashbery's paradoxical conceptualization, the effort to transcend career represents the very strategy by which it is advanced, even as its advancement is perpetually foiled by renewed efforts to transcend it. The ironic imagining of career in *Some Trees* haunts Ashbery's oeuvre as a whole. As he claims in "Houseboat Days," published twenty years later, "To praise this, blame that, / Leads one subtly away from the beginning, where / We must stay, in motion" (*JACP* 515).

Ashbery was working in New York in 1955, "writing and editing college textbooks," when he wrote "The Instruction Manual," which, along with "As You Know"—another poem concerned with instruction and involving escape from an institution—was one of the last to be included in *Some Trees*: Shoptaw notes that "neither poem appears in an early table of contents."[53] "I never actually wrote an instruction manual," Ashbery recalls in an interview, "but I wrote the poem in an office of McGraw-Hill in New York."[54] That he fabricates the idea of writing an "instruction manual" stresses Ashbery's particular interest in the notion of the *gradus* that haunts "The Hero" and *Some Trees* as a whole. That interest is also reflected in the way the title stands in an intriguingly antithetical relation to the poem: it directs our attention to an obscure textbook that has not yet been written, while the majority of the poem is taken up with a rhapsodic description of Guadalajara. The title serves to assign priority to a specifically professional scene of writing, and it evokes career through the oblique reference, via the textbook or "manual," to the notion of the *gradus*. As the poem bears out, though, Ashbery's progress is anything but linear; instead he drifts between an imperative to write from which he seeks to escape and a fantasized escape limited in turn by the imperative to write.[55] As he remarks in the passage from "Some Words" quoted above, "you will have to think of your career / Not live it," and the concept of the *gradus* is well-suited to Ashbery's sense of abstraction from life, for it positions him, in this case, at a remove from the practical "uses of the new metal." Not only does the manual, like the poetic career, reflect Ashbery's distance from his own life, but—again like the career—his distance from other people as well:

> I look down into the street and see people, each walking with an inner peace,
> And envy them—they are so far away from me!
> Not one of them has to worry about getting out this manual on schedule.
> (*JACP* 5–6)

The structure of the poem follows the "reality-dream-reality structure of the greater romantic lyric," as Perloff has noted.[56] Ashbery alludes to his McGraw-Hill office in the poem's opening lines, which present the speaker "looking out of a window of the building" wishing he "did not have to write the instruction manual on the uses of a new metal." The speaker fancies that he sees, "under the press" of having to get the manual "out . . . on schedule," the city of Guadalajara. The middle section of the poem presents an imaginary tour of the city, rendered in a language of rapturous emotion:

> But I fancy I see, under the press of having to write the instruction manual,
> Your public square, city, with its elaborate little bandstand!
> The band is playing *Scheherazade* by Rimsky-Korsakov.
> Around stand the flower girls, handing out rose- and lemon-colored flowers,
> Each attractive in her rose-and-blue striped dress (Oh! such shades of rose and blue),
> And nearby is the little white booth where women in green serve you green and yellow fruit.

The framing narrative returns at the end of the poem, as the exotic reverie ends:

> What more is there to do, except stay? And that we cannot do.
> And as the last breeze freshens the top of the weathered old tower, I turn my gaze
> Back to the instruction manual which has made me dream of Guadalajara.
> (*JACP* 6–8)

The dual structure of the poem neatly reflects Ashbery's ambivalence about career. It compels his departure from it—the "press" of producing the manual "on schedule" has "made [him] dream of Guadalajara"—even as it compels his return to it.

Significantly, however, the departure and return are finally illusory. The deliberateness with which Ashbery dutifully "turn[s]" his "gaze / Back to the instruction manual" in the poem's closing lines suggests that the career never lets him go, and the copiousness of the description of Guadalajara may itself be read as the result of a professional imperative to produce writing that follows him even into his dreams. That the two worlds of the poem differ from each other less than the clear transitions between reality and dream might at first suggest is borne out by Ashbery's incorporation of a double for himself in the midst of his reverie:

> An old woman in gray sits there, fanning herself with a palm leaf fan.
> She welcomes us to her patio, and offers us a cooling drink.
> "My son is in Mexico City," she says. "He would welcome you too
> If he were here. But his job is with a bank there.
> Look, here is a photograph of him."
> And a dark-skinned lad with pearly teeth grins out at us from the
>   worn leather frame.

It is in keeping with the Oedipal paradigm evoked throughout *Some Trees* that Ashbery should present himself in the image of a double who is introduced as a "son." Like the "dark-skinned lad" in the picture, Ashbery is not actually present "here" in Guadalajara, but is "there," working at a "job" in the "City." The old woman's son serves to remind Ashbery of his responsibilities: directly upon viewing the picture, he realizes that "it is getting late / And we must catch a view of the city, before we leave, from a good high place." Just as the woman's son parallels Ashbery, so the "good high place" to which Ashbery adjourns following his visit parallels his perspective back at the office, where he sits "look[ing] down" at the "far away" people in the street below.

The effect of these parallels is to point up Ashbery's awareness of the complex interdependence of "inside" and "outside," tradition and avant-garde, in the context of a post-1945 American literary culture that frames the prize-winning first book as a site of production in which these oppositions collapse: the outsider becomes an insider whose appeal derives from his status as an outsider; the vanguard is absorbed into the pseudo-tradition of the prize "series" whose prestige is bound up with its connection to the vanguard. Writing "The Instruction Manual" instead of the instruction manual he's supposed to be writing, walking the streets of Guadalajara while sitting in a New York office, abandoning his schedule only to insist on returning on time, Ashbery aligns himself with the establishment even as he rebels against it.

His position in the poem not only evokes a sense of resignation to the status quo in which the institution, symbolized here by the publishing house of McGraw-Hill, conditions even the space beyond it, but it also evokes a sense of the way in which the temporal and spatial strictures of the workplace can enable creativity, since it is "the instruction manual which has *made me dream* of Guadalajara" (my italics), a connection emphasized in the last line of the poem. Similarly, if the instruction manual, as a vehicle for the transmission of a set of normative practices, makes a ready figure for tradition, then we can see how tradition instigates Ashbery's opposition, just as his opposition will eventually be absorbed by the tradition in turn. This dialectical movement is reflected in the ironic process through which rebelling against writing the instruction manual leads to writing "The Instruction Manual." Ashbery's ambivalence about career is reflected not only in the poem's two worlds, but also in the thematization of beginning, which the imperative to conform and the imperative to avoid conformity dramatized in those worlds cooperate to privilege. Like his Guadalajaran double, Ashbery "grins out at us" from within the "frame" of his professional career, which he returns to at the end of the poem, only to begin again.

4

From *Firstborn* to *Vita Nova*
Louise Glück's Born-Again Professionalism

The fundamental experience of the writer is helplessness.
This does not mean to distinguish writing from being alive:
it means to correct the fantasy that creative work is an ongoing
record of the triumph of volition, that the writer is someone who has
the good luck to be able to do what he or she wishes to do: to
confidently and regularly imprint his being on a sheet of paper.
—Louise Glück, "The Education of the Poet"

In 1968 Louise Glück published *Firstborn*, her first book of poems, when she was just twenty-five years old. Poetic debuts had appeared during the 1950s and '60s from poets who were still younger: Adrienne Rich was twenty-one when she published *A Change of World* in 1950, and James Tate was twenty-four when *The Lost Pilot* came out in 1967. But if Glück's age does not by itself evoke her ambition, a glance at the copyright page of *Firstborn* will leave little doubt about it. Studying poetry under Leonie Adams and Stanley Kunitz at the School of General Studies at Columbia University, she worked assiduously toward the publication of her debut, as more than half of the poems in the book were published beforehand in a variety of magazines. Three poems had previously appeared in the *New Yorker*, and two each in the *Atlantic Monthly* and the *Nation*. Another eight poems had appeared in journals that were scarcely less prestigious: *Poetry, Salmagundi, Tri-Quarterly*, and the *Yale Review*. Her spartan dedication— "To my teacher"—attests to the specifically professional terms on which she pursued her ambition in the way it highlights a notion of formal train-ing even as it secrets the terms of that training—who is the teacher, and what exactly did he or she teach?—behind a veil of anonymity. The title of the volume reflects the conflicting imperatives of literary professionalism:

the poetic birth announced in *Firstborn* is also a death, as its implicit evocation of child sacrifice suggests. The word initiates the narration of the normative career at the same time that it declares the impossibility of doing so.

Like many of the poetic debuts of the post-1945 period, the volume opens with a poem about a journey. The speaker sits across from a man, woman, and child on a train. They are asleep for "the whole ride," but though they scarcely move, the speaker cannot help but study them with a kind of rising disgust that comes across, for example, in the description of the man's "barren / Skull" laying on the armrest and the "kid" who "Got his head between his mama's legs and slept." Their stillness registers not as peacefulness, nor even as the heavy slumber of exhaustion, but as a "paralysis preceding death." What small movements appear in the poem are captured in the last line, which yokes the woman's sexuality together with the child's uncleanliness:

And they sat—as though paralysis preceding death
Had nailed them there. The track bent south.
I saw her pulsing crotch . . . the lice rooted in that baby's hair.[1]

It is characteristic of Glück's uniquely severe enactment of the contradictory impulses of professionalism that the poem should seem to be at odds with itself on several levels. The poem's opening phrase, "Across from me," stresses the proximity of the speaker to the other passengers in the scene even as it puts distance between them by presenting their relationship under the aspect of opposition. Its steep enjambments; its two quatrains that have been compressed into one dense stanza; and its colon, ellipsis, and dash reflect a mode of textual production that is also a mode of reduction: at virtually every turn, parts of an earlier draft of the poem seem to have been cut away. The same goes for the poem's evocation of eros: as Lynn Keller observes, if "the pulsing of the crotch in this poem suggests sexual arousal," then it also reflects a "horrifying lack of control over her sexual desires." There is also a tension between the implicit mobility of the train—"The track bent south"—and the immobility, relative to one another, of the passengers, who seem to be "nailed" in place.

The motionless tableau before the speaker includes "Mister," a mother, and a "kid": together they evoke the familial context, organized around the age-old "metaphor of childbirth which seems never to die," as Glück puts it, that so often serves as a backdrop to her reflections on poetic vocation (and which, as we saw in the last chapter, Ashbery's reflections on intergenerational relationships also invoke) (*PT* 3). The position of the child's head "between his mama's legs" evokes the idea of birth, a notion further reinforced by the verb "Got." Consistent with the poem's logic of negation, the child appears to reject its own life. As Keller remarks, "the child . . . desires to press back toward the womb and prenatal weightless unconsciousness."[2] The emphasis on "paralysis" suggests that the ambivalent beginning that the poem makes represents a permanent state: much like Sisyphus in "The Mountain," Glück's work, the poem seems to suggest, must start over and over. With such leadoff poems from post-1945 debuts in mind as Sylvia Plath's "The Manor Garden," Amiri Baraka's "Preface to a Twenty Volume Suicide Note," or John Ashbery's "Two Scenes," it should come as no surprise that "The Chicago Train" reflects on Glück's conflicted embrace of the normative career path. Both "hungry for praise and ashamed of that," as she puts it in "The Education of the Poet," the path toward "distinction" is no sooner projected in her work than it is vehemently denied (*PT* 10).

Frank Bidart observes that "a little collection could be made of the negative things that Gluck has said about herself. This is not an attempt to charm; it is part of the poems' air of astringency, of applying the same disabused intelligence to the self that the self applies to the world."[3] This negative impulse represents for Glück the operation of will: "The only real exercise of will is negative: we have toward what we write the power of veto" (*PT* 3). As Bidart suggests, this impulse is present throughout Gluck's work, and it represents one important index to her professionalism, for the professional is likewise required to train on herself "the same disabused intelligence" that she employs on the job. That is to say that Glück's uncompromisingly critical perspective evokes precisely the rational self-discipline that underpins professional authority and autonomy. That impulse governs Gluck's poetic career: "Each book I've written has culminated in a conscious diagnostic act, a swearing off" (*PT* 17). Taking this principle into consideration, it becomes difficult to view her career as a steady forward progress—much though, for Glück, that is something devoutly to be wished. What foils the progress of the developmental narrative she desires is the unreliability of her *materia poetica*—which she sometimes figures as moments of "illumination," but more often and less grandly calls "material" or "matter"—as when she wryly exclaims in "Vita Nova," "O Blizzard, / be a brave dog—this is / all material; you'll wake up / in a different world, / you will eat again, you will grow up into a poet!"[4] She describes the opposition between the "unbroken line" of the ideal poetic career and the instability of such "material" succinctly in her essay "On T. S.

Eliot": her "mind," like Eliot's, "with its hunger for meaning and disposition to awe, its craving for the path, the continuum, the unbroken line, for
what is final, immutable, cannot sustain itself on matter and natural process" (*PT* 21). "The path to the hidden world," she writes in another context, tracing out another permutation of the same fundamental opposition
between "mind" and "matter," "is not inscribed by the will" (*PT* 7).

If, then, we cannot quite describe her career as a "developmental triumph," as Tony Hoagland does, neither can we describe it in terms of an
abject stasis.[5] As the contradictions of "The Chicago Train" suggest, Glück's
career follows the paradoxical logic of an ongoing process of beginning that
Ashbery articulates in "Houseboat Days": proceeding "away from the beginning," "We must stay" there, nevertheless, "in motion." As I suggested
in chapter 2, this logic is invoked in different ways by a number of post-1945
American poets with diverse affiliations, from Ashbery and Baraka to Michael Palmer and Lyn Hejinian. (Hejinian's sense of having "undertake[n]
a completely new project with each book I've written" very nearly echoes
Glück's claim, quoted above, about beginning anew in the wake of the
"conscious diagnostic act" that follows "each book" in her career.)[6] The special clarity with which Glück formulates this logic helps to shed light on its
presence in the way that her contemporaries represent their poetic careers.
What for other poets is apt to appear as a fairly unruly, though crucial,
process of self-reinvention registers in Glück's work as a strictly observed
regimen: while each book "culminates" in a "conscious diagnostic act" that
points the way forward to the next volume through a progressive transcendence of limitations, that "diagnostic act" is also "a swearing off" that marks
a movement of return, through a process of purgation, toward the book
with which she began her career and her initial motives for writing poetry.
As I have argued in previous chapters, the conflict between technicality and
indetermination that underlies the contradictory career logic evident here
leads to a powerful emphasis on beginning. But for Glück, the thematization of what Ashbery calls "the mooring of starting out" that is so often
expressed explicitly in post-1945 debuts persists with a kind of austere regularity throughout her oeuvre, which it represents as a series of beginnings.

Turning from my focus on first books to a consideration of Glück's work
over the first eight books of her career, I seek in this chapter not only to
offer a detailed reading of a poet whose work, though widely acclaimed,
remains surprisingly understudied, but also to continue to shed light both
on the nature of the poetic career and the moment of beginning—
formalized in the prize-winning debut—that has increasingly come to define it. I argue that Glück's work exhibits with unique clarity the obsession

with vocational integrity that propels the privileging of the first book as a special site of production within the culture of post-1945 American poetry.

The persistence of Glück's pattern of self-reinitiation reflects the roots of literary professionalism in the Calvinist theology of election, which demanded an endless practice of self-examination driven by constant awareness of innate depravity: "The Puritan must always be vigilant, for even those who achieve a crisis conversion are not assured of salvation. A perfect assurance, in fact, is considered a sign of the unelect."[7] The "crisis conversion," in other words, initiates a state of ongoing vocational anxiety that cannot be resolved, despite the fact that for the Puritan (as for Glück) settling the question of vocation—elect or reprobate?—may be seen as life's single most important concern. Glück's example drives home the point that the representation of career in the era of the first-book prize is hardly a simple or perfunctory reaction to poetry's institutionalization in the academy, and still less a convenient strategy of self-promotion. Rather, the complexity with which the theme of regeneration is articulated in Glück's poetry bespeaks the resourcefulness of a poet prompted by remarkable self-discipline to return time and again to the question of the authenticity of vocation.

Adam Smith isolates what Glück calls "distinction" as the primary motive for literary professionalism:

> To excel in any profession, in which but few arrive at mediocrity, is the most decisive mark of what is called genius or superior talents. The public admiration which attends upon such distinguished abilities makes always a part of their reward. It makes a considerable part of that reward in the profession of physic; a still greater perhaps in that of law; *in poetry and philosophy it makes almost the whole.*"[8]

Glück reiterates Smith's point with a blunt precision and a frequency that are telling in themselves: acting as if she were her own Bourdieu, she refuses to allow her motives to take cover in a loftier or more convenient conception of inspiration than her experience warrants. She writes, for example, in "On Courage," of the way D. H. Lawrence can seem "weirdly daring (and, by inference, courageous) in [his] apparent disdain for poetry's single reward, namely approval" (*PT* 24). This "disdain" is only "apparent" because, for Glück, the desire for "approval," "poetry's single reward," must always retain priority in any accurate account of a poet's motives for writing, even if, like Lawrence, he seems to view such approval with contempt.

Glück's view that the desire for approval that serves as poetry's central motive and reward may often take the form of an "apparent" contempt for approval is founded upon an insight into the vicissitudes of her own sense of ambition. The same tension that animates the representation of beginning in her poetry also animates the account of her passion for distinction in "The Education of the Poet." She begins by describing a taste for language she discovered early. Having started reading poems "at four or five or six," Glück finds herself drawn to "the sort of sentence" that enacts a "paradox." But that preference for paradoxical sentences makes for a conflict, she explains, because she is "born into an environment in which the right of any family member to complete the sentence of another" is "assumed"; this assumption spoils the "sweetness of paradox," which inheres in the surprise of its ending. She responds therefore with "silence. Sulky silence, since I never stopped wanting deferential attention. I was bent on personal distinction, which was linked in my mind, to the making of sentences." Even though distinction is "linked . . . to the making of sentences," she pursues it, paradoxically, by maintaining a resolute "silence," or rather, "sulky silence"—that is, a performance of silence that is poised on the brink of speech (*PT* 4–5).

The same dynamic in play here, according to which Glück tries to distinguish herself by eradicating every sign of her desire to distinguish herself, shows up again later in the essay: "Hungry as I was for praise, I was also proud and could not bear to ask for it, to seem to need it" (*PT* 8). And yet again, in the sentence I quoted earlier: "Like most people hungry for praise and ashamed of that, of any hunger, I alternated between contempt for the world that judged me and lacerating self-hatred." That Glück reiterates the point in this way exemplifies her professional self-discipline— her ability to train her "disabused intelligence" relentlessly on herself— even as it stresses the essentially antithetical nature of her conception of her poetic calling, which is motivated by a desire for praise which itself serves as grounds for shame.

But Glück's exploration of vocational ambivalence is not restricted to her prose. Consider how resolutely she takes up the subject in a pair of linked poems from *The Triumph of Achilles*. Daniel Morris interprets "A Parable" conjointly with the poem that precedes it in the volume, "The Mountain," for both poems, he suggests, allow Glück to "explore . . . her own aspirations for glory."[9] In these poems, Morris observes, "Glück symbolizes her desire for literary accomplishment by having her main speaker scale a mountain, such as Parnassus would be within the Greek classical tradition. Both poems graft a personal narrative upon archetypal stories recounting desire for individual attainment."[10] Not only do these poems figure the poetic career by means of the image of the mountain, they also articulate an ambivalence that, as the permanence of their respective "archetypal" contexts implies, figures as a fundamental, unchanging aspect of her sense of vocation.

In "A Parable," that archetypal context is the story of David and Goliath. The poem begins by describing David as an unlikely hero: at first he is only a "nobody, making his way from one plain to another," who "picks up a small stone among the cold, unspecified / rocks of the hillside." The opening describes David's unconsciousness of his destiny by stressing the arbitrariness with which he "picks up [the] small stone" that will serve as the weapon with which he brings down Goliath, who appears in the second stanza as "the beast . . . / towering above the childish shepherd." Upon vanquishing Goliath, "David / lifts his hand: then it is his, the hushed, / completed kingdom":

Fellow Jews, to plot a hero's journey
is to trace a mountain: hero to god, god to ruler.
At the precipice, the moment we don't want to hear about—
the stone is gone; now
the hand is the weapon.[11]

The tension at the heart of Glück's sense of vocation is elaborated through David's transformation from a "nobody" to a "King," which depends upon a curious combination of accident—evident in his random choice of "a small stone among the cold, unspecified / rocks"—and design—evident in the lifting of "his hand" to take credit for Goliath's defeat and so take possession of the "completed kingdom." The poem replays this transformation in miniature in its account of what happens at the "precipice," which is "the moment we don't want to hear about" because it is the moment at which the "stone"—an emblem of fate that stresses David's innocence of the desire for heroic distinction—disappears, and "the hand," which he raises in a gesture of self-acknowledgment, is "now" recognizable as "the weapon."

The poem illuminates the primacy of the hunger for attainment in Glück's conception of her calling. In a way characteristic of the confessional mode she employs when she writes of the poetic career, she refuses to ignore "the moment we don't want to hear about" and instead exposes it as the moment at which the "journey" that formerly appeared to be a function of destiny is revealed, instead, to be a function of desire. Translated into the terms of professionalism, the career, fittingly imaged in the contradictory movements up and down a mountain, is figured as the product of the contradictory imperatives of indetermination, which governs David's fortuitous selection of a stone at the beginning, and technicality, which governs the act of will whereby he brings down Goliath and gains a kingdom at the end. As is typical in Glück's work, the preoccupation with approval that career signifies is registered in conjunction with a troubling lack of human feeling, as if to feel nothing but "desire" for distinction were ultimately to feel "nothing" at all: the poem closes with an image of King David gazing across "the shining city of Jerusalem / into the face of Bathsheba" where he "perceives his own amplified desire." "At heart," Glück adds, "he feels nothing."

As Morris suggests, "A Parable" takes up the same theme as "The Mountain," and it does so largely in the same terms: not only do both poems explore the issue of "attainment" against the backdrop of ancient myth (David and Goliath in "A Parable," Sisyphus in "The Mountain"), but also they share a focus on the images of the "mountain," the "hand," and the "stone." The action of "The Mountain" takes place in a classroom—an appropriate setting, to be sure, for a poem about professionalism, since it symbolizes the professional market that generates the contradictory demands that structure the poetic career. The poem unfolds in two movements. In the first, Glück offers her students a view of the "artist's life" as "a life / of endless labor," a point she illustrates through "the story of Sisyphus, how he was doomed to push / a rock up a mountain, knowing nothing / would come of this effort." The life of the artist appears here under the aspect of indetermination. "There is joy in this, in the artist's life," Glück explains, precisely because "nothing" comes of the "effort," which is "endless" because it is made for its own sake. The second part of the poem contradicts the first:

> Why do I lie
> to these children? They aren't listening,
> they aren't deceived, their fingers
> tapping at the wooden desks—
> So I retract
> the myth; I tell them it occurs
> in hell, and that the artist lies
> because he is obsessed with attainment,
> that he perceives the summit
> as that place where he will live forever,
> a place about to be
> transformed by his burden . . .

If the figure of the artist in the first version of the myth performed his labor for its own sake, in the second, he does so in order to win glory. The artist knows "nothing / would come" of his "effort" in the first scenario, but in the second, by contrast, he looks forward to the prospect of "transform[ation]." The "endless" labor of the artist in Glück's initial account is replaced in the end by a career motivated by the prospect of a particular goal—the "summit," "that place where he will live forever."[12]

Two versions of career are being elaborated here, and the process by which the latter comes to supplant the former is itself an instance of the double movement that governs Glück's career. At the turning point in the poem, there is what she calls in "The Education of the Poet" a "conscious diagnostic act," through which she comes to see her initial explanation of the artist's life as a "lie." There follows, then, "a swearing off" whereby she "retract[s] / the myth." Much though the contrasts I have mentioned may seem to suggest that the vision of the artist's life offered at the end of the poem marks an advance beyond the vision offered at the beginning, that is by no means the case, for the logic of Glück's career, evident in the way the poem pivots from one story to another, combines a progressive impulse with an impulse of return. That is why, in spite of Glück's retraction, the new version of the myth leaves so much of the original intact. The first myth is a "lie," for instance, but how different could its replacement be, given its blunt insistence that "the artist lies"? Similarly, the second version of the myth "occurs / in hell," but to say so is only to make explicit what seems true, implicitly, in the first version, in which Sisyphus is "doomed" to a "life of endless labor"—endless and also, since "nothing" comes of "this effort," meaningless. The myth of Sisyphus serves as a suitable back-drop for both of the poem's accounts of the path of the artist: on the whole, the poem amplifies the Sisyphian theme of repetition, for though it advances from one career story to another, it also, in a way that is itself consistent with the contradictory logic of Glück's career, returns in the end to the story with which it began.

The stories of vocation that Glück offers her students in "The Mountain" resemble those she elaborates in "The Education of the Poet." Her vocational ambivalence, as we have already seen, is bound up with an obsession with "attainment" that both propels her on her career path and leads her to put that path in question. Not only does "attainment" prompt mixed feelings, but it is also represented in the essay as the product of mixed motives. Consider the contrasting accounts Glück offers in the essay of her reasons for writing. On the one hand, she observes, "My mother was the judge," and "it was her approval I lived on" when she read her daughter's poems, stories, and essays. She stresses the same point later on: "I was sufficiently addicted to my mother's approval to want to shine at something she held in high esteem" (*PT* 6, 8). But this judgment, usually delivered with great precision and no softening by Glück's mother, is exactly what is excluded in another account of the poet's motives in the same essay: "It is very strange to want so much what cannot be achieved in life," she writes. "For those of us attempting dialogue with the great dead . . . the judgment we wait for is made by the unborn; we can never, in our lifetimes, know it." In this alternative take on poetic achievement, the "judgment" Glück "lives on," which she receives in the first account from her mother, is instead to be "made by the unborn" in a future she will never know (*PT* 4).

It could be objected that there is no conflict in the motives for achievement Glück describes here, on the grounds that she might have outgrown her addiction to her mother's judgment and thus come into her desire for the approval of future readers later on. But while I do not mean to suggest that Glück did not change as she grew up, she nevertheless emphasizes her precocity and her aspirations to the highest levels of achievement from a young age a great deal in the essay. Already at "four or five or six" years old, she thinks of the poets she reads as her "companions," and more tellingly, as her "predecessors"—a word that locates the young poet within a continuum that includes "the great dead" and, by implication, "the unborn" (*PT* 4). Further on in the essay, she describes again a sense of connection with "the tradition of my language"—poets such as Shakespeare, Blake, Keats, Yeats, and Eliot. Here she uses the metaphor of the "dialogue with the great dead" explicitly: "I read early, and wanted, from a very early age, to speak in return" (*PT* 7). With this emphatically "early" sense of ambition in view, it becomes clear that both of the contradictory motives that drive Glück to achieve, and to seek judgment for that achievement—motives she links to her mother, and, alternatively, to the "unborn" readers of the future—have been present from the beginning.

Just as Glück offers contradictory accounts of the origins of her poetic ambition, so she also offers opposing accounts of the origins of her literary abilities. Her emphasis on her precocity shows in her persistent stress on the remarkable earliness with which her gifts appeared. Who but a born poet would possess, "early on, a very strong sense that there was no point to speech if speech did not precisely articulate perception"? Likewise, she writes coherent quatrains using the rhyme scheme and alternating meter of the ballad stanza at the age of five: the poem, quoted in full in the essay and framed as evidence of her "preoccupation with syntax," ends, "If robins went out coasting, / They slid down, crying whee, / If all this happened to be true / Then where would people be?" (*PT* 8). She also describes an "argument I had with someone's mother when I was eight or nine" about a poem she had written and recited that "involved a metrical reversal in the last line" (*PT* 9).

But if this discourse of precocity—with its precise notation of age, its supporting evidence, and its resounding accentuation of earliness—suggests that Glück the poet was born not made, it is counterbalanced by a discourse of improvement, which emphasizes the impact of her parents on her growth. Both parents, for instance, serve as models for Glück: both "admired intellectual accomplishment," and while her mother served as "the judge," her father, who "wanted to be a writer," served as "the inspired thinker." Similarly, while her mother "read to us, then taught us to read very early" so that before the age of three she "was well-grounded in the Greek myths," her father "told stories" that "were wholly invented," and also stories that "revised history"—a form that resonates with the preoccupation with mythic analogy that informs much of Glück's poetry. On the view elaborated here, Glück appears as a poet who benefited greatly from the ambitious educational regimen imposed upon her by her parents, who "raised her to aspire to glorious achievement." At the same time, however, she appears as the opposite—a prodigy whose preoccupation with syntax and feeling of kinship with the likes of William Blake and T. S. Eliot suggest that she would have attempted "dialogue with the Great Dead" regardless of her parents' encouragements (*PT* 5–7).

What is notable about the essay is not, I should make clear, that Glück's artistic beginnings reflect a combination of learned skill and natural talent, but rather that her account presses each of these bases for achievement to an extreme that makes the other seem all but irrelevant, for in them we can see the primary impulses of professionalism, which are not only different, but contradictory. Those impulses continue to govern Glück's representation of the "Education of the Poet" as she turns from her beginnings to her apprenticeship. Her gratitude toward her teachers at the School of General Studies at Columbia, Leonie Adams and, later, Stanley Kunitz, reflects a belief that the poetic career is predicated upon the development of acquirable skills: "the whole experience of apprenticeship," she writes, "seems to me beyond value." She benefits on a pragmatic level from her teachers' "scrutiny" of her poems, as well as from the examples they set of a kind of "persistence" over time that Glück images as a "steady upward labor." And yet the reason she values this exemplary "persistence" points to the impossibility of envisioning the career in terms of a "steady" ascent (terms that clearly recall the symbol of the mountain in "The Mountain" and "A Parable"), for she needs it, she explains, in order to survive hiatuses that would seem to rule out a career altogether. From the moment a poem is finished, "the poet, from that point, isn't a poet anymore, simply someone who wishes to be one" (*PT* 14-16). In the same vein, she writes that "the fundamental experience of the writer is helplessness," for "creative work" is not "an ongoing record of the triumph of volition," but an affair of chance. In other words, the mastery of the art of poetry (a possibility she stresses by referring to Kunitz in the essay as "the Master")[13] toward which Glück would seem to advance by serving out her "apprenticeship" is portrayed as a realistic goal, and at the same time as a fantasy, for the word "'Poet' . . . names an aspiration, not an occupation" (*PT* 3).

The reason that the contradictory impulses of professionalism animate not only Glück's account of her obsession with "attainment," but also her accounts of both her motives for writing and her aptitude for poetry, is itself bound up with the ideology of professionalism. That ideology, as I noted earlier, posits a mystical connection between a person and her work, on the principle that the professional is what she does. This formulation of identity encourages the comprehensive saturation of the self in all of its aspects by the same fundamental logic. That equation between self and work explains, for example, why Glück fears that the cure for her anorexia at the hands of her psychoanalyst will *also* affect her ability to write poetry: "I'd turn to my doctor with the old accusation: he'd make me so well, so whole, I'd never write again" (*PT* 12). The fear rests on the assumption that to "tamper with the mechanism," as Glück puts it, that produces anorexia would also be to tamper with the mechanism that generates her ambition and inspires her to write. In the same way, when she claims to be "hungry for praise and ashamed of that fact," she employs the metaphor of hunger deliberately, in order to imply a connection between her hunger for praise, the denial of which issues in a sense of radical detachment from the world, and her hunger for food, the denial of which issues in a similar sense of detachment from the body.

Glück makes the connection between writing and anorexia explicit in "The Deviation," the fourth section of "Dedication to Hunger" from *Descending Figure*:

It begins quietly
in certain female children:
the fear of death, taking as its form
dedication to hunger,
because a woman's body
is a grave; it will accept

anything. I remember
lying in bed at night
touching the soft, digressive breasts,
touching, at fifteen,
the interfering flesh
that I would sacrifice
until the limbs were free
of blossom and subterfuge: I felt
what I feel now, aligning these words—
it is the same need to perfect,
of which death is the mere byproduct.[14]

The poem traces a paradoxical course. Anorexia, in "The Education of the Poet," represents a negative strategy of self-fashioning involving the denial of "all forms of dependency" as a way to "establish a self with clear boundaries." But "the tragedy of anorexia," she goes on to explain, is "that its intent is not self-destructive, though its outcome so often is." This is because the renunciation of "dependency" on food is "impossible to sustain by mere act of will," and so "anorexia proves not the soul's superiority to but its dependence on flesh" (*PT* 10–11). In "The Deviation," the soul's ultimate "dependence on flesh" is reflected in the return, at the end of the poem, of the very prospect of "death" that the speaker attempts to escape, through her "dedication to hunger," at the beginning.

The poem amplifies the account of anorexia in "The Education of the Poet" by elaborating an opposition between form and nature. The equation of the "body" with the "grave" in the fifth and sixth lines of the poem rests on the idea that because the death of the body is inevitable, the body itself functions as a symbol for the "grave" for which it is destined. This metonymic connection between body and grave is overlaid by a metaphorical one: the "woman's body / *is* a grave" because "it will accept anything." The "mere act of will" through which Glück dedicates herself to "hunger" is aligned with the idea of "form" here: it stands opposed to the natural processes represented by the empty void of the "grave" that symbolizes the formlessness of "death," the growth of the "interfering flesh" of the body, and the unruly sexuality evoked in the images of the "woman's body" that "will accept / anything," the "digressive breasts," and the "blossom and subterfuge" of the "limbs."

The poem relates the opposition between the discipline of "form" and the natural processes associated with the body to an opposition between order and language. This relationship is explicitly alluded to at the end of the poem, where Glück claims to "feel" the "same need to perfect" in "aligning these words" that she felt renouncing "death" by renouncing the body's needs and desires. It is also present in the equation of the "body" with the "grave," which calls up the idea of writing through its connection to the inscription of words, a connection reinforced through a pun on "graph." Just as Glück attempts to "perfect" the body by sacrificing it, even to the death, so she would "perfect" her poetry by means of a strategy of negation through which the text, like the "digressive," "interfering," and indiscriminately "accept[ing]" body, would ultimately be effaced altogether. Of course, as Glück observes, anorexia proves the "soul's . . . dependence on the flesh," and the radical ascesis to which she would subject her poems must finally stop short of total erasure. But while these disciplinary impulses must themselves be kept in check, no matter how distasteful the notion of compromise may be to Glück's self-denying temperament, they nevertheless reflect the profoundly negative impulse that motivates her writing. Indeed, the poem itself would seem to have undergone precisely the kind of purgation it describes, since, as Lisa Sewell accurately observes, "Glück's style and diction correspond to the expected contours of a so-called anorexic aesthetic. The language is spare, the lines are short—there is little 'blossom' or 'subterfuge' in the passage."[15]

The cost of practicing the sort of aesthetic discipline Glück describes in "The Deviation,"—the severity of which is stressed through its analogousness to the self-destructive illness of anorexia—is, I suggested earlier, the poet's awareness of her ambition, and the attitude of indifference that her ambition fosters. "The Deviation" offers a clear example of how that indifference emerges. The "fear of death" prompts an extreme effort of renunciation, the result of which is the transformation of death from a natural, human "fear" into a "mere byproduct" of that very same effort. The strategy of ascesis, in other words, through which Glück would attain distinction, assumes in the end an importance superior to the "fear of death" that spawned it in the first place. Art takes priority over experience, and the poetic career takes priority over life in a way that resonates with the imperative Ashbery describes in "Some Words," which defines the career as that which can only be thought of, not lived: "you will have to think of your career / Not live it."

As Brian Henry observes, "What would be problematic for many poets—the near-fetishization of a life, the determination to 'use' one's life for the purposes of art—has become natural for Glück."[16] Not only is this severe pragmatism "natural" for her, its problematic effects are obsessively documented in her work. For example, the same process by which "aligning these words" assumes such a great importance that "death" itself becomes a "mere byproduct" in "The Deviation" governs the transformation of "love" into "use" in "Nest." The poem is about starting over. In a dream, the speaker watches a bird "making / efforts to survive / on what remained to it." Like the bird, at first the speaker has "nothing to build with." But the arrival of spring evokes a sense of promise that enables her to take stock of the available "materials." The joy she takes in making this new beginning does not serve as an end in itself, however, and the poem turns as it closes from an appreciation of "each thing" in the newly renovated world to a confession of a will for attainment that defines value according to utility:

> And I remember accurately
> the sequence of my responses,
> my eyes fixing on each thing
> from the shelter of the hidden self:
>
> first, *I love it.*
> Then, *I can use it.*[17]

In "On Stanley Kunitz," Glück makes the connection between her pragmatism and her vocation clear: "Like all people with a powerful sense of vocation, I was concerned with what I could use" (*PT* 108).

But what is particularly disturbing for Glück is not so much that her "Demonic Ambition," as she describes it in "The Winged Horse," should entail the conversion of experience into material for poetry, a conversion more or less inevitable for any artist, but rather that that conversion enforces a sense of detachment from experience and from other human beings.[18] Glück's questioning of her capacity for feeling anything other than the force of her own calling comes through, for instance, in "The Wish," one of the poems from *Meadowlands* that takes the form of a dialogue between a husband and wife. "What do you think I wished," asks the wife. "I don't know," the husband replies: "That I'd come back, / that we'd somehow be together in the end." But his guesses underestimate Glück's poetic ambition, which, as her brutally honest response reflects, takes precedence over not only the prospect of the husband's return, but even the idea that "we'd somehow be together in the end," a vision that, in its vagueness, would seem to offer few grounds for rejection. But the wife is on a different wavelength altogether, and she does not scruple to tell a truth that wounds them both in different ways: "I wished for what I always wish for," she says simply. "I wished for another poem."[19] The response is meant to sting the unfaithful husband for his assumption that his wife's wishes would continue to revolve around him. Looking back over the poem, one can see the wife setting her cutting remark up in advance: first she asks him what he thinks she wished, and then she sets him straight. But her response is also a self-rebuke, a painful admission that her desires are "always" set apart from the common run of human affections represented by the husband's focus on reconciliation.

Glück's awareness of the potential to prioritize artistic ambition over human feeling, evident in "The Wish," is a central concern of her essay "The Forbidden." There she reflects on the ways in which several poets— Linda McCarriston, Sharon Olds, Carolyn Forché, Martha Rhodes, and Frank Bidart—engage the theme of guilt. "Dark truth has become unnervingly popular," she observes, and she goes on to explain how McCarriston's book, *Eva-Mary*, fails in her estimation because its "dark truth," incest, is represented with a moral simplicity—"all guilt absorbed by agents of suppression and all nobility divided among the helpless victims"—that betrays "the delight of the ambitious artist at discovering terrain this promising." This "delight," by Glück's reasoning, so overrides the sense of "anguish" that the materials call for that "the voice speaking suffers no dilemma toward the past, never falters in its judgments," and thus maintains a disappointingly clear division between "the heroes and villains." She contrasts *Eva-Mary* with Forché's book, *The Country between Us*. What is notable is that Glück likes Forché's book more than McCarriston's, but *not* on the grounds that Forché is innocent of the artistic ambition on which McCarriston's shortcomings are founded. On the contrary, it turns out that that ambition, evident in the "delight" in the discovery of "promising" new material, is a force Glück tellingly assumes to be constant in poetry, even when the material—incest, and in Forché's case, political upheaval—ought to exclude any response approaching to "delight." So it is that Forché's strength derives not from moral purity, but from her willingness to voice a sense of "complicity" in the "injustice" she describes, a complicity that stems from her interest in using it to further her career: "Unlike McCarriston's, Forché's speaker is suspect; the poems' extraordinary drama derives equally from rage at injustice . . . and the recurring question of complicity, since it is to the poet's distinct advantage that this reality continue" (*PT* 55).

What Glück appreciates in Forché, then, is precisely the confession of the professional ambition for "attainment," and the sense of detachment from suffering that it can provoke, that Glück herself is given to confessing. But I should emphasize that the value of registering the full extent of her ambition is not that it serves as an apology for it. That confession is a form of discipline meant to keep "Demonic Ambition" in check, and its use consists not so much in improving anyone's impression of her morality, but in avoiding the failings of an art founded on ambition alone. For ambition operates through a force of will that, by itself, produces art that lacks authenticity, much like McCarriston's does in Glück's account: "*Eva-Mary* is limited by McCarriston's managerial interventions, her insistence on a single rigid interpretation; limited, in a sense, by excess will" (*PT* 63).

The importance of limiting will as a way of counteracting ambition and its tendency toward "excess will" is the subject of "On Impoverishment." The last essay in *Proofs and Theories*, it returns to the first, "The Education of the Poet," and it reconsiders the book's first sentence: "The fundamental experience of the writer is helplessness" (*PT* 3). Whereas that "helplessness" had at first seemed lamentable, in "On Impoverishment" it represents an important literary resource. Glück reflects on the rhythms of her poetic career, the periods of silence she has had to endure between books:

> To teach myself hope, I began, thirty years ago, to chart periods of silence in the same way that I dated poems. And I have repeatedly seen long silence end in speech. Moreover, the speech, the writing that begins after such a siege, differs always from what went before, and in ways I couldn't through act of will accomplish. And this happens even when outward circumstances don't change at all. Some work is done through suffering, through impoverishment, through the involuntary relinquishing of a self. (*PT* 133)

At every turn in this passage, Glück defends this submission to "impoverishment" against the impulse to turn it into a routine that may be accomplished on demand. That is why, for instance, she stresses that the growth that takes place is not a function of a change in "outward circumstances": to suggest that this sort of change could have an effect would be to invite an attempt to will growth by simply changing those "circumstances" on schedule between books. The danger for the artist, she goes on to explain, of a "life made entirely of will," is that it "expresses itself in too prompt, too superficial adjustments of what can, in the external environment, be manipulated, or in a cautious clinging to those habits and forms which, because they are not crucial, cannot, in being lost, do much damage" (*PT* 133–34). Will, aligned with discipline and form in such poems as "The Deviation," is also aligned here with surface, while "impoverishment" is aligned with depth.

Here we can glimpse Glück's romanticism, which, as the trope of "impoverishment" itself suggests, has roots in Emerson: "And yet is the God the native of these bleak rocks. . . . We must hold hard to this poverty, however scandalous, and by more vigorous self-recoveries, after the sallies of action, possess our axis more firmly."[20] Like Emerson, whose reluctance about embracing "poverty" comes across in the image of "bleak rocks," Glück would rather muster continuous "sallies of action," but experience has taught her the value of "impoverishment," and as a result her career is structured as a series of "self-recoveries."[21] Legible here are the contradictory impulses of professionalism, which call for the acquirement and application of expertise on the one hand, and on the other hand, for precisely the opposite—the inexplicable revitalization attendant upon the "involuntary relinquishing of a self"—since the authority of the artist and the authenticity of the work of art cannot stand on will alone.

I have suggested that these imperatives account for the thematization of beginning that we have seen in post-1945 debuts. With that connection in mind, it is notable that Glück's strategy of "impoverishment" produces a "yield" that she figures as a moment of regeneration: "Realize, then, that impoverishment is also a teacher, unique in its capacity to renew, and that its yield, when it ends, is a passionate openness which in turn re-invests the world with meaning. What I remember of such moments is gratitude: the fact of being born immerses us in the world without conveying the daily immensity of that gift." To become aware of the "immensity" of the "gift" of "being born," as Glück goes on to explain, is to be given a "sense of the significance of the original gift," and so, in a sense, to be born anew. Always alert to the tendency of ambition to turn knowledge to its immediate practical advantage, she is careful to warn against making a "policy" of the paradoxical principle she advocates, for "when response becomes policy it has ceased to engage directly with circumstance" (*PT* 134). Glück's strategy of self-relinquishment and recovery is borne out in the representation of career in her poetry, which replays the moment of beginning with a remarkable regularity. In this, her career attests to the particular power of the stance of the beginner, which stems from the way it harnesses the authority inherent in both of professionalism's contradictory imperatives.

It is fitting that Glück describes her emergence from "impoverishment" in terms of "being born," for as I mentioned earlier, her reflections on the poetic calling tend to occur within the context of the family even as they hark back to the Puritan mindset that lies behind Emerson's remarks on "poverty" and regeneration. Turning back to Glück's early poetry, we can see that "All Hallows," the leadoff poem in her second collection, *The House on the Marshland*, revisits the idea of birth that is elaborated in "The Chicago Train" from *Firstborn*. The poem "is about bearing a child," as Helen Vendler suggests, even as it is "saturated by the poet's sense of her own birth."[22]

> This is the barrenness
> of harvest or pestilence.
> And the wife leaning out the window
> with her hand extended, as in payment,
> and the seeds,
> distinct, gold, calling
> *Come here*
> *Come here, little one*
>
> And the soul creeps out of the tree.[23]

The poem is fraught with ambivalence about the poetic calling, imaged here in the literal "calling" of the child-soul "out of the tree": the "barrenness" (which recalls the "barren skull" of "Mister" from "The Chicago Train") is of either "harvest or pestilence," and similarly the woman's voice can be heard either as a kindly, maternal one, or, as Vendler suggests, as an "evil" one.[24] The image of the "hand extended" in "payment" also evokes that ambivalence. Recall that in "A Parable," David "lifts his hand" to take possession of the kingdom: it is a gesture of self-acknowledgment, and it transforms "the hand" into a "weapon." Here in "All Hallows" the image functions in a similar way. It is the sign of Glück's hunger for distinction; as such, it also embodies the price—the "payment" mentioned here—of that distinction, for what is most unbearable to Glück is that her hunger should be made apparent at all: "hungry as I was for praise, I was also proud and could not bear to ask for it, to seem to need it" (*PT* 8).

In the opening poems of Glück's third and fourth collections, that vocational ambivalence appears to increase in severity. New life dies all too quickly in "The Drowned Children," the first poem in *Descending Figure*. The poem reinitiates her career by imagining another problematic birth. As in "The Chicago Train," the birth appears to occur in reverse: Vendler points out that the children "resume the fetal condition—blind, weightless, suspended in water" as they drown and are bequeathed to the maternal "dark arms" of the pond.[25] And as in "All Hallows," Glück incorporates the notion of the poetic vocation into the poem through the literal calling with which the poem ends: "*Come home, come home, lost / in the waters, blue and permanent.*"[26] "Mock Orange" from her next book, *The Triumph of Achilles,* turns from the "metaphor of childbirth" employed in Glück's first three books to the "sexual drama," which, as Edward Said notes, "more than any other image conveys the novelty, as well as the nexus of intention, circumstance, and force that always characterizes a beginning."[27] In "Mock Orange," sexual desire—which, as "The Deviation" bears out, is always in Glück analogous to the hunger for distinction that drives her vocation—emerges not in the "calling" we saw in "All Hallows" and "The Drowned Children," but rather in the inchoate "cry that always escapes, / the low, humiliating / premise of union." Like the notion of "calling," the "cry" recurs throughout Glück's work. Together they characterize the two sides of Glück's ambivalence: while "calling" evokes an exalted notion of the poetic vocation, the image of the "cry" evokes vocation as undisciplined hunger.[28]

"Parodos" opens *Ararat,* the first of the four book-length sequences Glück wrote during the 1990s. The poem is suffused with a subtle tension between life and death, speech and silence. Like Eliot's Prufrock, who finds it impossible to say just what he means, Glück seems to be impelled by language—that indeterminate "grave" that "will accept anything"—on a course of perpetual self-redefinition that resembles the structure of her career:

> Long ago, I was wounded.
> I learned
> to exist, in reaction,
> out of touch
> with the world: I'll tell you
> what I meant to be—
> a device that listened.
> Not inert: still.
> A piece of wood. A stone.

The "unspecified wound" that life deals to the speaker, as Paul Breslin remarks, produces a response that is "thanatic: she seeks to become as much like inanimate matter as a sentient human being can." And yet the repeated efforts of qualification—she is "not inert" but "still," like "a piece of wood," but then again she is "inert" after all, like "a stone"—reflect an indubitable liveliness. The aggressive assertion "I'll tell you" harks back to the opening words of "The Drowned Children," "You see," and it looks forward to "The Wild Iris," where Glück is likewise at pains to articulate and confirm a particular relationship between speaker and audience: "Hear me out," she enjoins the reader, and "I tell you I could speak again."[29] Repeatedly calling, crying, demanding to be heard, and declaring her intent to make a declaration, Glück's leadoff poems show a pattern of insistent address that reflects the intensity of her desire to "speak again."

But for all its intensity, that desire has been persistently checked by a contrary desire to be "a device that listened." "Parodos" breaks from the attempt at self-definition, asking, "Why should I tire myself, debating, arguing?" But it returns to stage another such attempt in the final stanza. It, too, proves incomplete:

> I was born to a vocation:
> to bear witness
> to the great mysteries.
> Now that I've seen both
> birth and death, I know
> to the dark nature these
> are proofs, not
> mysteries—[30]

Breslin suggests that Glück "describes her 'vocation' (a bit too portentously, but it's one of a very few weak moments in an extraordinary book) as bearing 'witness / to the great mysteries,' which she names as 'birth and death.' "[31] The portentousness of the description is important. Like the weighty assertion of purpose in the first stanza, the claim to vocation here is voiced with a bold assurance that is ironic, for it is set forth in order to be undermined. Contra Breslin, "birth and death" are clearly *not* the "great mysteries" Glück refers to, since she "now" claims to "know / to the dark nature" that "these / are proofs, not / mysteries." Much like the first stanza, this stanza reflects contrary impulses. Glück seems to want to solidify a notion of vocation: this she accomplishes by rededicating herself to the vocation of "witness" that she "was born to." At the same time, however, her newly acquired knowledge of "birth and death," which has entailed a shift in their status from "mysteries" to "proofs," resonates with the "learn[ing]" process she invokes in the first stanza and points rather to a sense of vocation that is constantly in flux.

Just as the speaker of "Parodos" claims to have "seen both birth and death," so the speaker of "The Wild Iris," the title poem of Glück's next collection, claims "to remember / passage from the other world" into a new life that permits her to "speak again," since "whatever / returns from oblivion returns / to find a voice."[32] It begins by evoking an end that marks a new beginning:

> At the end of my suffering
> there was a door.
>
> Hear me out: that which you call death
> I remember.

The poem offers another take on the career pattern Glück discusses in "On Impoverishment." At first glance, it seems to suggest simply that she rediscovers her "voice" cyclically, just as the wild iris returns perennially. But the poem is shadowed by doubt. "To remember death is to know it is not final," Breslin remarks.[33] And as Glück explains in "On Impoverishment," the value of the experience of self-relinquishment, its "yield," depends crucially on feeling that it *is* final: "The condition demands resistance at the outset; to treat impoverishment as a prerequisite to wealth, to turn it into a kind of fraternity hazing, is to deny the experience. It must be feared and resisted; it must exhaust all available resources, since its essence is defeat" (*PT* 133). The analogy between poet and flower cannot hold, for the flower's memory of death must always function as a kind of resource, a sign that there will always be a door at the end of suffering. And yet, though Glück's conception of her career does not allow her the comfort of assured rebirth, she has nevertheless "repeatedly seen long silence end in speech," as she puts it in "On Impoverishment." Glück is again thinking of her career in two ways at once: the "I" in the poem imagines it as a continuity that the "you" of the poem—who "call[s]" the flower's dormancy "death," perhaps out of her "fear" of "being / a soul and unable / to speak"—cannot accept. (We can see here another example of the logic of contradiction elaborated in "The Deviation." A "fear" of silence generates an impulse of self-renunciation, according to which surviving without a voice is "call[ed]" "death." In this way, the speech—literally a "call[ing]"— whose production ensures the continuation of the career also, paradoxically, marks its termination.) The cyclical renewal of "voice" described in the poem is neither a fantasy for Glück, nor a reality, but a combination of both.

I want to conclude by discussing Glück's most direct articulations of the theme of renewal—the two title poems from *Vita Nova* that, "as if to emphasize the circularity implicit in the very idea of *re*newal," as Sandra

Gilbert remarks, are positioned at the beginning and end of the collection. But even as these two poems reinforce the theme of beginning that we have been examining, they also problematize it, for they offer conflicting perspectives on the new life Glück has begun. This conflict is visible even in the title they share. It alludes to Dante's *Vita Nuova*, which, like Glück's book, concerns the "mingled lamentation and transfiguration associated with the loss of a beloved," as Gilbert puts it, and yet, as the substitution of the Latinate "Nova" for the Italian "Nuova" suggests, it also separates itself from Dante.[34] And further, since its declaration of a fresh start is at the same time a return to medieval Florence and ancient Rome, the title puts the whole concept of the new itself in question from the beginning.

The poem with which the collection opens evokes the cyclical return of spring:

> The spring of the year; young men buying tickets for the ferryboats.
> Laughter, because the air is full of apple blossoms.
>
> When I woke up, I realized I was capable of the same feeling.
>
> I remember sounds like that from my childhood,
> laughter for no cause, simply because the world is beautiful,
> something like that.[35]

"Vita Nova" claims to rediscover a particular capacity for "feeling" by way of "childhood" memories. Glück's skepticism of the possibility of her rebirth comes through in the way she tempers her confidence in her memory. The laughter she remembers is only "like" the laughter she hears in her dream, and the spirit of exultation with which she observes that "the world is beautiful" is undercut by her throwaway qualification—"something like that." This pattern of qualification continues throughout the poem. For example, "Crucial / sounds or gestures" from the past seem to direct her career path, for they are "like a track laid down before the larger themes," but that "track" remains "unused, buried" for reasons Glück does not explain: it is as if the "track" exists only to be forgotten. Similarly, the image of her "mother / holding out a plate of little cakes"—an image that recalls "the wife leaning out the window / with her hand extended, as in payment" from "All Hallows"—is "changed / in no detail" and is the more "vivid" to Glück for being "intact," and yet it remains unchanged only "as far as I remember." This suspicion of memory reflects Glück's "recognition of mortality—the recognition that we live in time," as James Longenbach suggests.[36] That recognition runs counter to the Wordsworthian myth of redemption through memory that the poem explores—explores, that is, and then abandons: "Surely spring has been returned to me," the poem concludes, "this time / not as a lover but a messenger of death."

The book ends with a very different "Vita Nova." In this regard, the structure of *Vita Nova* represents a departure from the sort of closure achieved in *Ararat*, in which the last poem, "First Memory," circles back to the first, "Parodos," by reiterating its first sentence—"Long ago, I was wounded"; this movement of return marks an advance in insight, whereby Glück comes to understand that the "pain" of the wound means not that she was "not loved," but that *she* loved.[37] In *Vita Nova* there is no circling back, and therefore no way to gauge an advance: the last poem's tone, its subject, its procedure, all differ from those of the first. It does retain, though, the opening poem's skepticism of the possibility of new life. In the first "Vita Nova," Glück "retract[s] the myth" of memory, much as she retracts the myth of Sisyphus in "The Mountain," and interprets renewal itself as a "messenger of death" in the end. In the second "Vita Nova," she expresses her hopes with a naive enthusiasm—"you'll wake up / in a different world"—and glib simplicity—"*I thought my life was over and my heart was broken. / Then I moved to Cambridge*"—that make the idea of a new life seem deeply suspect.

Whereas the first "Vita Nova" is all terse declaration, the second is loaded with questions both comedic and pathetic. The poem represents an attempt to interpret a "splitting up dream" in which a divorced couple is "fighting over who would keep / the dog, / Blizzard." The "splitting up dream" refers, on one level, to a dream about a couple that is breaking up, but it also refers to a dream that is itself falling apart: an ideal of cohesion is breaking down, a perception of life is going to pieces. That notion of "splitting up" is the keynote of the poem, which, in its sustained, frantic confusion, itself may be said to split or depart from the controlled minimalism of Glück's own earlier poetry. "You tell me / what that name means," the speaker demands, in reference to "the dog, / Blizzard," in an ironic inversion of the formula Glück employs in several of her poems of beginning—the insistent "I tell you" of "Mock Orange," "Parodos," and "The Wild Iris." Similarly, the loathing of sexual desire that figures prominently in such poems as "The Chicago Train" and "Mock Orange" is handled a good deal less anxiously: Blizzard "was / a cross between / something big and fluffy / and a dachshund. Does this have to be / the male and female / genitalia?" Or consider the contrast between the evocation of anorexia in "The Deviation," where the "sacrifice" of "interfering flesh" is made out of a "need to perfect," and its evocation in "Vita Nova": "Poor Blizzard, / why was he a dog? He barely touched / the hummus in his dogfood dish."[38]

The poem also takes up the question of the subordination of life to art that recurs throughout Glück's poetry, but in a new register. In "Mirror Image" from *Ararat*, for instance, her exploration of this question proceeds grimly toward a severe self-chastisement:

> Tonight I saw myself in the dark window as
> the image of my father, whose life
> was spent like this,
> thinking of death, to the exclusion
> of other sensual matters,
> so in the end that life
> was easy to give up, since
> it contained nothing . . .[39]

In "Vita Nova," Glück's tone is obviously less solemn, and she seems to take comfort in—rather than decry—the idea of converting life into "material" for poetry:

> Blizzard,
> Daddy needs you; Daddy's heart is empty,
> not because he's leaving Mommy but because
> the kind of love he wants Mommy
> doesn't have, Mommy's
> too ironic—Mommy wouldn't do
> the rhumba in the driveway. Or
> is this wrong. Supposing
> I'm the dog, as in
> my child-self, unconsolable because
> completely pre-verbal? With
> anorexia! O Blizzard,
> be a brave dog—this is
> all material; you'll wake up
> in a different world,
> you will eat again, you will grow up into a poet!

Henry observes, "Again, the sense that Glück exhaustively mines memory and experience for her poetry comes to the fore,"[40] and that sense arises in conjunction with an abstraction from "memory and experience" that limits the life of the emotions. "Daddy's heart is empty," but so, implicitly, is "Mommy's," for she "doesn't have" the "kind of love he wants," and she's "too ironic" to "do / the rhumba in the driveway." The alternative interpretation of the dream, in which the speaker is the dog, reinforces the idea that Glück lives to write. Thus, in effect, she tells herself to "be a brave dog" during this difficult time of "splitting up," for "this is all material" that will be of use later, when she "grow[s] up into a poet!"

Glück consoles herself with the prospect of beginning a poetic career, which functions here as a sort of compensation for life's losses. The path forward that she invokes in "Vita Nova" represents a claim to authority derived from the conversion of those losses into the "material" necessary for her future work. And yet the overt sentimentality and the uncharacteristic bathos in the poem—"Never / will I forget your face, your frantic human eyes / swollen with tears"—reflect a self-consciousness that problematizes that claim on the future. The poem could also be read as a caricature of the motif of rebirth that resounds throughout her career, and thus a claim to the authority produced by the strategy of self-critique. Certainly there is a conspicuous ease present in the solution she discovers to what seemed a life-ending heartbreak: *I thought my life was over and my heart was broken. / Then I moved to Cambridge.*

The tonal complexity of the poem allows Glück to capture once again the sense of vocational ambivalence that we have seen throughout her work, and the poetic career accordingly appears here as both a certainty and an absurdity. As I have suggested, the conflicting impulses in evidence here produce an emphasis on beginning—the "Vita Nova" of the title— that focuses the tension between them without resolving it. Glück's many beginnings allow us to appreciate the dynamic character of that moment. That she has returned to it over the course of her career with an almost systematic regularity is not, however, merely a sign of literary professionalism. It is also a reflection of the rigor of attention and imaginative power with which she has explored the (necessarily) contradictory logic of her vocation.

Conclusion
Making Introductions

At a little distance from their customary location on the fringes of the poems collected in a first book, otherwise familiar presentational devices and conventions such as the acknowledgments, notes, contest rules, and preface are apt to seem anxious, extravagant, curiously stylized. Cy Twombly, Anselm Kiefer, Alain Badiou, Merytamun, Tutankhaman, Giacomo Leopardi, Basho, Joseph Kosuth, Maurice Blanchot, Giorgio Agamben, Ted Berrigan, Adam Zagajewski, W. G. Sebald, and Ovid appear together in the multilingual "Notes" to James McCorkle's *Evidences*.[1] Rules for the Crab Orchard Series in Poetry First Book Award recommend a spring clip or plain file folder ("no paper clips or staples please") for postal submissions, while online submissions, which must arrive no later than "11:59:59 PM," should take the first eight letters of the manuscript title as the file name ("either lower or upper case is fine") and spell out punctuation marks without spaces, so that "if your manuscript was titled 'Poems!' your file would be titled 'poemsexc' for 'Poems exclamation point.'"[2] In the introduction to *Things Are Happening*, Gerald Stern praises Joshua Beckman's poems as "direct, clear, modest, wondrous, affectionate, hopeful," "courageous," "tenacious," "direct, non-ironic, passionate," "modest, trusting, noncombative," "tender, reverential, trusting, sane," "believing," "hopeful," "realistic," and "not special, symbolic, scholarly, exclusionary, digressive, arch, or encoded," "dithering or magisterial or magical," "innocent," "naïve," or "pessimistic," while noting in addition that Beckman's influences include not only James Schuyler and Frank O'Hara, "but also Spicer and Lorca and Whitman and Berrigan and Hart Crane. And Creeley and Snyder and Zukofsky and a little Roethke, and a little Mandelstam. Even a little Pound."[3]

Exploring first books at the turn of the millennium, my conclusion extends the history and analysis of American debut culture begun in chapter 1, albeit from a slightly different angle. Though I offer an interpretation of Allison Adelle Hedge Coke's "The Change," which opens her first book, *Dog Road Woman* (1997), to close my discussion, and I glance beforehand at other recent first books, my emphasis falls for the most part on poetry's paratexts—Gérard Genette's term for the assemblage of "accompanying productions" that surround the primary text and "ensure the text's presence in the world, its 'reception' and consumption in the form (nowadays, at least) of a book."[4] Such features play a crucial role in constructing the first book of poetry as a unique literary artifact, one that can be differentiated from other productions—chapbooks, pamphlets, MFA theses, groups of poems published in anthologies or magazines, second books, and so on—which can be (and sometimes are) treated as poetic debuts. What Virginia Jackson has influentially said of lyric might also be said of the first book: "To be lyric is to be read as lyric—and to be read as lyric is to be printed and framed as lyric."[5] The appearance of John Ashbery's *Some Trees* in the Yale Series, for instance, points to the efficacy of the paratexts that enabled it to be "printed and framed" as a first book three years after his *Turandot and Other Poems* was published by Tibor de Nagy in 1953. One might also think of Marianne Moore's *Observations*, commonly referred to as her "first book," but described in the colophon as a "reprint of 'Poems,' published in London in 1921 by the Egoist Press" (*BMM* 49); of suppressed first books like Lyn Hejinian's *The Grreat Adventure*, which she burned all but "very, very few copies of" soon after it was published in 1972; or of revised and expanded first books like Wallace Stevens's *Harmonium*, which appeared twice in substantially different editions published eight years apart. Examples like these highlight the extent to which the first book of poetry is always also a work of fiction, one that can be conceptualized and presented in different ways to suit a variety of interests and occasions.

Not only do paratexts help to define the debut against other productions within an author's oeuvre, but they also define it against first books from other presses, in other series, chosen by other judges and editors, and published under the auspices of other prizes. Of course all texts are presented using "accompanying productions" of various kinds: neither submission guidelines, nor acknowledgments, nor introductions are unique to first books of poetry. But any account of the rise of the first book would be incomplete without paying some attention to the often peculiarly elaborate paratextual framework used to stage the poetic debut. The sheer number of first book prizes and series, each of which boasts its own distinctive mission, rules, history, and format, virtually ensures that the paratextual intensification of the first book is apt to be particularly thoroughgoing. The myriad forms of affiliation afforded by first-book paratexts present an opportunity to reap the rewards of identification and alignment with the figure of the debut poet and the first book, the very embodiments of aesthetic autonomy and disinterested activity, insofar as youth is symbolically opposed to power in Bourdieu's reading of the field of cultural production. In this way, paratexts also highlight the way in which the poetic debut can be seen as a means of promoting poetry within the ranks of literary and artistic practices in general: first-book paratexts offer the poetry establishment the opportunity to appear as an ardent supporter of new work and an advocate for the individual talent. Far from the perfunctory exercises one might expect, the paratexts of first books are loaded with the sort of energy and idiosyncrasy that betoken substantial investment in their value.

In focusing on paratexts, I aim to shed light on the extent to which the strategies of self-representation discussed throughout this book are coordinated with and dependent upon the efforts of the other figures and organizations involved in the publication of the debut. To focus on first-book paratexts is in this way to invoke the debut author neither as the purely autonomous creator of romanticism (though the paratexts of a prize-winning debut are characteristically geared toward constructing just this mythic figure), nor as a mere product of the disciplinary discourses of the system (though debut paratexts also tend to provide ample evidence of the author's complex ties to the various institutions and communities that constitute her milieu), but rather as a figure who inevitably both shapes and is shaped by evolving conditions of literary production. A "zone not only of transition but also of *transaction*," as Genette observes,[6] the paratext usefully highlights the reductiveness of conceiving the author as either free agent or function of ideology, for it attests repeatedly and explicitly to the centrality of exchange in the production of authorship: judges thank poets and poets thank judges; contest rules are energetically set forth and quietly revamped; epigraphs pay homage to and take liberties with canonical texts.

Focusing on the liminal space that mediates relations between poet and literary system highlights the way in which the first book continues to serve as the site of a complex set of activities geared toward the legitimation of poets, judges, prizes, poetry magazines, sponsoring institutions, and even certain schools, styles, and modes of poetry. Insofar as it promotes specific credentials while at the same time conjuring up the image of the poet as inspired genius, the paratextual apparatus that typifies the contemporary prize-winning debut—but also, perhaps to a lesser extent, debuts published without prizes—can be seen to serve much the same purposes as the rhetoric of beginning in post-1945 poetic debuts. Ironically, the paths of many of the more successful contemporary poets are apt to involve more than one first-book prize, and the presentational strategies poets often adopt to launch their own careers converge with those they use to launch the careers of others.

Even before a prize-winning debut appears in print, contemporary submission guidelines and contest rules call up an ethos of professional rigor that is as daunting for its complexity as it is commendable for its promotion of fairness. In this specialized discursive sphere even the word "guidelines" can be fatally misleading: a disclaimer included on the website for the Robert Dana / Anhinga Prize states that "every year many entries are disqualified for reasons that have little or nothing to do with the quality of the poetry—simply because they have not followed contest guidelines." It then goes on to offer a stern warning to the inexperienced contestant: "the term 'guidelines' in this context means the same thing as 'requirements'!"[7] In a similar vein, the Tupelo Press website advises prospective entrants to "consider exploring the work of the poets we have published" before entering a contest, but the putative Tupelo house aesthetic—as exemplified either by previous winners selected by changing panels of dozens of judges or by the description provided ("technical virtuosity combined with abundant imagination; memorable, vivid imagery and strikingly musical approaches to language; willingness to take risks; and penetrating insights into human experience")—offers little in the way of either deterrence or encouragement, except, perhaps, to the savviest of contest participants.[8] Long lists of previous winners, runners-up, finalists, and semifinalists—sometimes with city and state of residence energetically noted—abound, evoking a sense that the prestige of winning is both restricted to the few and shared by the many. The "Ethics Statement" of the Council of Literary Magazines and Presses is usually quoted in full. Descriptions of contest procedures are particularly nuanced: preferred font, pagination, envelope size, reading-fee payment method, submission and notification deadlines, revision policy, and manuscript recycling policy are all routinely and exhaustively laid out. All the fine print makes for important, if not especially exciting, reading for the prospective debut poet. If its copiousness evokes the encroachments of institutional routine on literary labor, it also provides evidence of a continuing dedication to the idea of poetry as a properly self-regulated domain of disinterested activity.

First-book contest rules and guidelines not only affirm aesthetic autonomy, but they also dictate the shape and size of book-length collections. Manuscripts are typically required to fall between forty-eight and one hundred pages in length, with different prizes setting different limits: 50–84 pages for the Patricia Bibby First Book Award, 48–70 pages for the Trio Award for First or Second Book, 48–64 pages for the Yale prize, and so on. Granting that some such limits are to be expected given the small budgets on which most poetry publishers operate, it is worth noting that many well-known twentieth-century debuts published before the advent of the first-book prize era would have been disqualified: first books by H. D., T. S. Eliot, Robinson Jeffers, Louise Bogan, Weldon Kees, and Robert Lowell would have fallen short, while those of Conrad Aiken, Wallace Stevens, e. e. cummings, Countee Cullen, and John Crowe Ransom would have run too long. Rules commonly require that there be "no more than one poem on each page," using phrasing that seems bound to produce the mistaken impression that no poem should be *longer* than one page. (The guidelines for Pavement Saw Press's prize even take the trouble to stipulate that the "manuscript can contain pieces longer than one page" in anticipation of such a misunderstanding.)[9] That this ambiguity—or, rather, appearance of ambiguity—is usually allowed to stand, in a discourse otherwise saturated with detailed qualification, is telling. Along with the publishing credits that are customarily allowed through the ostensibly blind selection process, the rule that no two poems begin on the same page of the manuscript, the length limits placed on the book as a whole, and even the required table of contents, this ambiguity subtly reflects the privileging of lyric over other poetic modes. The first book seems to set the tone for a poet's subsequent publications in this regard: most new collections observe more or less the same conventions with regard to overall length and pagination. Contests for first *or* second books, such as those offered by Omnidawn, Tupelo, Perugia, Switchback, Pavement Saw, and Trio House, directly reinforce the tendency for subsequent books to take after the first, since the same rules apply to both types of manuscript.

The conventional acknowledgments page places the lyricism of the prize-winning first book in the service of the making of the author as a credentialed professional. The list form in which such acknowledgments are presented is itself significant, for it serves as a reminder that many of the poems collected in the table of contents once stood alone. It also exerts a rationalizing effect on the production of poetic authority insofar as it defines recognition in terms of quantity: the sheer number of prebook publications, often visually accentuated by giving each poem or periodical its own line in a vertical arrangement on the page, becomes a source of legitimacy in its own right. Of course, the poet is not the only one being recognized. Acknowledgments in a first book confer additional prestige on journals and magazines for their willingness to present work by poets who have yet to publish a book. Thanking editors for permission to reprint previously published work also reinforces the validity of the judge's selection by evoking the field of poetic production under the sign of a consensus in which the tastes of a variety of publications, often covering a range of formats and fields of interest, are seen to converge in the work of a new poet, thus evoking aesthetic judgment as an objective quantity.

Debut acknowledgments usually include not only previous publications in magazines, newspapers, and anthologies but also an unusually wide-ranging gallery of foundations, colonies, schools, fellowships, editors, family members, teachers, and friends. Laurie Ann Guerrero's acknowledgments in her Andrés Montoya-prize-winning *A Tongue in the Mouth of the Dying* fill up four pages as she thanks no fewer than 146 institutions, organizations, groups, and individuals for various kinds of help and support.[10] However genuine the author's gratitude, there is also a clear advantage in dropping names in this way, an advantage that even the most disinterested poets can ill afford to ignore in a field as surprisingly crowded as that of contemporary poetry. As Genette wryly observes, "An author who has so many friends of both sexes cannot be completely bad."[11] That acknowledgment of previous publications appears as a fairly standard *requirement* for submissions to first-book contests (including the Lexi Rudnitsky First Book Prize, the APR / Honickman First Book Prize, the Cleveland State University Poetry Center First Book Award, the A. Poulin Jr. Poetry Prize, and the Yale Younger Poets Prize, to take half a dozen at random) sheds light on the degree to which the legitimacy of the prize-winning debut depends on a group effort promising rewards for all involved.

The conventional introduction to the post-1945 debut recapitulates and reinforces the functions of the submission guidelines and acknowledgments. It epitomizes the principle of recognition between fellow practitioners that underpins professional autonomy, and it validates that recognition by laying out a rationale for selection. The style of the introduction typically reflects the judge's contradictory role as both guardian of tradition and advocate for the individual talent, though the ratio between these two discursive strands has gradually shifted over the last half century. If, as George Bradley remarks, "Auden uses his Yale introductions to give a short course in poetry," exploring the role of the "pastoral genre in our technological age" and sketching "the attractions and dangers of surrealism," later judges have been increasingly inclined toward purely enthusiastic support.[12]

Before the Auden years, introductions to books in the Yale Series—then the only ongoing first-book contest for poetry—incorporated a biographical sketch that later became isolated, as a matter of course, in a note about the author usually located in the back matter, on the jacket flap, or on the back cover of the book. This adjustment highlights a difference between the relatively casual reflections of Archibald MacLeish and Stephen Vincent Benét, on the one hand, and the high seriousness of the "course in poetry" Auden offered during his tenure, on the other. The relaxed tone of MacLeish's account of "Miss [Eve] Merriam," for example, as "a Philadelphian who now lives in Baltimore, having spent seven or eight years in New York in between" is of a piece with his genially understated prediction that she "may very well survive."[13] The air of easygoing sociability that characterizes Benét's biographical summaries often registers as a penchant for in-jokes that mock the outmoded tastes of others. "Mr. Weismiller differs from the poets who write very pretty little verses on gardens and would be hard put to it to tell the difference between an elm and a beech," he writes in the introduction to *The Deer Come Down*, distancing the Yale Series aesthetic from genteel verse. He strikes a similar note when he mocks the celebration of modern industrialism one finds in the likes of Carl Sandburg as the "'O Grandmother Dynamo, what great big wheels you have!' school" in the introduction to *Theory of Flight*.[14]

If the disentanglement of the author's note from the editor's introduction may be seen as a reflection of the mid-century rise of a New Critical preference for separating the analysis of poetry from its biographical contexts, it can also be seen as a reflection of Auden's personal reluctance to turn the introduction into a kind of advertisement. "These introductions always sound awful," he wrote to Davidson when he first came on board as editor, "and the whole idea that a new poet should be introduced by an older one as if he were a debutante or a new face cream, deplorable and false."[15] After publishing Joan Murray's *Poems* in 1947 without an introduction, Auden found it in himself to supply one for each of the subsequent volumes he chose, but his distaste for the role of the promoter plays out in the muted tone of his praise and his almost total absorption in the discussion of weighty questions about art, history, and society rather than the poems at hand. His foreword to James Wright's *The Green Wall*, for example, uses Wright's epigraph, "Adam Lay Ibounden," as a point of departure for discussing the "characteristics of an age." These he derives by pondering such questions as "What is the essential difference between man and all the other creatures, animal, vegetable, and mineral?" and "What is the nature and human significance of time?" What little attention Wright's poetry receives ironically arises from Auden's explanation of why it's not worth attending to in a foreword: "I have not said anything about the quality of Mr. Wright's poems because assertions have no point without proofs, and the only proof in this case is reading." Contenting himself with "one or two quotations to illustrate his handling of imagery and rhythm and the variety of his concerns," Auden simply quotes three passages by way of conclusion without offering any further comment.[16]

On the evidence of their forewords of the 1960s and '70s, Dudley Fitts and Stanley Kunitz would seem to share, by and large, their predecessor's taste for and inclination toward restraint. In the foreword to Jack Gilbert's *Views of Jeopardy*, for example, Fitts observes that "anyone dealing from day to day with masses of new poetry in manuscript knows how often technical competence is marred by the cult of a different and false Orpheus, the Genius of Outpouring. The ritual prescribes only strength of feeling: anything goes, if it is 'felt' and 'true'; one has only to utter it, and there is a poem."[17] In a passage reminiscent of Auden's criticism of Ashbery's supposed lapses into eccentricity for its own sake in *Some Trees*, Fitts offers Gilbert a mild chastisement: "His concessions to unbridled emotion are relatively few, and it is worth noting that they generally weaken his structure when they occur."[18] Kunitz's touch is gentler still, though he, too, airs his misgivings, as when he reminds Olga Broumas not to overdo it in the foreword to *Beginning with O*: "Now and then I detect a note of stridency in her voice, a hint of doctrinal overkill, and I am tempted to remind her of Yeats's dictum that we make out of our quarrel with others, rhetoric; out of the quarrel with ourselves, poetry."[19]

This politely yet openly critical strain, which reflects the judge's role as cultural gatekeeper, disappears almost entirely from the prefatorial discourse of the poetic debut by the turn of the millennium. If judges still occasionally take on the grand themes to which Auden gravitated ("emboldened," as Genette explains, by a sense of surplus authority generated by (relative) fame and the unique sense of occasion defined by "responding to a request"),[20] they also tend to promote books at more length and with much more energy than Auden, and to avoid even the sort of moderate criticism applied by Fitts and Kunitz above. This development is unmistakably bound up with the multiplication of first-book prizes for poetry over the past fifty years. The handful of contests that existed by 1960 has grown to more than fifty by James English's count.[21] Introducing new poets as a first-book prize judge clearly counts as a professional credential, and it enables the poet to occupy a special position on the cultural field that confirms advanced status within the existing hierarchy while at the same time challenging the status quo. But in the context of such wild proliferation, it also places substantial pressure on judges to differentiate their selections from others and negotiate new modes of self-presentation that preserve vocational authenticity within a heavily institutionalized field of production.

The challenges of making introductions in this context are manifold, beginning with the "unbalanced and even shaky situation of communication" constituted by the preface itself. Jorge Luis Borges sarcastically considered advance commentary on a book the reader had not yet read to be "somewhat impossible."[22] Quoting out of context what can so easily be read in context a few pages hence can seem as superfluous as evaluating the genius of a contemporary artist in the space of a few paragraphs is presumptuous. Further, promotion of the selected work in a contest scenario is always legible as self-promotion, since complimenting the poet's prowess is tantamount to praising the judge's taste. Add to these inherent difficulties the challenge of making endorsements stick when the sheer number of prizes can mean introducing first books on multiple occasions, in consecutive years, or even in the same year through different contests. For example, Louise Glück selected and introduced Spencer Reese's *The Clerk's Tale* for the Kathryn Bakeless Prize and Peter Streckfus's *The Cuckoo* for the Yale Younger Poets Prize in 2004, and 1994 saw the publication of Alison Hawthorne Deming's *Science and Other Poems* and Kim Addonizio's *The Philosopher's Club*— Gerald Stern's choices for the Walt Whitman Award and the A. Poulin Jr. Award, respectively.

Contemporary prefatorial discourse responds to these challenges with tactics and strategies that pay homage to tradition and affirm establishment norms while also asserting the judge's poethood over against the routinizing ethos of the literary system and championing the work of the next generation. The rhetoric of institutional critique typifies the debut preface, though it is always limited by the judge's own participation in the contest and the fact of the prize selection itself. If Auden, Fitts, Kunitz, and other mid-century prize judges could still afford to criticize aspects of the work they selected, the contemporary prize judge has little choice, given all the competition, but to criticize the system as a whole while celebrating the debut selected. "One of the most annoying things about judging literary contests like the Bakeless Prize is the near impossibility of offering credible praise. Given the overload of superlatives on book-jacket-scapes and reader resistance to this overpainted scenery, it is almost impossible to describe in unclichéd terms the virtues of a collection," writes Carol Muske-Dukes in the foreword to Miranda Field's *Swallow*. "One of the most gratifying things about judging literary contests like the Bakeless Prize, however," she continues, "is simply getting to read, every blue moon or so, a first collection that really is groundbreaking and dazzling."[23] Such a procedure draws attention to the fine line judges often have to walk: Muske-Dukes distances herself from a field so crowded with talent that "superlatives" have been disabled, and then invokes those superlatives anyway on the basis that *Swallow* is the exception that proves the rule. "Every blue moon or so" is well calibrated to the occasion, since it evokes a sense of rarity appropriate to a prize-winning first book while also describing the scandalous frequency— every two or three years—with which she and other poet-judges are often called upon to introduce another "groundbreaking," "dazzling" debut. Caught in the same double bind, Glück writes resignedly in the introduction to Dana Levin's *In the Surgical Theater* of the "well-documented and scrutinized arena" that is "current American literary life," in which "a lit trail from the MFA programs through the multiple journals" defines the career of the debut poet in advance. Levin succeeds in spite of the system: "it is rare," Glück continues, "to encounter so substantially, and for the first time, so mature a gift."[24] That such judgments ignore or talk around the fact that the Bakeless and APR / Honickman are awarded on an annual basis, that Muske-Dukes and Glück will be called upon to introduce other exceptional talents sooner rather than later, or that four dozen or so other first-book awards for poetry are awarded every year, is not a shortcoming of their introductions but an unavoidable pitfall of contemporary first-book prize culture.

Another way in which prefatorial discourse mounts a resistance to the standardizing ethos of the prize bureaucracy and also distinguishes judge, debut poet, and prize alike from the many others in the field is its lyrical turn. The restrained tone and analytic procedures that typify introductions from earlier in the era of the first-book prize have given way to a language that seems extravagant by comparison. Auden may have inquired into large questions of time and identity in the passage from his foreword to Wright's *The Green Wall* quoted above, but Robert Creeley's discussion of the same matters in his introduction to Ann Marie Macari's *Ivory Cradle* raises the rhetorical ante considerably, evoking a vivid sense of apocalyptic crisis as it strains against the limits of its occasion: "The shatter and dislocation of our common world, its bitter habits of authority, the persistent loss of identifying place, all that one recalls now as 'existentialism,' made the singular fact of 'person' loom with an extraordinary scale upon the surface of that earth we had so presumed to know."[25] Kunitz describes the intersection of the material world and consciousness in Robert Hass's *Field Guide* this way: "Natural universe and moral universe coincide for him, centered in a nexus of personal affections"; Jorie Graham describes the same intersection in McCorkle's *Evidences* like this: "That the poem moves from phenomenological perception to the literal world of ray and eel-grass, of swarm, transparent spawn, silt and mudflows, toxins, slow spillage, dampnesses, seepages, in the very next lines, is typical of its spirit-knowledge of how mysteriously, organically and effortlessly, the abstract courses down the tiniest slope of thought to pick up, carry, and be carried by, its material grains."[26] Not all prefatorial lyricism unfolds on such an elaborate scale. That a great deal of it does, though, suggests that it can be understood to serve a number of functions related to its occasion, including promoting the first book, adding distinction to the prize, and affirming, under cover of the promotional motive, that the writer is a poet first and prize judge second.[27]

This is not to say that contemporary debut introductions are wholly given over to such poetic flights; they also engage in familiar forms of literary analysis—sorting out influences, appraising aspects of a poet's style, and remarking on recurrent thematic concerns. The strategy of equivocation that typifies judges' comments on the prize industry characterizes their evaluation of poets' specific virtues as well. Technical accomplishment and learning are often marked negatively as evidence of the unfortunate effects of the all-too-systematic education so many poets ostensibly receive in undergraduate and graduate creative writing programs. In the winning volume, however, these qualities are redeemed through a fortunate combination with their opposites—those virtues that are not susceptible to standardization, such as "lived experience," "heart," and "daring." So it is, for example, that Thomas Lux praises Keetje Kuipers for having "learned her trade" and used its "tools" to "get under the reader's skin, into the reader's heart," while also absorbing "many influences" in a "voice" that is nevertheless "entirely her own." Elizabeth Spires writes that Janice N. Harrington "is a celebratory poet who *sees* with the fresh, wondering eye of a child, but *knows* with the mind and heart of an adult." For Philip Levine the "dazzling new talent whose language seizes [him], who makes [his] hair stand on end," is the debut poet "whose voice" both "owes nothing to anyone and everything to the greats of the past."[28] Crossing registers from formal mastery to heart and soul, from maturity to playfulness, and from tradition to originality, representative passages such as these describe the crossing from inspired prophecy to discerning appraisal enacted in the movement between the lyrical and critical strands in prefatorial discourse. In other words, the ratio between technicality and indetermination that informs the ideology of professionalism defines the self-presentation of contemporary first-book prize judge and debut poet alike.

As we have seen in earlier chapters, these conflicting imperatives often issue in representations of career that privilege a thematic of beginning, a tendency that continues unabated in contemporary poetic debuts. The titles of a number of recent first books feature an emphasis on birth, youth, and onset in the manner of the titles listed in the introduction and chapter 2: *Living in the Resurrection* (Tony Crunk, 1995), *The New Intimacy* (Barbara Cully, 1997), *Apprentice of Fever* (Richard Tayson, 1998), *Ivory Cradle* (Anne Marie Macari, 2000), *Earliest Worlds* (Eleni Sikelianos, 2001), *Gravedigger's Birthday* (B. J. Ward, 2002), *The Room Where I Was Born* (Brian Teare, 2003), *The Green Girls* (John Blair, 2003), *Birthmark* (Jon Pineda, 2004), *Morning Prayer* (Eve Grubin, 2006), *The New Year of Yellow* (Matthew Lippman, 2007), *The Morning* (Roger Snell, 2008), *It Is Daylight* (Arda Collins, 2009), *The Waker's Corridor* (Jonathan Thirkield, 2009), *Born in the Cavity of Sunsets* (Michael Luis Medrano, 2009), *The Beginning of the Fields* (Angela Shaw, 2009), *To Light Out* (Karen Weiser, 2010), and *Juvenilia* (Ken Chen, 2010). Among leadoff poems, the theme of beginning remains fairly common and is often strikingly explicit. The last line of Crystal Bacon's "Elegy with a Glass of Whiskey in Its Hand" announces that "the words will wait, are waiting, to be born"; the speaker of John Blair's "The Cicada" wants "to crawl headfirst into a dirt-warm womb / to sleep, to wait seventeen years, to emerge again"; Paul LeGault's "Madeleine" opens with the order to "leave / open the book of your arrival"; the first line of Erin Elizabeth Smith's "The Mulberry Trees" declares "We have to start somewhere"; the surrealistic opening claim of Matthias Svalina's "Creation Myth" is "In the beginning, everyone looked like Larry Bird."[29] The titles of opening poems often evoke beginnings of one kind or another: "New Science," "Opening Up," "Beginnings," "AA," "Youth," "Forecasts," "Preludio," "The First Biome," "Greeting," "Primer for Non-Native Speakers," "Decampment," "Origin and Ash," "New Cairo," "Drawing for Absolute Beginners," "In the Beginning," "Waking in Antibes," "March Morning," "Christmas Morning," "Generation," "In the Garden," "Philadelphia, 1976," "Foreplay," "New Year's Eve 2000," "We Didn't Start the Fire," and "Vestibule" are drawn from debuts by Priscilla Sneff, Jeredith Merrin, Nomi Stone, Shelley Stenhouse, Jason Whitmarsh, Sabrina Dalla Valle, Katie Umans, Matthew Schwartz, Philip Metres, Travis Mossotti, Tina Chang, Matthew Shenoda, Monica Youn, Jill Alexander Essbaum, Mary Jo Bang, David Tucker, Tony Crunk, Suji Kwok Kim, Jay Hopler, Ryan Teitman, Paige Ackerson-Kiely, Daisy Fried, Will Schutt, and Daniel Albergotti, respectively. Such persistence is particularly surprising given that poets inhabit a "universe in which to exist is to differ," as Bourdieu puts it: "newcomers" must "assert their difference, get it known and recognized, get themselves known and recognized ('make a name for themselves') by endeavoring to impose new modes of thought and expression" (*FCP* 58). It also helps to account for the proliferation of debut prizes over the past sixty years—for it attests to the continuing symbolic power of youth and the prestige of the new that such prizes capitalize on and, on a still broader level, to the enduring value of autonomy in the field of cultural production, insofar as the thematic of beginning signals independence from the establishment.

I want to conclude with a reading of Hedge Coke's "The Change," a poem that offers a powerful and ambitious illustration of the complex pre-occupation with autonomy that drives the rise of the first book after World War II. The opening poem in her American Book Award-winning 1997 debut, *Dog Road Woman*, "The Change" narrates a kind of fall from a time "Thirteen years ago,   before bulk barns   and / fifth gear diesel tractors," when the speaker and her husband, "as married to the fields as we were to each other," farmed tobacco together.[30] It is a time "Before the year dusters sprayed / malathion over our clustered bodies," "before anyone had seen / automated machines that top and prime," and "before the encroachment of / big business in the Reagan era / and the slow murder of method / from a hundred years before." It is also a time punctuated by moments of beauty, as when she describes how the tobacco "leaves hung down / like butterfly wings, though / sometimes the color of luna moths, or Carolina parakeets," and it is marked in general by a profound sense of being "content and free." But despite the appeal of the way things were, it does not appear as a prelapsarian paradise: they toil in "one hundred fifteen degree   summer / heat," roll "eight-inch balls" of tar off of their arms after work, and remember the selling of their "ancestors as slaves in the Middle East." This refusal of idealization reflects Hedge Coke's pragmatic sense of the provisional nature of autonomy—the concern that focuses the poem's conclusion.

Hedge Coke describes "The Change" through a series of before-and-after images as she comes to the turning point cited in the title:

> Then they came and changed things
> and you left me for a fancy white girl
> and I waited on the land
> until you brought her back
> in that brand new white Trans Am,
> purchased from our crop,   you gave her
> and left her waiting in a motel.

The infidelity is loaded with political and historical resonances. The "fancy white girl" clearly anticipates the "brand new white Trans Am," which, in turn, is linked to the theme of mechanization even as it conjures up the displacement of indigenous peoples through (trans-American) colonial expansion. In this way, the husband's betrayal serves as the model for other kinds of failure and decline; it also gives us a clue to the sort of integrity to which Hedge Coke aspires, but which she does not claim to possess. Keeping her knowledge of the infidelity secret until she leaves, the speaker withdraws "down the dirt path   by the empty fields" to a "shack" with "cardboard windows" and a rotten floor. Perched "at hilltop,   where I could / see out across all the fields," the speaker declares her independence from her marriage, industrialization, and the debased culture of modern "America" as a whole:

> I heard you remarried
> and went into automated farming
> and kept up with America.
> I watched all of you   from the hill
> and I waited for the lavender blooms
> to return   and when it was spring
> even the blooms   had turned white.
> I rolled up my bedroll,   remembering before,
> when the fields were like waves on a green ocean,
> and turned away,   away from the change
> and corruption of big business on small farms
> of traditional agricultural people,   and sharecroppers.

The sense of isolation described here resonates in a number of ways with that of earlier poets who, like Hedge Coke, are interested in finding ways to lay claim to the autonomy that underpins poetic authority. Her travel on a "dirt path" to a solitary position on the "hill" harks back to such debut poems of arrival as Donald Hall's "Apology," in which the pursuit of "singleness" leads the speaker to "climb the mountain / Which is my own choice," just as her turning "away,   away" recalls Richard Howard's "Sandusky–New York," in which the speaker "follow[s] himself away, away" from his origins in order to make a new start. "The Change" also recalls Gary Snyder's "Mid-August at Sourdough Mountain Lookout," a poem with which it has more in common than those by Hall and Howard, but that has not yet been mentioned here. The leadoff poem of *Riprap* (a title that evokes career as "a cobble of stone laid on steep, slick rock to make a trail for horses in the mountains"), Snyder's poem closes with the speaker "Drinking cold snow-water from a tin cup / Looking down for miles / Through high still air."[31]

As we have seen throughout this study, the poetic career tends to take shape through the effort made to resist conformity, though since career itself inevitably embodies an ethos of conformity, each new "dirt path," as Hedge Coke puts it, must be abandoned in turn. So it is that, having left her farm for life alone in the house on the hill, she rolls up her "bedroll" again in preparation for yet another leave-taking. Interestingly, the impetus behind these abandonments derives from her fidelity to the past, as the link between packing up to leave and "remembering before," contrasting notions that share a line of verse, suggest. Here, as in Ashbery's "The Instruction Manual," for example, among other debut poems, moving on represents a strategy for maintaining a connection to origins, an irony powerfully captured in the poem's final lines. There again the speaker turns

> Away,   so that I could always   hold this concise image
> of before   that   time   and it
> floods   my memory.

Turning away from the past is what enables the speaker to fix it, to "hold" onto it as a "concise image," though the empty spaces that break up all three of the final lines suggest the tenuousness of that "hold" as well as the susceptibility of the "concise image" to change. That it "floods" the "memory" that inspires the poem itself is borne out by the recurrent, hyperbolic emphasis on humidity, which appears early on in the description of "air so thick with moisture / you drink as you breathe" and then again in the account of working in the fields while "drinking air   which poured / through our pores." The word "floods" not only suggests a fortunate inundation by the past, but also the destructive force dramatized in mythic flood narratives. Consistent with the contradictory logic that permeates the representation of the trajectories discussed throughout this study, Hedge Coke opens her first book by imagining tradition as a past whose recuperation is inseparable from its dissolution: turning "away" from it precisely in order to be more fully immersed in it, she frames a moment of transition and ends the poem poised to begin anew.

Notes

Introduction: The History of the Poetic Career

1. Arnold Rampersad, *The Life of Langston Hughes, Volume I: 1902–1941, I, Too, Sing America* (New York: Oxford University Press, 1986), 48.
2. Of course, there have been a number of poets, including Alexander Pope, Mary Robinson, Lord Byron, Henry Wadsworth Longfellow, Elizabeth Barrett Browning, and Robert Frost, among others, whose income from publishing poetry was substantial, but even in such exceptional cases, the money poetry made was supplemented by patronage (Pope and Robinson), inheritance (Byron and Barrett Browning), and day jobs (Longfellow and Frost). William Charvat provides a succinct overview of the ways in which American poets have supported themselves in "The Popularization of Poetry," collected in *The Profession of Authorship in America, 1800–1870*, ed. Matthew J. Bruccoli (1968; repr., New York: Columbia University Press, 1992), 100–5.
3. Patrick Cheney, "'Jog On, Jog On': European Career Paths," in *European Literary Careers: The Author from Antiquity to the Renaissance*, ed. Patrick Cheney and Frederick A. de Armas (Toronto: University of Toronto Press, 2002), 3. Recent studies that deal with the idea of the twentieth-century American poetic career include Libbie Rifkin's *Career Moves: Olson, Creeley, Zukofsky, Berrigan, and the American Avant-Garde* (Madison: University of Wisconsin Press, 2000) and Andrew Mossin's *Male Subjectivity and Poetic Form in "New American" Poetry* (New York: Palgrave Macmillan, 2010). The qualification in Cheney's claim implies a recognition of critical works that have begun the exploration of career in the sense that he is promoting—a sense in which it figures as something more than a convenient synonym for "development," "life," or "oeuvre" and serves instead as a complex term whose study demands attention to patterns of stylistic, generic, and thematic change, traditional models of development, and strategies of self-presentation linked to a writer's social, psychological, and economic circumstances. Influential examples of such studies include Jerome Christensen, "Byron's Career: The Speculative Stage," *English Literary History* 52.1 (Spring 1985): 59–84 and *Practicing Enlightenment: Hume and the Formation of a Literary Career* (Madison: University of Wisconsin Press, 1987); John Guillory, "The Father's House: *Samson Agonistes* in Its Historical Moment," in *Re-Membering Milton: Essays on the Texts and Traditions*, ed. Mary Nyquist and Margaret W. Ferguson (New

York: Methuen, 1987), 148–76; Lee Erickson, "The Egoism of Authorship: Words-worth's Poetic Career," *Journal of English and Germanic Philology* 89.1 (January 1990): 37–50; Scott Rambuss, *Spencer's Secret Career* (Cambridge: Cambridge University Press, 1993); and Ann Baynes Coiro, "Fable and Old Song: *Samson Agonistes* and the Idea of a Poetic Career," *Milton Studies* 36 (1998): 123–52. For a list of works engaged in "career criticism," see below, note 6.

4. Louis Menand, *Discovering Modernism: T. S. Eliot and His Context* (New York: Oxford University Press, 1986), 117.

5. Fred Moramarco provides a list of Ashbery's "life metaphors" as an appendix to "Coming Full Circle: John Ashbery's Later Poetry," *The Tribe of John: Ashbery and Contemporary Poetry*, ed. Susan M. Schultz (Tuscaloosa: University of Alabama Press, 1995), 39, 52–59.

6. Cheney, "'Jog On, Jog On,'" 3. A recent "essential bibliography" lists Helgerson, *Self-Crowned Laureates: Spenser, Jonson, Milton, and the Literary System* (Berkeley: University of California Press, 1983); Lawrence Lipking, *The Life of the Poet: Beginning and Ending Poetic Careers* (Chicago: University of Chicago Press, 1981); and Cheney's "books on Marlowe, Spenser, and Shakespeare." Philip Hardie and Helen Moore, "Introduction: Literary Careers—Classical Models and Their Receptions," in *Classical Literary Careers*, ed. Philip Hardie and Helen Moore (Cambridge: Cambridge University Press, 2010), 1. Cheney's books include *Spenser's Famous Flight: A Renaissance Idea of a Literary Career* (Toronto: University of Toronto Press, 1993); *Marlowe's Counterfeit Profession: Ovid, Spenser, and Counter-Nationhood* (Toronto: University of Toronto Press, 1997); *Shakespeare, National Poet-Playwright* (Cambridge: Cambridge University Press, 2004); *Shakespeare's Literary Authorship* (Cambridge: Cambridge University Press, 2008); and *Marlowe's Republican Authorship: Lucan, Liberty, and the Sublime* (Basingstoke, UK: Palgrave Macmillan, 2009).

7. Cheney, "'Jog On, Jog On,'" 12. For all its familiarity, the "literary career" can be surprisingly difficult to define, as Cheney's reflections suggest: "By 'literary career,' what do we mean? In trying to define this complex idea, we might not find it unwise to resort to what Walter Bagehot said of nation-building in 1887: 'We know what it is when you do not ask us, but we cannot very quickly explain or define it.'" Ibid., 4.

8. For an excellent discussion of the "story of the Fall into professionalism," see Bruce Robbins, *Secular Vocations: Intellectuals, Professionalism, Culture* (London: Verso, 1993).

9. Andrew Goldstone provides an insightful discussion of the relative nature of autonomy in *Fictions of Autonomy: Modernism from Wilde to de Man* (New York: Oxford University Press, 2013).

10. Stephen Greenblatt, *Renaissance Self-Fashioning: From More to Shakespeare* (Chicago: University of Chicago Press, 1980), 9.

11. Cheney, "'Jog On, Jog On,'" 9; Hardie and Moore, "Introduction," 2.

12. In a valuable study of twentieth-century poetry and capitalism, Christopher Nealon notes that this sort of betrayal, which prompts a range of guilty reactions in contemporary poetry, has been largely ignored in the poetry criticism of the last fifty years. *The Matter of Capital: Poetry and Crisis in the American Century* (Cambridge, MA: Harvard University Press, 2011), 9-10.

13. Anis Shivani's *Against the Workshop: Provocations, Polemics, Controversies* (Huntsville: Texas Review Press, 2011) is a recent example of the anti-establishment, anti-careerist

critique that runs through much of the journalistic coverage of contemporary poetry, a critique that always ironically implicates the critic.

14. Bourdieu observes that "a position-taking changes, even when the position remains identical, whenever there is change in the universe of options that are simultaneously offered for producers and consumers to choose from. The meaning of a work (artistic, literary, philosophical, etc.) changes automatically with each change in the field within which it is situated for the spectator or reader" (*FCP* 30–31).

15. John Guillory, "Bourdieu's Refusal," *Modern Language Quarterly* 58, no. 4 (December 1997): 394.

16. Langdon Hammer discusses the implications of Plath's "incalculable" debt to her mother in the context of this letter in "Plath's Lives: Poetry, Professionalism, and the Culture of the School," *Representations* 75 (Summer 2001): 72.

17. Guillory, "Refusal," 397.

18. Lipking, *Life of the Poet*, viii.

19. Lipking, "Inventing a Life—A Personal View of Literary Careers," in *Classical Literary Careers*, 299.

20. *The Foucault Reader*, ed. Paul Rabinow (New York: Vintage, 2010), 103, 118.

21. "This book," Helgerson claims, "is about . . . three poets whose ambition preceded and determined their work, three poets who strove to achieve a major literary career and said so." *Self-Crowned Laureates*, 1. Similarly, Lipking observes that "Keats' ability to grow, like Milton's, depends on a vision of his future self." *Life of the Poet*, 4. The titles of both Helen Vendler's book and Edward Said's clearly give prominence to the initial moment in careers. See Helen Vendler, *Coming of Age as a Poet* (Cambridge, MA: Harvard University Press, 2003) and Edward Said, *Beginnings: Intention and Method* (1975; repr., New York: Columbia University Press, 1985).

22. The first book decides the contest "between career and noncareer." Said, *Beginnings*, 236. As Jim Harrison writes, "Nothing . . . equals the first book," that "tenuous justification of what you insisted was your calling." "Introduction," *The Shape of the Journey: New and Collected Poems* (Port Townsend, WA: Copper Canyon Press, 1998), 3.

23. Said claims that "the writer's life, his career, and his text form a system of relationships whose configuration *in real human time* becomes progressively stronger (i.e., more distinct, more individualized and exacerbated)." *Beginnings*, 227.

24. Magali Sarfatti Larson, *The Rise of Professionalism: A Sociological Analysis* (Berkeley: University of California Press, 1977), 229.

25. Guillory, "The Father's House," 150.

26. Joseph Farrell, "Greek Lives and Roman Careers in the Classical *Vita* Tradition," in *European Literary Careers*, 24.

27. Patrick Cheney, "Spenser's Pastorals: *The Shepheardes Calendar* and *Colin Clouts Come Home Againe*," in *The Cambridge Companion to Spenser*, ed. Andrew Hadfield (Cambridge: Cambridge University Press, 2001), 79–80.

28. Farrell, "Greek Lives," 24–25.

29. Ibid., 36.

30. Cheney, "'Jog On, Jog On,'" 9.

31. Spenser, *The Faerie Queen*, bk. 1, pr. 1.

32. John Milton, *An Apology for Smectymnuus* in *John Milton: Selected Prose*, ed. C. A. Patrides (Columbia: University of Missouri Press, 1985), 62.

33. See Alexander Pope, "A Discourse on Pastoral Poetry," in *The Poems of Alexander Pope*, ed. John Butt (New Haven, CT: Yale University Press, 1963), 119–23.

34. See, for example, Roy Gibson and Catherine Steel, "The Indistinct Literary Careers of Cicero and Pliny the Younger" and Patrick Cheney, "Did Shakespeare Have a Literary Career?" in *Classical Literary Careers*.

35. Said, *Beginnings*, 227. While this claim usefully captures the substance of the difference between vocation and career, it is worth noting that the terms also overlap with one another. Christensen follows M. H. Abrams in asserting that "vocation has a 'high' romantic sense . . . which adheres to the Augustinian, radically Protestant conception of the spirit's progress." Christensen, "Byron's Career," 61. That Augustinian conception of spiritual progress, however, is derived from the same "classical, primarily Virgilian" conception of vocation from which the romantics are typically supposed to depart. For this reason, both the classical and romantic conceptions of vocation, like the classical and romantic conceptions of career, involve the notion of progress, and Wordsworth's portrayal of the "Growth of the Poet's Mind" in *The Prelude* retains the principle of development implicit in Virgil's path from pastoral to epic. The difference between classical and romantic models, then, has to do with the kind of progress being evoked: the normative vocational trajectory produced by "imitating a ritual progress" contrasts with the often conspicuously indeterminate forms of personal "Growth" in which Wordsworth and the romantics tend to be invested.

    I use "vocation" and "career" interchangeably in this study, while also remaining mindful that "career" and "vocation," along with "election" and "profession," can be understood to depend on one another in a hierarchical series in which "election" is verified by "vocation," "vocation" is verified by "profession" (where "profession" marks a step downward from the spiritual passion associated with "vocation" to the concrete, worldly conditions and exercise of personal agency connected with professional labor), and "profession" is verified by "career," understood here simply as the series of successes (and failures) that define the working life. For more on the distinction between vocation and profession, see Max Weber's "Science as a Vocation" in *The Vocation Lectures*, ed. David Owen and Tracy B. Strong, trans. Rodney Livingstone (Indianapolis, IN: Hackett, 2004), 1–31. For Weber's discussion of the way in which successful work over the course of a career "creates the certainty of salvation," see *The Protestant Ethic and the "Spirit" of Capitalism and Other Writings*, ed. and trans. Peter Baehr and Gordon C. Wells (1905; repr., New York: Penguin, 2002), especially 67–202. For an excellent overview of the "spiritualization of work" as it pertains to the rise of professionalism in the nineteenth century, see Alan Mintz, "Ideas and Institutions," in *George Eliot and the Novel of Vocation* (Cambridge, MA: Harvard University Press, 1978), 1–20.

36. Raymond Williams, *Culture and Society: 1780–1950* (1958; repr., New York: Columbia University Press, 1983), 32; Samuel Taylor Coleridge, *The Major Works*, ed. H. J. Jackson (New York: Oxford University Press, 1985), 274. William Hazlitt claimed that "Professional Art is a contradiction in terms. Art is genius, and genius cannot belong to a profession." Quoted in David Bromwich, *Hazlitt: The Mind of a Critic* (1983; repr., New Haven, CT: Yale University Press, 1999), 119. Similarly, Sir Egerton Brydges observed that "it is a vile evil that literature is become so much a trade all over Europe." Quoted in Williams, *Culture and Society*, 35.

37. Robin Valenza, *Literature, Language, and the Rise of the Intellectual Disciplines in Britain, 1680–1820* (Cambridge: Cambridge University Press, 2009), 148.

38. Williams, *Culture and Society*, 36. Williams is careful to note that this reaction is "not merely a professional one. It is also (and this has been of the greatest subsequent importance) an emphasis on the embodiment in art of certain human values, capacities, energies, which the development of society towards an industrial civilization was felt to be threatening or even destroying. The element of professional protest is undoubtedly there, but the larger issue is the opposition on general human grounds to the kind of civilization that was being inaugurated."

39. See "The Conditions of Authorship in 1820," in Charvat, *Profession of Authorship*, 29–48.

40. Linda Zionkowski, *Men's Work: Gender, Class, and the Professionalization of Poetry, 1660–1784* (New York: Palgrave Macmillan, 2001), 7.

41. As Everard H. King suggests, Edwin "provided the fundamental pattern of the poetic life which many poets of the late eighteenth and early nineteenth centuries knowingly adopted in their personal lives and imitated in various ways in their autobiographical compositions." *James Beattie's "The Minstrel" and the Origins of Romantic Autobiography* (Lewiston, NY: Edwin Mellen Press, 1992), vii.

42. See M. H. Abrams, *Natural Supernaturalism* (New York: W. W. Norton, 1973), 385–90, 418–27.

43. *Shelley's Poetry and Prose*, ed. Donald H. Reiman and Sharon B. Powers (New York: W. W. Norton, 1977), 93–95.

44. For a valuable analysis of the way in which sincerity—as in the sincerity of the sense of vocation in Shelley's poem—"can be saved only by its careful abandonment," see Deborah Forbes, *Sincerity's Shadow: Self-Consciousness in British Romantic and Mid-Twentieth-Century American Poetry* (Cambridge, MA: Harvard University Press, 2004), 189.

45. Larson, *Rise of Professionalism*, 41.

46. Clifford Siskin, *The Work of Writing: Literature and Social Change in Britain* (Baltimore: Johns Hopkins University Press, 1998), 116.

47. Jonathan Freedman, *Professions of Taste: Henry James, British Aestheticism, and Commodity Culture* (Stanford, CA: Stanford University Press, 1990), 55.

48. For an excellent discussion of the complex connections between modernist literature and professionalism, see Thomas Strychacz, *Modernism, Mass Culture, and Professionalism* (Cambridge: Cambridge University Press, 1993).

49. Stanley Fish makes the same claim: "while in other disciplines anti-professionalism requires a conscious effort to detach the commodity from the social and cultural contexts in which it seems inextricably embedded, in literary [activities] . . . the commodity is defined by its independence of those same contexts, and anti-professionalism is the very content of the profession itself." "Anti-Professionalism," *New Literary History* 17, no. 1 (Autumn 1985): 99.

50. Edmund S. Morgan, *Visible Saints: The History of a Puritan Idea* (Ithaca, NY: Cornell University Press, 1965), 70.

51. Bruce Kimball, *The "True Professional Ideal" in America: A History* (Lanham, MD: Rowman and Littlefield, 1992), 2, 27.

52. "There is no more important point to be made about English Romantic poetry" than that it is "a kind of religious poetry, and the religion is in the Protestant line" observes Harold Bloom in *The Visionary Company* (Ithaca, NY: Cornell University Press,

1974), xvii. See also Abrams, *Natural Supernaturalism* and Elisa New, *The Regenerate Lyric: Theology and Innovation in American Poetry* (Cambridge: Cambridge University Press, 1993).

53. Charvat, *Profession of Authorship*, 3, 101. Strychacz rightly points out that "twentieth century creative writers require no higher education, are subject to no system of credentialing, and do not possess the automatic prestige accorded to the traditional professions (law, medicine) or to those working in scientific fields of knowledge," and he adds that "creative writing seems different in kind, and created for significantly different ends, than the bodies of formal knowledge that grant authority to professional groups," 25, 29–30.

54. John Keats to J. A. Hessey, October 8, 1818, in *Letters of John Keats*, ed. Robert Gittings (New York: Oxford University Press, 1970), 156, quoted in Williams, *Culture and Society*, 44.

55. See Eliot Friedson, "Formal Knowledge, Power, and the Professions" in *Professional Powers: A Study of the Institutionalization of Formal Knowledge* (Chicago: University of Chicago Press, 1988), 1–19.

56. Frank Lentricchia, *Modernist Quartet* (Cambridge: Cambridge University Press, 1994), 56.

57. Max Weber, *The Protestant Ethic and the Spirit of Capitalism*, trans. Talcott Parsons (New York: Scribner's, 1958), 117, quoted in Guillory, "The Father's House," 149.

58. "Interview with Donald Hall," in *A Marianne Moore Reader* (New York: Viking, 1961), 256.

Chapter 1: Apprentices to Chance Event

1. James Longenbach, *Wallace Stevens: The Plain Sense of Things* (New York: Oxford University Press, 1991), 16.

2. Burton J. Bledstein, *The Culture of Professionalism: The Middle Class and the Development of Higher Education in America* (New York: W. W. Norton, 1976), 184, 19.

3. Larson, *Rise of Professionalism*, 42.

4. Bledstein, *Culture of Professionalism*, 68, 111–12.

5. Larson, *Rise of Professionalism*, 229.

6. Longenbach, *Plain Sense of Things*, 15.

7. Bledstein, *Culture of Professionalism*, 160.

8. See Larson, *Rise of Professionalism*, 41–42.

9. Longenbach, *Plain Sense of Things*, 17.

10. Menand, *Discovering Modernism*, 117.

11. Samuel Longfellow, ed., *Life of Henry Wadsworth Longfellow*, vol. 1 (Boston: Ticknor and Company, 1886), 56.

12. Matthew Gartner, "Becoming Longfellow: Work, Manhood, and Poetry," *American Literature* 72.1 (March 2000): 74, 76; Henry Wadsworth Longfellow, *Voices of the Night* (Cambridge, MA: John Owen, 1849), ix, x, xiii, xv; Jill Anderson, "'Be Up and Doing': Henry Wadsworth Longfellow and Poetic Labor," *Journal of American Studies* 37.1 (April 2003): 15, 3. John Timberman Newcomb corroborates this view of Longfellow and the Fireside group in general: "But the more success these poets enjoyed in the world, the more completely they effaced worldly arenas of achievement from their verse," *Would Poetry Disappear? American Verse and the Crisis of Modernity* (Athens: University of Ohio Press, 2004), 24.

13. Newcomb, *Would Poetry Disappear?*, 4, 49.

14. Ibid., 61, 136–37, 54, 55, 48–49.

15. Writing of the death of George Santayana in 1952, Stevens observed, "It is difficult for a man whose whole life is thought to continue as a poet. The reason (like the law, which is only a form of the reason) is a jealous mistress" (*SP* 69).

16. John Guillory, *Cultural Capital: The Problem of Literary Canon Formation* (Chicago: University of Chicago Press, 1993), 146, 143.

17. As Charles Altieri suggests, "In this volume Stevens was obsessed with being adequate to his historical moment, a moment defined by the triumph of an essentially secular and typically empiricist worldview." This puts Stevens in a double bind: "How could he develop stylistic traits that acknowledged modern skepticism about traditional values yet nonetheless possessed the ability to redirect that skepticism to accord with the capacities of imagination that poetry might display?" Whereas I focus on this sense of impasse as the occasion of a specifically vocational anxiety that is the recurrent and central concern of first books, for Altieri it prompts anxieties about the existence of value in general in a modern world replete with the "terrifying force of fact." *Wallace Stevens and the Demands of Modernity: Toward a Phenomenology of Value* (Ithaca, NY: Cornell University Press, 2013), 47.

18. Harold Bloom, *Wallace Stevens: The Poems of Our Climate* (Ithaca, NY: Cornell University Press, 1977), 70. Stevens is fairly explicit about his need to mock what he also would embrace in a letter to William Carlos Williams from 1918: "I spare you the whole-souled burblings in the park, the leaves, lilacs, tulips and so on. Such things are unmanly and non-Prussian and, of course, a fellow must pooh-pooh something, even if it happens to be something he rather fancies, you know," quoted in Milton J. Bates, *Wallace Stevens: A Mythology of Self* (Berkeley: University of California Press, 1985), 87. See Bates's "Burgher, Fop, and Clown" for a useful discussion of the way in which Stevens's poetic personae complicate the legend of his divided life in *Mythology of Self*, 83–126.

19. William W. Bevis, "The Arrangement of *Harmonium*," *English Literary History* 37, no. 3 (September 1970): 470.

20. Paul Rosenfeld, "Another Pierrot," *Men Seen: Twenty-Four Modern Authors* (New York: Dial, 1925), quoted in Charles Doyle, ed. *Wallace Stevens: The Critical Heritage* (New York: Routledge, 1985), 74.

21. William Carlos Williams, *Imaginations*, ed. Webster Schott (New York: New Directions, 1970), 15.

22. See Stevens's letter to Harriet Monroe of August 24, 1922, in which he explains that "it will not be possible for me to do anything new in the interim" between the time of the letter and the deadline for completion of the manuscript, which was set at November 1, 1922. Stevens had already known of the deadline for a few weeks when he wrote and was finished editing the manuscript on November 18, 1922 (*WSL* 228, 232).

23. Lentricchia, *Modernist Quartet*, 147.

24. Eleanor Cook, *Poetry, Word-Play, and Word-War in Wallace Stevens* (Princeton, NJ: Princeton University Press, 1988), 113; John Hollander, *Melodious Guile: Fictive Pattern in Poetic Language* (New Haven, CT: Yale University Press, 1990), 78.

25. B. J. Leggett, *Early Stevens: The Nietzschean Intertext* (Durham, NC: Duke University Press, 1992), 63; Eleanor Cook, *A Reader's Guide to Wallace Stevens* (Princeton, NJ: Princeton University Press, 2007), 86.

26. Altieri, *Wallace Stevens*, 82–83.

27. Cook, *Word-War in Wallace Stevens*, 25.
28. Bevis, "Arrangement of *Harmonium*," 467–68.
29. Robert Buttel, "Teasing the Reader into *Harmonium*," *Texas Studies in Literature and Language* 25, no. 4 (Winter 1983): 85.
30. Altieri, *Wallace Stevens*, 55.
31. Richard Blessing, *Wallace Stevens' "Whole Harmonium"* (Syracuse: Syracuse University Press, 1970), 11; Michel Benamou, *Wallace Stevens and the Symbolist Imagination* (Princeton: Princeton University Press, 1972), 94; Harold Bloom, *Wallace Stevens: The Poems of Our Climate* (Ithaca: Cornell University Press, 1977), 128; Mervyn Nicholson, "The Riddle of the Firecat," *The Wallace Stevens Journal* 22, no. 2 (Fall 1998): 138.
32. Edward Ragg makes a similar point regarding Stevens's anxieties over the publication of *Harmonium*: "Perhaps Stevens preferred his anecdotes in a paradoxically *unpublished* state," *Wallace Stevens and the Aesthetics of Abstraction* (Cambridge: Cambridge University Press, 2010), 32.
33. In Altieri's account, the poem deploys allegory in a way that "facilitate[s] a mode of generating value not available if we insist on decoding meanings." Offering no "resolutions for our uncertainties," the poem teaches a kind of negative capability—a way to "position ourselves to heed those aspects of human life that are subjected to forces beyond our control," *Wallace Stevens*, 57–58.
34. Bloom provides a useful list: *The Man with the Blue Guitar*, "Poetry Is a Destructive Force," "Lions of Sweden," "The Sun This March," "Puella Parvula," and "An Ordinary Evening in New Haven." *Poems of Our Climate*, 174.
35. Eleanor Cook reads "clatter" as "chatter" in *Word-War in Wallace Stevens*, 29. Her note that "clattering" is "not usually a sound made by bucks, who more often graze or gallop," makes Stevens's interest in it as a representation of speech seem more deliberate. *Reader's Guide*, 31.
36. Leggett, *Early Stevens*, 207.
37. Louis L. Martz, "'From the Journal of Crispin': An Early Version of 'The Comedian as the Letter C,'" in *Wallace Stevens: A Celebration*, ed. Frank Doggett and Robert Buttell (Princeton, NJ: Princeton University Press, 1980), 3.
38. Siobhan Phillips, *The Poetics of the Everyday: Creative Repetition in Modern American Verse* (New York: Columbia University Press, 2010), 77.
39. Cook, *Word-War in Wallace Stevens*, 73.
40. Bloom, *Poems of Our Climate*, 75.
41. New, *Regenerate Lyric*, 72–73.
42. In 1897, Stevens's father wrote to Wallace that "the afflatus" or poetic inspiration in evidence in the poems Stevens had been sending to his mother, "was not serious." Joan Richardson persuasively suggests that the word "afflatus" "was still resounding in [Stevens's] mind" in the years leading up to the publication of *Harmonium*. She claims that Stevens attempts to "negate the judgment of long ago" in "Negation," which features a "creator" who is "overwhelmed / By an afflatus that persists." *Wallace Stevens: The Early Years, 1879–1923* (New York: William Morrow, 1986), 487–88. I think Richardson's biographical reading of "afflatus" can also be applied to these lines from the "Comedian." Garrett's "reproach" is, for Stevens, "contained" in the word "afflatus" itself, a judgment that impacts Stevens's sense of vocation throughout his life, just as in the "Comedian" it is what "first drove Crispin to his wandering" even as it inspires "these bland excursions into time to come."

43. Cook, *Reader's Guide*, 77.

44. Bloom, *Poems of Our Climate*, 57.

45. Langdon Hammer, *Hart Crane and Allen Tate: Janus-Faced Modernism* (Princeton, NJ: Princeton University Press, 1993), 12.

46. Ellen Levy, *Criminal Ingenuity: Moore, Cornell, Ashbery, and the Struggle between the Arts* (New York: Oxford University Press, 2011), 35, 42.

47. Menand, *Discovering Modernism*, 117.

48. Yvor Winters to Marianne Moore, June 6, 1921, Rosenbach Collection, quoted in Robin G. Schulze, *The Web of Friendship: Marianne Moore and Wallace Stevens* (Ann Arbor: University of Michigan Press, 1995), 41.

49. Menand, *Discovering Modernism*, 145–46.

50. See Schulze's discussion of this pattern in *Becoming Marianne Moore*, 23–24.

51. Morgan, *Visible Saints*, 70.

52. Bonnie Costello, *Marianne Moore: Imaginary Possessions* (Cambridge, MA: Harvard University Press, 1981), 166. See also David Bromwich, " 'That Weapon, Self-Protectiveness': Notes on a Friendship," *Skeptical Music: Essays on Modern Poetry* (Chicago: University of Chicago Press, 2001), 102–15.

53. "Flight" is a commonplace reference to the literary career; see Cheney, *Spenser's Famous Flight*.

54. John Slatin, *The Savage's Romance: The Poetry of Marianne Moore* (University Park, PA: Penn State University Press, 1986), 33.

55. According to Leavell, Mary's criticism, which "has horrified readers of Moore's letters," is "a prime example of Mary's 'saying yes by a thousand no's' "—a mode of expression rooted in her penchant for "Scotch-Irish indirection." On this reading, respect for her daughter's achievement is ironically embedded in the negative judgment of her style. Leavell's interpretation helps to account for the tone of Moore's claim that she "could publish a book anytime," which would not be in keeping with her characteristic humility unless the boast was meant playfully. Linda Leavell, *Holding On Upside Down: The Life and Work of Marianne Moore* (New York: Farrar, Straus, and Giroux, 2013), 134–35.

56. Sandra M. Gilbert and Susan Gubar, *No Man's Land: The Place of the Woman Writer in the Twentieth Century*, vol. 3, *Letters from the Front* (New Haven, CT: Yale University Press, 1994), 102.

57. George Kateb, *Emerson and Self-Reliance* (Lanham, MD: Rowman and Littlefield Publishers, 2002), 152–53.

58. *Ralph Waldo Emerson: Collected Essays and Poems* (New York: Library of America, 1996), 414.

59. Ibid., 403.

60. In a related discussion of the poem as "a tale about the effectiveness of indirection and the folly of elitist indifference," Cristanne Miller sees a potential in the poem to "contain a disguised self-portrait" in which Moore appears as "an underdog"—the "poor fool" in the poem who "enjoys a weapon of great power in his imaginative, inconsequential manner and wit." *Cultures of Modernism: Marianne Moore, Mina Loy, and Else Lasker-Schüler* (Ann Arbor: University of Michigan Press, 2005), 9, 11.

61. Costello, *Imaginary Possessions*, 225.

62. *Ralph Waldo Emerson: Essays and Poems*, 271.

63. Leavell, *Holding On Upside Down*, 126–27.

64. The image of the labyrinth figures in the Calvinist conception of vocation, as Perry Miller points out: "Calvin had wisely advised caution in promising divine assurance, since predestination takes place in the inmost recesses of divine wisdom, where the careless intruder may obtain no satisfaction, 'but will enter a labyrinth from which he shall find no way to depart.'" Perry Miller, *The New England Mind: The Seventeenth Century* (New York: Macmillan, 1939), 370. For more on Moore's relationship to the Calvinist tradition see Jeredith Merrin, "Sites of Struggle: Marianne Moore and American Calvinism" in *The Calvinist Roots of the Modern Era*, ed. Aliki Barnstone, Michael Tomasek Manson, and Carol J. Singly (Hanover, NH: University Press of New England, 1997), 91–106.

65. Charles Molesworth, *Marianne Moore: A Literary Life* (Boston: Northeastern University Press, 1991), 114. Leavell notes that Moore sent the poem to her brother Warner "well before she began calling herself Rat," but suggests nevertheless that it is a "self-portrait predicting the kind of poet Moore would be." *Holding On Upside Down*, 127.

66. T. S. Eliot, *Collected Poems, 1909–1962* (London: Faber and Faber, 1963), 5.

67. Brian Reed, *Hart Crane: After His Lights* (Tuscaloosa: University of Alabama Press, 2007), 17, 40, 58.

68. Ibid., 109.

69. New, *Regenerate Lyric*, 187.

70. Bonnie Costello, "The 'Feminine' Language of Marianne Moore," in *Women and Language in Literature and Society*, ed. Sally McConnell-Ginet, Ruth Borker, and Nelly Furman (New York: Praeger, 1980), 225.

71. "Crane's 'whirling spout' represented the all-consuming experience of acknowledgment which seemed to him the one proper subject of poetry and the sustaining condition of life. His dream of rescue was a story about the restoration of relationship between persons. He had no other subject." Allen Grossman, "Hart Crane and Poetry: A Consideration of Crane's Intense Poetics," in *Modern Critical Views: Hart Crane*, ed. Harold Bloom (New York: Chelsea House Publishers, 1986), 240.

72. As John T. Irwin notes, the "number of words in the first two stanzas that can also refer to writing metrical verse" stresses the point "that it is a *poet* imagining his own death." *Hart Crane's Poetry: "Appolinaire Lived in Paris, I Live in Cleveland, Ohio"* (Baltimore, MD: Johns Hopkins University Press, 2011), 283.

73. Walter Pater, *The Renaissance: Studies in Art and Poetry*, ed. Donald L. Hill (Berkeley: University of California Press, 1980), 188–89.

74. Ibid., 188, 190.

75. In his discussion of "Possessions," Irwin also observes that the "sexual drive is seen as something excessive, humiliatingly painful, and possibly self-destructive but also as the libidinal energy that drives [Crane's] creativity." *Hart Crane's Poetry*, 285.

76. Hammer, *Hart Crane and Allen Tate*, 51.

77. Bromwich, *Skeptical Music*, 46. There is also a pun on "thrust"; perhaps Jean Toomer, who called the poem "a deep, thrusting, dense, organized, strong, passionate, luminous, and ecstatic poem," heard the same wordplay. Part of his response to the poem is quoted in *O My Land, My Friends* (New York: Four Walls Eight Windows, 1997), 163–64.

78. This analysis is indebted to Bromwich's insight that "the idea of counting such moments is bound to be false; they are really one moment 'that stays / As though prepared.'" *Skeptical Music*, 47.

79. A similar moment occurs in "Praise for an Urn," in which the image of the "slant moon" in the third stanza prefigures that of the "insistent clock" that appears in the fourth (*HCCP* 7).

80. Alfred Hanley, *Hart Crane's Holy Vision: White Buildings* (Pittsburgh, PA: Duquesne University Press, 1981), 21.

81. Alan Trachtenberg, introduction to *Hart Crane: A Collection of Critical Essays* (Englewood Cliffs, NJ: Prentice-Hall, 1982), 6.

82. Ibid.

83. Pater, *The Renaissance*, 187–88.

84. Hammer, *Hart Crane and Allen Tate*, 128.

85. "You already know, I think, that my work for the past two years (those meagre drops!) has been more influenced by Eliot than any other modern" (*HCL* 117).

86. Harold Bloom, "Hart Crane's Gnosis," in *Agon: Towards a Theory of Revisionism* (New York: Oxford University Press, 1982), 258.

87. In the well-known letter to Yvor Winters of 1927, Crane complains of Edmund Wilson's remark (in an omnibus review in the *New Republic*) that poets shouldn't be "so 'professional.'" Crane is clearly reluctant to accept the label, but he does accept it, with qualifications: he claims that if he does appear to be a professional, it is because life circumstances that were beyond his control forced him to professionalize (*HCL* 336).

88. Larson, *Rise of Professionalism*, 32.

89. "Above all else the ideology supporting professional training emphasizes theory and abstract concepts." Eliot Freidson, *Professionalism: The Third Logic* (Chicago: University of Chicago Press, 2001), 95.

90. "The monopolistic goal of the professional project, which demands regulation and control of access to the professional market on the supply side, contradicts, therefore, the democratization potential inherent in the expansion of professional markets and in the challenge to corporate privileges." Larson, *Rise of Professionalism*, 51. Hammer sees the presence of "democratizing and elitist drives" illustrated in "Crane's sense of himself as the privileged, individual possessor of a collective vision." Hammer, *Hart Crane and Allen Tate*, 9.

91. "The strength of [the professional's] inner character, the permanence of his inner continuity," Bledstein suggests, "correspond[s] to the outer continuity of the career." *Culture of Professionalism*, 158.

92. Grossman, "Crane's Intense Poetics," 224–25.

93. Irwin suggests that "caper" can also be read to suggest a "prance," rather than a prank or a stunt, and he concludes that "capering is an image of that sexual excess Crane claims in 'Legend' is the inevitable accompaniment of his tragically joyful poetic song." *Hart Crane's Poetry*, 249.

Chapter 2: "Poets of the First Book, Writers of Promise"

1. Harvey Shapiro, "Some Notes Are Familiar," *New York Times*, January 14, 1962.

2. Gerald Graff, *Professing Literature: An Institutional History* (Chicago: University of Chicago Press, 1987), 145.

3. For example, Charles Bernstein observes that the "use of standard patterns of syntax and exposition effectively rebroadcast, often at a subliminal level, the basic constitutive elements of the social structure" in *Content's Dream: Essays 1975–1984* (Los Angeles: Sun and Moon Press, 1986), 59–60.

4. James Longenbach, *Modern Poetry after Modernism* (New York: Oxford University Press, 1997), 5–6. For Langdon Hammer's critique of the "breakthrough narrative," see "Robert Lowell's Breakdown," in *Hart Crane and Allen Tate*, 211–32 and "Plath's Lives," *Representations* 75 (Summer 2001): 61–88.

5. Christopher Beach, *Poetic Culture: Contemporary American Poetry between Community and Institution* (Evanston, IL: Northwestern University Press, 1999); Paul Breslin, *The Psycho-Political Muse: American Poetry since the Fifties* (Chicago: University of Chicago Press, 1987); Michael Davidson, *Guys Like Us: Citing Masculinity in Cold War Poetics* (Chicago: University of Chicago Press, 2004); Alan Golding, *From Outlaw to Classic: Canons in American Poetry* (Madison: University of Wisconsin Press, 1995); Libbie Rifkin, *Career Moves: Olson, Creeley, Zukofsky, Berrigan, and the American Avant-Garde* (Madison: University of Wisconsin Press, 2000).

6. Michael Davidson offers a ready example in his discussion of the ethos of competition that characterizes the San Francisco Renaissance: "Poets often had recourse to rather exclusive and exclusionist rituals that belied their democratic social ideals. The bohemian bar life of the 1950s was a competitive arena in which many of the power struggles of the dominant culture were acted out in microcosm." *The San Francisco Renaissance* (Cambridge: Cambridge University Press, 1989), xi. Thinking along similar lines, Golding asks, "Isn't Language writing merely set to occupy the very center that it claims to critique, set to become another 'field' within the larger field of recent American poetry?" Golding, *From Outlaw to Classic*, 145.

7. I borrow the phrase "official verse culture" from Bernstein, according to whom it encompasses "the poetry publishing and reviewing practices of the *New York Times*, the *Nation*, *American Poetry Review*, *New York Review of Books*, the *New Yorker*, *Poetry* (Chicago), *Antaeus*, *Parnassus*, Atheneum Press, all the major trade publishers, [and] the poetry series of almost all the major university presses. . . . Add to this the ideologically motivated selection of the vast majority of poets teaching in university writing and literature programs and of poets taught in such programs as well as the interlocking accreditation of these selections through prizes and awards judged by these same individuals." *Content's Dream*, 247–48.

8. Jed Rasula, *Syncopations: The Stress of Innovation in Contemporary American Poetry* (Tuscaloosa: University of Alabama Press, 2004), 7.

9. I have adapted the phrasing of Jennifer Ashton in her useful overview of "Poetry of the Twenty-First Century: The First Decade," where she speaks of the "intensification of commitment to the self" in lyric poetry as "an intensification so great that even opposition to it becomes a form of it." *The Cambridge Companion to American Poetry since 1945*, ed. Jennifer Ashton (Cambridge: Cambridge University Press, 2013), 220. For more on what Walter Kalaidjian describes as countercultural poetry's "oppositional *dependence* on the very traditions it repudiate[s]," see Kalaidjian, *Languages of Liberation: The Social Text in Contemporary American Poetry* (New York: Columbia University Press, 1989), 7. In a discussion of the "vertiginously dialectical mobilization of the distinction between 'inside' and 'outside'" in post-1945 culture in general, Mark McGurl cites Walter Ong's *The Barbarian Within* (New York: Macmillan, 1962) as an important early description of this phenomenon. McGurl, *The Program Era: Postwar Fiction and the Rise of Creative Writing* (Cambridge, MA: Harvard University Press, 2009), 197.

10. McGurl, *Program Era*, ix, xi.

11. Ibid., 74, 27.

12. Ibid., 5, 29.
13. Paul Alexander, *Rough Magic: A Biography of Sylvia Plath* (1991; repr., Cambridge, MA: Da Capo, 1999), 305.
14. Linda Wagner-Martin, *Sylvia Plath: A Biography* (New York: Simon and Schuster, 1987), 40.
15. James F. English observes that arts prizes now number "well over one hundred thousand" in "Winning the Culture Game: Prizes, Awards, and the Rules of Art," *New Literary History* 33:1 (Winter 2002): 129.
16. Peter Davison, "Discovering Young Poets," *Atlantic Monthly,* June 1998, 103.
17. Wagner-Martin, *Sylvia Plath*, 96.
18. Davison, "Discovering Young Poets," 103.
19. Alexander, *Rough Magic*, 208, 250; *UJSP*, 689, 492.
20. Sylvia Plath, *The Colossus and Other Poems* (1962; repr., New York: Vintage, 1968), 20.
21. The intensity of Plath's excitement over Hughes's prize-winning debut also comes across in a letter to her mother: "The big, brown envelope came from Harper's today. Very exciting. A huge blue contract to sign with hundreds of little bylaws" (*LH* 303).
22. James F. English, *The Economy of Prestige* (Cambridge, MA: Harvard University Press, 2005), 51.
23. Louis Simpson, "Poets in Isolation," *Hudson Review* 6, no. 4 (Autumn 1957): 458.
24. Edward M. Cifelli, *John Ciardi: A Biography* (Fayetteville: University of Arkansas Press, 1997), 132.
25. Constance Carrier, *The Middle Voice*, New Poetry Series (Denver, CO: A. Swallow, 1955); Poets of Today, 8 vols. (New York: Scribner's, 1954–61).
26. J. Donald Adams, "Speaking of Books," *New York Times*, May 24, 1953.
27. George Bradley, introduction to *The Yale Younger Poets Anthology*, ed. George Bradley (New Haven, CT: Yale University Press, 1998), lxxiv.
28. The books are David Wagoner's *Dry Sun, Dry Wind* (1953), W. Walker Gibson's *Reckless Spenders* (1954), John Woods's *Deaths at Paragon, Indiana* (1955), and Neil Weiss's *Changes of Garments* (1956).
29. Bruce Wilcox, interview by author, September 14, 2006.
30. J. Donald Adams, "Speaking of Books," *New York Times*, May 24, 1953.
31. Eda Lou Walton, "Younger Voices," *Poetry* 43, no. 12 (March 1954): 343.
32. W. S. Merwin, "Something of His Own to Say," *New York Times*, October 6, 1957.
33. Paul Engle, "Praise to Poets and Presses," *Chicago Daily Tribune*, August 5, 1956; "Poets Keeping Their Private Skies Inviolate," *Chicago Daily Tribune*, December 15, 1957.
34. J. Donald Adams, "Speaking of Books," *New York Times*, May 16, 1954.
35. William Meredith, "A Lot of Poems and a Bit of Theory," *Hudson Review* 7, no. 4 (Winter 1955): 594.
36. Thomas Lask, "Books of the Times: Firsts," *New York Times*, August 15, 1970.
37. *New York Times*, November 8, 1951; October 23, 1960; November 17, 1960; September 1, 1963; September 9, 1967; January 25, 1970; August 15, 1970.
38. Alfred Alvarez, "Poetry Chronicle," *Partisan Review* 25, no. 4 (Fall 1958): 604.
39. Frank O'Hara, "Rare Modern," *Poetry* 89, no. 5 (February 1957): 313; Hayden Carruth, "Four New Books," *Poetry* 93, no. 2 (November 1958): 107.
40. Jack Gilbert, "Perspective He Would Mutter Going to Bed," in *Views of Jeopardy* (New Haven, CT: Yale University Press, 1958), 2, quoted in John Simon, "More Brass Than Enduring," *Hudson Review* 15, no. 3 (Autumn 1962): 456.

41. John Thompson, "A Catalogue of Poets," *Hudson Review* 13, no. 4 (Winter 1960–61): 623.

42. James Dickey, "Toward a Solitary Joy," *Hudson Review* 14, no. 4 (Winter 1961–62): 609.

43. F. O. Matthiessen, introduction to *Fingerboard*, by Marshall Schacht (New York: Twayne, 1949), 5.

44. Harvey Shapiro, "Some Notes Are Familiar," *New York Times*, January 14, 1962.

45. Michael Goldman, "Reawakened Into Life," *New York Times*, December 8, 1968.

46. William Arrowsmith, "Nine New Poets," *Hudson Review* 9, no. 2 (Summer 1956): 289–97. Matthiessen anticipates this trend in the opening to his introduction to *Fingerboard*: "Introducing this first collection of poems by Marshall Schacht, I am deprived of the phrase usual to such occasions. This is not a promising book," 5.

47. Donald Hall, "A Diet of Dissatisfaction," *Poetry* 87, no. 5 (February 1956): 301–2.

48. Donald Justice, *Collected Poems* (New York: Alfred A. Knopf, 2006), 5–6. Additional examples include Donald Hall's "On a Birthday," in *Exiles and Marriages* (New York: Viking, 1955), 77; Norma Farber's "The Hatch," in *The Hatch: Poems*, Poets of Today 2 (New York: Charles Scribner's Sons, 1955), 21; Walter Stone's "Poeta Nascitur," in *Poems 1955–1958,* Poets of Today 6 (New York: Charles Scribner's Sons, 1959), 158–59; and Jean Valentine's "New York, April 27, 1962" in *Dream Barker*, Yale Series of Younger Poets (New Haven, CT: Yale University Press, 1965), 26.

49. Plath, *The Colossus*, 3. Plath writes in her journal of her distaste for "The Earthenware Head," which was "once, in England, my 'best poem,'" but is now "too fancy, glassy, patchy & rigid—it embarrasses me now—with its ten elaborate epithets for head in 5 verses" (*UJSP* 399). This embarrassment over the artificiality of her poetry surfaces in "The Winter Ship" from *The Colossus* in the image of the "red and orange barges," which "list and blister / Shackled to the dock, outmoded, gaudy, / And apparently indestructible," 44.

50. Jo Gill, "*The Colossus* and *Crossing the Water*," in *The Cambridge Companion to Sylvia Plath*, ed. Jo Gill (New York: Cambridge University Press, 2006), 96–97.

51. Theodore Holmes, "The Letter Killeth," in *The Harvest and the Scythe: Poems*, Poets of Today 4 (New York: Charles Scribner's Sons, 1957), 76; Donald Finkel, "An Esthetic of Imitation," in *The Clothing's New Emperor and Other Poems*, Poets of Today 6, (New York: Charles Scribner's Sons, 1959), 85; X. J. Kennedy, "Ars Poetica," in *Nude Descending a Staircase* (Garden City, NY: Doubleday, 1961), 53.

52. Longenbach, *Modern Poetry*, 125.

53. Richard Howard, *Quantities / Damages: Early Poems* (Middletown, CT: Wesleyan University Press, 1984), 3.

54. This sort of language is tellingly common among leadoff poems during the era of the first-book prize. John Hollander's "Icarus Before Knossos," positions the poet somewhere between youth and age: "No longer being young . . . ; Not yet being old." *The Crackling of Thorns* (New Haven, CT: Yale University Press, 1958), 2. William Heyen's opening poem, "Winter Solstice," locates the speaker in a similar state of limbo: ". . . neither in / nor out / of any life." *Depth of Field* (Baton Rouge: Louisiana State University Press, 1970), 5. In "Perpetual Motion," the leadoff poem of Tony Hoagland's debut, the speaker appears "With my foot upon the gas, / between the future and the past." *Sweet Ruin* (Madison: University of Wisconsin Press, 1993), 4.

55. Charles G. Bell, *Songs for a New America*, Indiana University Poetry Series (Bloomington: Indiana University Press, 1953), 71.

56. Said, *Beginnings*, 33.

57. Robert Pack, *The Irony of Joy: Poems*, Poets of Today 2 (New York: Charles Scriber's Sons, 1955), 87.

58. Henry Taylor's debut begins with a poem about his college "Latin master" entitled—appropriately enough for a beginning—"In Medias Res." Taylor learns "tact" and "Vergil's verses" from his teacher, and he memorizes "the motto of the University of Chicago: / *Let knowledge grow from more to more / And so be human life enriched*." The poem concludes with the speaker poised at the beginning of his adult career, his "diploma in [his] hand," ready now to leave "love and [his] Latin book behind." *The Horse Show at Midnight* (Baton Rouge: Louisiana State University Press, 1966), 3.

59. *Walt Whitman: Complete Poetry and Collected Prose*, ed. Justin Kaplan (New York: Library of America, 1982), 1326.

60. Stanley Plumly, *In the Outer Dark* (Baton Rouge: Louisiana State University Press, 1970), 50.

61. Donald Hall, "Six Poets in Search of a Lawyer," in *Exiles and Marriages*, 61.

62. The glowing review in *Time* quoted precisely these lines from "Six Poets in Search of a Lawyer" before concluding by nominating him (unofficially) for the Pulitzer. See "Time's Sweet Praise" in *The Day I Was Older: On the Poetry of Donald Hall*, ed. Liam Rector (Santa Cruz, CA: Storyline Press, 1989), 204–5.

63. Hall, *Exiles and Marriages*, 11.

64. Harvey Shapiro's "The Dark Wood" is another debut poem of arrival in which the poet is likewise positioned at the foot of a mountain. Noting that the "voyager discovers nothing new / Unless" he "Keep[s] to his shining origin," he distinguishes himself from "those, upon whatever slope / Who wake to know the child gone" and who therefore "cannot find / The form that will remember them." Borrowing the image of the "dark wood" that precedes the mountain of salvation from Dante's *Inferno*, the poem concludes with the speaker poised on the brink of his journey: "I make what images I can, / Staring into that dark wood." *The Eye*, New Poetry Series (Denver, CO: Alan Swallow, 1953), 10.

65. Howard, *Quantities / Damages*, 71.

66. Jed Rasula, *The American Poetry Wax Museum: Reality Effects, 1940–1990* (Urbana, IL: National Council of Teachers of English, 1996), 68. For a valuable discussion of the way in which "contemporary writers of color can best be understood in terms we have developed for the analysis of the avant-garde," see Timothy Yu, *Race and the Avant-Garde: Experimental and Asian American Poetry since 1965* (Stanford, CA: Stanford University Press, 2011), 2.

67. Just as the academic insiders presented themselves as rebels, so the rebels often turned out to be academics: "After the smoke of ill repute associated with 'Howl' cleared away, it turned out that the 'know-nothing' upstarts were a platoon of bibliophiles and wandering scholars." Rasula, *American Poetry Wax Museum*, 238, 246.

68. Greenblatt, *Renaissance Self-Fashioning*, 9. As Gillian White astutely suggests, "theories of lyric reading are especially exciting for the promise they hold out to scholars to see what opens up in the realization that the 'lyric' tradition against which an avant-garde antilyricism has posited itself (whether implicitly or explicitly) never existed in the first place." *Lyric Shame: The "Lyric" Subject of Contemporary American Poetry* (Cambridge, MA: Harvard University Press, 2014), 16.

69. In a related discussion of the "absorption of Language poetry into the academy," Marjorie Perloff acknowledges that the passage from "outlaw to classic" is inevitable: "no

avant-garde cenacle can keep up its momentum for three decades." Yet she denies this knowledge of the "temporal" limits of avant-garde "momentum" to the Language poets themselves: "Surely the founders of the Language movement could not have anticipated that, within twenty years, the case against 'the natural look,' the authoritative Cartesian subject, the transparency of meaning, and the use of 'old-fashioned lineation' (much less meter) rather than the 'new sentence' would become mere items to be ticked off on the 'How To Make It New' list, that the 'innovative' writing produced in the Workshop . . . would become just as tedious and formulaic as the Workshop poetry it had once spurned." I think the rhetoric of beginning and concern with career that animates both mainstream and countercultural first books suggests more awareness of the half-life of countercultural opposition on the part of the Language poets than Perloff gives them credit for. Perloff, "Avant-Garde Tradition and the Individual Talent: The Case of Language Poetry," *Revue Française d'Études Américaines* 103 (February 2005): 132.

70. For an insightful discussion of Baraka's "poetics of turning away"—an ongoing effort of self-reinvention rooted in "an Emersonian pragmatist aversion to conformity" that is also particularly relevant to Moore, Ashbery, and Glück, among the poets included in this study—see Andrew Epstein, *Beautiful Enemies: Friendship and Postwar American Poetry* (New York: Oxford University Press, 2006), 166.

71. Amiri Baraka [LeRoi Jones], *Preface to a Twenty Volume Suicide Note* (New York: Totem Press, 1961), 5.

72. Houston A. Baker, *Afro-American Poetics: Revisions of Harlem and the Black Aesthetic* (Madison: University of Wisconsin Press, 1988), 120, 118.

73. Nikki Giovanni, *Black Feeling Black Talk* (repr. 1994; Detroit, MI: Broadside Press, 1970), 1.

74. Ibid., 18.

75. Henry Louis Gates, *The Signifying Monkey: A Theory of African-American Literary Criticism* (New York: Oxford University Press, 1988), 78.

76. Lyn Hejinian, *The Language of Inquiry* (Berkeley: University of California Press, 2000), 171.

77. Ibid., 191.

78. Lyn Hejinian, *My Life and My Life in the Nineties* (Middletown, CT: Wesleyan University Press, 2013), 138.

79. Michael Davidson, *The Mutabilities & The Foul Papers* (Berkeley, CA: Sand Dollar Books, 1976), 13.

80. Bob Perelman, *Braille* (Ithaca, NY: Ithaca House, 1975), 1.

81. Hejinian, *Inquiry*, 43.

82. Michael Palmer, *Blake's Newton* (Los Angeles: Black Sparrow Press, 1972), 9.

83. "Now I a fourfold vision see," begins the last stanza, which concludes: "May God us keep / From a single vision, and Newton's sleep!" *The Selected Poems of William Blake* (Hertfordshire, UK: Wordsworth Editions, 1994), 148.

84. Marjorie Perloff, *Differentials: Poetry, Poetics, Pedagogy* (Tuscaloosa: University of Alabama Press, 2004), 158.

85. Ai, *Cruelty* (Boston: Houghton Mifflin, 1973), 1.

86. Alfred Corn, *All Roads at Once* (New York: Viking, 1976), 1, 83.

87. John Yau, *Crossing Canal Street* (Binghamton, NY: Bellevue Press, 1976); Dorothy Wang, *Thinking Its Presence: Form, Race, and Subjectivity in Contemporary Asian Poetry* (Stanford, CA: Stanford University Press, 2014), 177.

88. Yusef Komunyakaa, *Pleasure Dome: New and Collected Poems* (Middletown, CT: Wesleyan University Press, 2001), 47.

89. J. D. McClatchy, *Scenes from Another Life* (New York: George Braziller, 1981), 13.

90. Wyatt Prunty, *The Times Between* (Baltimore, MD: Johns Hopkins University Press, 1982), 3.

91. Alice Fulton, *Dance Script with Electric Ballerina* (Philadelphia: University of Pennsylvania Press, 1983), 4.

92. Thylias Moss, *Hosiery Seams on a Bowlegged Woman* (Cleveland, OH: Cleveland State University Poetry Center, 1983), 5.

93. Rachel Hadas, *Slow Transparency* (Middletown, CT: Wesleyan University Press, 1984), 3.

94. Mark Halliday, *Little Star* (New York: William Morrow, 1987), 15.

Chapter 3: "Everything Has a Schedule"

1. Edward Brunner, *Cold War Poetry: The Social Text in the Fifties Poem* (Urbana: University of Illinois Press, 2000), 76.

2. W. H. Auden to Eugene Davidson, quoted in George Bradley, introduction to *Yale Younger Poets*, lxviii.

3. Ibid.

4. Ibid., lxix.

5. W. H. Auden, foreword to *Some Trees*, by John Ashbery. Yale Series of Younger Poets (New Haven, CT: Yale University Press, 1956), 16.

6. W. H. Auden to Frank O'Hara, June 3, 1955, quoted in Marjorie Perloff, *The Poetics of Indeterminacy* (1981; repr., Evanston, IL: Northwestern University Press, 1999), 249–50.

7. David Kermani, *John Ashbery: A Comprehensive Bibliography* (New York: Garland Publishing, 1976), 6.

8. William Arrowsmith, "Nine New Poets," 294.

9. Donald Hall, "Oddities and Sestinas," *Saturday Review*, June 16, 1956.

10. David Lehman, *The Last Avant-Garde: The Making of the New York School of Poets* (New York: Scribner's, 1998), 5.

11. David Herd, *John Ashbery and American Poetry* (New York: Palgrave, 2000), 2.

12. Vernon Shetley, *After the Death of Poetry: Poet and Audience in Contemporary America* (Durham, NC: Duke University Press, 1993), 103–34.

13. John Koethe, "An Interview with John Ashbery," *SubStance* 37/38 (1983): 179.

14. John Ashbery, introduction to *The Collected Poems of Frank O'Hara*, ed. Donald Allen (Berkeley: University of California Press, 1995), ix.

15. Davidson, *Guys Like Us*, 50–54.

16. Levy, *Criminal Ingenuity*, 160.

17. Bledstein, *Culture of Professionalism*, 19.

18. Larson, *Rise of Professionalism*, 229.

19. Lehman, *Last Avant-Garde*, 119.

20. Hammer, "Plath's Lives," 66.

21. Bradley, introduction to *Yale Younger Poets*, lxi.

22. English, *Economy of Prestige*, 145.

23. Andrew DuBois, *Ashbery's Forms of Attention* (Tuscaloosa: University of Alabama Press, 2006), 4–8.

24. Richard Howard, *Alone with America: Essay on the Art of Poetry in the United States since 1950* (1969; repr., New York: Atheneum, 1980), 30.

25. Cleanth Brooks and Robert Penn Warren, *Understanding Poetry*, rev. ed. (New York: Henry Holt, 1950), 1. In a valuable discussion of Ashbery's formal poems, Joseph Conte suggests that form has priority over content: "Ashbery's use of [the sestina, the canzone, and the pantoum] does not constitute an endorsement of 'form as superimposed.' He does not have a preexisting subject matter to which poetic structure is applied; rather, he employs elaborate forms—or, occasionally, goofy titles—as exploratory or generative devices." *Unending Design: The Forms of Postmodern Poetry* (Ithaca, NY: Cornell University Press, 1991), 174.

26. Brunner, *Cold War Poetry*, 161.

27. John Shoptaw, *On the Outside Looking Out: John Ashbery's Poetry* (Cambridge, MA: Harvard University Press, 1994), 2.

28. Brooks and Warren, *Understanding Poetry*, xlix.

29. Claude Rawson, "Bards, Boardrooms, and Blackboards: John Ashbery, Wallace Stevens, and the Academicization of Poetry" in *On Modern Poetry: Essays Presented to Donald Davie*, ed. Vereen Bell and Laurence Lerner (Nashville, TN: Vanderbilt University Press, 1988), 181.

30. O'Hara, "Rare Modern," 312–13.

31. For a useful examination of the relation between Ashbery's status as an outsider and his homosexuality in the context of *Some Trees*, see Catherine Imbriglio, " 'Our Days Put On Such Reticence': The Rhetoric of the Closet in John Ashbery's *Some Trees*," *Contemporary Literature* 36, no. 2 (Summer 1995): 249–88.

32. Shetley, *Death of Poetry*, 104.

33. Herd, *John Ashbery*, 30.

34. Shetley, *Death of Poetry*, 106. Likewise attuned to the origins of the mid-century literary establishment in the modernist vanguard, Mark Silverberg makes a similar argument in *The New York School Poets and the Neo-Avant-Garde*, where he suggests that Ashbery and the other members of the New York School "created a position *between* the radical art of the historical avant-garde and the radical chic of the 1960s which turned 'revolutionary' gestures into marketable commodities." *The New York School Poets and the Neo-Avant-Garde: Between Radical Art and Radical Chic* (Farnham, UK: Ashgate, 2010), 33.

35. Shetley, *Death of Poetry*, 107, 130.

36. Herd, *John Ashbery*, 35, 41.

37. Bromwich, *Skeptical Music*, 185.

38. Nealon follows John Emil Vincent in suggesting that "it is at the level of the book, rather than the individual poem, where Ashbery makes himself most available to historically and culturally specific readings" that run against the grain of what he calls "the great theme of Ashbery criticism," namely "that his poems are about nothing, that they are textual rather than referential." Nealon, *Matter of Capital*, 74–75.

39. Shoptaw, *Outside Looking Out*, 20; Marjorie Perloff, " 'Fragments of a Buried Life': John Ashbery's Dream Songs," in *Beyond Amazement: New Essays on John Ashbery*, ed. David Lehman (Ithaca, NY: Cornell University Press, 1980), 77.

40. Nicholas Jenkins, "A Life of Beginnings," *New York Times*, January 4, 1998.

41. I adopt here Shoptaw's helpful sense of Ashbery as a poet crucially concerned with misrepresentation, which Shoptaw views "as an alternative to various interpretative

strategies that treat Ashbery's poetry as purely non-representational, self-referential, nonsensical, parodic, or deconstructive. Ashbery's poetry is all these things, but his misrepresentations do not as a consequence rule out meaning, expression, and representation; they renovate them." Shoptaw, *Outside Looking Out*, 2–3. Though Shoptaw notes the way the two stanzas in "Two Scenes" parallel one another, he does not view them, as I do, as an exemplary instance of the process of misrepresentation, appropriately placed at the opening of his first book and his career.

42. Ibid., 32, 20.
43. Ibid., 25.
44. Bloom, *Capable Imagination*, 170.
45. Shoptaw, *Outside Looking Out*, 25.
46. *Selected Poems of Ezra Pound* (New York: New Directions, 1957), 64; Eliot, *Collected Poems*, 66.
47. Shetley, *Death of Poetry*, 107.
48. Shoptaw, *Outside Looking Out*, 26.
49. Harold Bloom, *A Map of Misreading* (New York: Oxford, 1975), 56.
50. Ibid., 49, 59.
51. Shoptaw, *Outside Looking Out*, 35.
52. Ibid., 34–35.
53. Ibid., 36.
54. Sue Gangel, "John Ashbery," *American Poetry Observed: Poets on Their Work*, ed. Joe David Bellamy (Urbana: Illinois University Press, 1988), 18.
55. The structure of "The Instruction Manual" anticipates that of some of O'Hara's *Lunch Poems*. Levy shows how the Museum of Modern Art, where O'Hara worked, marks the beginning and ending of poems such as "The Day Lady Died," so that "the institutional displaces the formal." Levy, *Criminal Ingenuity*, 147–48. The same could be said of the constraints that Ashbery's position at McGraw Hill entails in "The Instruction Manual."
56. Perloff, " 'Fragments of a Buried Life,' " 75.

Chapter 4: From *Firstborn* to *Vita Nova*

1. Louise Glück, *Firstborn* (New York: New American Library, 1968), 3.
2. Lynn Keller, " 'Free / of Blossom and Subterfuge': Louise Glück and the Language of Renunciation," in *World, Self, Poem*, ed. Leonard M. Trawick (Kent, OH: Kent State University Press, 1990), 121.
3. Frank Bidart, "Louise Glück," in *On Louise Glück: Change What You See*, ed. Joanne Feit Diehl (Ann Arbor: University of Michigan Press, 2005), 23.
4. Louise Glück, *Vita Nova* (Hopewell, NJ: Ecco Press, 1999), 51.
5. Tony Hoagland, "Three Tenors: Glück, Hass, Pinsky, and the Deployment of Talent," *American Poetry Review* 32, no. 4 (July/August 2003): 41.
6. Hejinian, *Language of Inquiry*, 191.
7. Aliki Barnstone, "Mastering the Master: Emily Dickinson's Appropriation of Crisis Conversion," in *The Calvinist Roots of the Modern Era*, 150.
8. Adam Smith, *The Wealth of Nations* (1776), 119, quoted in Thomas Pfau, *Wordsworth's Profession: Form, Class, and the Logic of Early Romantic Cultural Production* (Stanford, CA: Stanford University Press, 1997), 26–27.

9. Daniel Morris, *The Poetry of Louise Glück: A Thematic Introduction* (Columbia: University of Missouri Press, 2006), 86.

10. Ibid., 91.

11. Louise Glück, *The Triumph of Achilles* (New York: Ecco Press, 1985), 45.

12. Ibid., 44.

13. Glück quotes in the essay a poem about Kunitz called "Four Dreams Concerning the Master" (*PT 13*).

14. Louise Glück, *Descending Figure* (New York: Ecco Press, 1980), 32.

15. Lisa Sewell, " 'In the End, the One Who Has Nothing Wins': Louise Glück and the Poetics of Anorexia," *Literature Interpretation Theory* 17 (2006): 55.

16. Brian Henry, "To Speak of Woe," *Kenyon Review* (Winter 2001): 168.

17. Glück, *Vita Nova*, 39.

18. Ibid., 31.

19. Glück, *Meadowlands* (Hopewell, NJ: Ecco Press, 1996), 58.

20. *Ralph Waldo Emerson: Essays and Poems*, 490.

21. That Glück's native inclination is to will her career is apparent in her attempt to reformulate "impoverishment," paradoxically, as a sort of activity: "passivity over time is, by definition, active. There exists, in other words, a form of action felt as helplessness, a form of will that exhibits, on the surface, none of the familiar dynamic properties of will" (*PT* 134).

22. Helen Vendler, *Part of Nature, Part of Us* (Cambridge, MA: Harvard University Press, 1980), 303.

23. Glück, *The House on the Marshland* (New York: Ecco Press, 1975), 3.

24. Vendler, *Part of Nature*, 304.

25. Ibid., 310.

26. Vendler suggestively links the words "blue" and "permanent" with ink. Ibid., 311.

27. Said, *Beginnings*, 46.

28. This contrast may be glimpsed in "Trillium," to provide one ready example. The poem takes the perspective of a newly reborn plant that broods on the fact that some power "calls" other "souls to exchange their lives." But that high, selfless calling cannot yet be understood by the plant, which "woke up ignorant in a forest . . . only a moment ago." Its utterances reflect its youthful "ignoran[ce]": "my sentences," it says, are "like cries strung together." Glück, *The Wild Iris*, (Hopewell, NJ: Ecco Press, 1992), 4.

29. Ibid., 1.

30. Louise Glück, *Ararat* (New York: Ecco Press, 1990), 15.

31. Paul Breslin, "Thanatos Turannos: The Poetry of Louise Glück," in *On Louise Glück*, 111.

32. Glück, *The Wild Iris*, 1.

33. Breslin, "Thanatos Turannos," 119.

34. Sandra M. Gilbert, "The Lamentations of the New," in *On Louise Glück*, 131.

35. Glück, *Vita Nova*, 1.

36. James Longenbach, "Louise Glück's Nine Lives," in *On Louise Glück*, 145.

37. Glück, *Ararat*, 68.

38. Glück, *Vita Nova*, 50.

39. Glück, *Ararat*, 63.

40. Henry, "To Speak of Woe," 172.

Conclusion

1. James McCorkle, *Evidences* (Port Townsend, WA: Copper Canyon Press, 2003), 109.
2. Southern Illinois University Press, Crab Orchard Series, "2013 First Book Award," http://craborchardreview.siu.edu/firstpo.html (accessed 22 July 2013).
3. Gerald Stern, introduction to *Things Are Happening*, by Joshua Beckman (Philadelphia: American Poetry Review, 1998), vii–xii.
4. Gérard Genette, *Paratexts: Thresholds of Interpretation*, trans. Jane E. Lewin (Cambridge: Cambridge University Press, 1997), 1.
5. Virginia Jackson, *Dickinson's Misery: A Theory of Lyric Reading* (Princeton, NJ: Princeton University Press, 2005), 6.
6. Genette, *Paratexts*, 2.
7. Anhinga Press, "The Robert Dana-Anhinga Prize for Poetry," http://www.anhinga.org/books/contest.cfm (accessed 22 July 2013).
8. Tupelo Press, "2013 First/Second Book Award Guidelines," http://www.tupelopress.org/first.php (accessed 22 July 2013).
9. Pavement Saw Press, "Transcontinental Poetry Award," http://www.tupelopress.org/first.php (accessed 22 July 2013).
10. Laurie Ann Guerrero, *A Tongue in the Mouth of the Dying* (Notre Dame, IN: University of Notre Dame Press, 2013), ix–xii.
11. Genette, *Paratexts*, 212. Like acknowledgments, notes glossing obscure or foreign terms, clarifying arcane references, and documenting allusions and quotations present an additional opportunity to advance the work of self-presentation with which debuts are often explicitly preoccupied. Notes not only help readers—including prize judges—to understand the poetry, but also to define the poet's position in the field of production through the various forms of affiliation and renunciation they articulate on the pretext provided by academic protocol. Notes can be seen to compliment the acknowledgments, which define the poet's position in relation to proximal figures, schools, and institutions, by ranging instead across disciplinary, geographical, and historical boundaries.
12. Bradley, introduction to *Yale Younger Poets*, lix.
13. Archibald MacLeish, foreword to *Family Circle*, by Eve Merriam (New Haven, CT: Yale University Press, 1946), 6.
14. Stephen Vincent Benét, foreword to *The Deer Come Down*, by Edward Weismiller (New Haven, CT: Yale University Press, 1936), 8; Benét, foreword to *Theory of Flight*, by Murial Rukeyser (New Haven, CT: Yale University Press, 1935), 5–6. For a later example of this more personal style of prefatorial discourse, see William Carlos Williams's brief introduction to Allen Ginsberg's *Howl and Other Poems* (1956; San Francisco, CA: City Lights, 2000), 7–8.
15. Quoted in Bradley, introduction to *Yale Younger Poets*, lix.
16. W. H. Auden, foreword to *The Green Wall*, by James Wright (New Haven, CT: Yale University Press, 1957), ix–xi, xiv–xvi. The introductory essays by John Hall Wheelock to the Poets of Today series are cut from the same cloth as Auden's forewords, as even the titles suggest: "A Critical Introduction," "The Poem in the Atomic Age," "The Process and the Poem," and "Man's Struggle to Understand."
17. Dudley Fitts, foreword to *Views of Jeopardy*, by Jack Gilbert (New Haven, CT: Yale University Press, 1962), viii.

18. Ibid., ix–x.
19. Stanley Kunitz, foreword to *Beginning with O*, by Olga Broumas (New Haven, CT: Yale University Press, 1977), xii. Other introductions to poetic debuts from the 1960s and '70s generally seem to follow suit. See, for example, first books in the Braziller Poetry Series, which often featured an introductory "note by Richard Howard," such as Cynthia Macdonald's *Amputations* (1972) or Frank Bidart's *Golden State* (1973).
20. Genette, *Paratexts*, 271.
21. English, *Economy of Prestige*, 139.
22. Genette, *Paratexts,* 237.
23. Carol Muske-Dukes, foreword to *Swallow*, by Miranda Field (New York: Houghton Mifflin, 2002), ix. It is worth noting that Muske-Dukes omits reflections on the problem of the overcrowded first-book prize field in her brief foreword to Malinda Markham's work, which she selected as co-winner of the 2001 Bakeless Prize, *Ninety-Five Nights of Listening* (New York: Houghton Mifflin, 2002), xi–xii. Of course such a gesture risks undermining the praise accorded to both, and it surprisingly suggests, against the grain of the familiar complaint she registers, that crowded as it is, the field needs still more first-book prizes.
24. Louise Glück, introduction to *In the Surgical Theatre*, by Dana Levin (Philadelphia: American Poetry Review, 1999), x.
25. Robert Creeley, introduction to *Ivory Cradle*, by Anne Marie Macari (Philadelphia: American Poetry Review, 2000), xii.
26. Stanley Kunitz, foreword to *Field Guide*, by Robert Hass (New Haven, CT: Yale University Press, 1973), xii; Jorie Graham, introduction to *Evidences*, xiii.
27. Take, for example, this vibrantly detailed account by James Dickey of the recurrent jungle setting in Talvikki Ansel's *My Shining Archipelago*: "Present always is the sense of expectancy, of something inexplicable and terrible about to happen, as various poisons refine in plants and the heads of serpents, the spider affixes another filament of itself to the huge web where the tarantula struggles, the dread clicking sound of billions of tiny razor jaws comes gradually to be heard: red hunger of the soldier ant multiplied beyond reason, unstoppable lava flow of insects, *La Marabunta*, stripping to skeletons all trees and animals on a fifty mile-front. In the saw-edged shadows of the sun, in the green night of her hammock, Ansel finds her own fraught calm." (New Haven, CT: Yale University Press, 1997), viii.
28. Thomas Lux, foreword to *Beautiful in the Mouth*, by Keetje Kuipers (Brockport, NY: Boa Editions, 2010), 9–10; Elizabeth Spires, foreword to *Even the Hollow My Body Made Is Gone*, by Janice N. Harrington (Brockport, NY: Boa Editions, 2007), 9; Philip Levine, foreword to *Late for Work*, by David Tucker (New York: Houghton Mifflin, 2006), ix.
29. Crystal Bacon, *Elegy with a Glass of Whiskey* (Rochester, NY: Boa Editions, 2004), 14; John Blair, *The Green Girls* (Warrensburg, MO: Pleiades Press, 2003), 4; Paul Le-Gault, *The Madeleine Poems* (Richmond, CA: Omnidawn Publishing, 2010), 15; Erin Elizabeth Smith, *The Fear of Being Found* (Savage, MN: Three Candles Press, 2008), 3; Matthias Svalina, *Destruction Myth* (Cleveland, OH: Cleveland State University Press, 2010), 3.
30. Allison Adelle Hedge Coke, *Dog Road Woman* (Minneapolis, MN: Coffee House Press, 1997), 3–7.
31. Gary Snyder, *Riprap and Cold Mountain Poems* (1959; San Francisco, CA: North Point Press, 1990), 1, 3.

Bibliography

Abrams, M. H. *Natural Supernaturalism*. New York: W. W. Norton, 1973.

Ai. *Cruelty*. Boston: Houghton Mifflin, 1973.

Alexander, Paul. *Rough Magic: A Biography of Sylvia Plath*. 1991. Reprint, Cambridge, MA: Da Capo Press, 1999.

Altieri, Charles. *Wallace Stevens and the Demands of Modernity: Toward a Phenomenology of Value*. Ithaca, NY: Cornell University Press, 2013.

Alvarez, Alfred. "Poetry Chronicle." *Partisan Review* 25, no. 4 (Fall 1958): 603–9.

Anderson, Jill. " 'Be Up and Doing': Henry Wadsworth Longfellow and Poetic Labor." *Journal of American Studies* 37, no. 1 (April 2003): 1–15.

Arrowsmith, William. "Nine New Poets." *Hudson Review* 9, no. 2 (Summer 1956): 289–97.

Ashbery, John. *Collected Poems 1956–1987*. Edited by Mark Ford. New York: Library of America, 2008.

———. Introduction to *The Collected Poems of Frank O'Hara*. Edited by Donald Allen. Berkeley: University of California Press, 1995.

Ashton, Jennifer. "Poetry of the Twenty-First Century: The First Decade." In *The Cambridge Companion to American Poetry since 1945*, 216–30. Edited by Jennifer Ashton. New York: Cambridge University Press, 2013.

Auden, W. H. Foreword to *The Green Wall*, by James Wright, ix–xvi. Yale Series of Younger Poets. New Haven, CT: Yale University Press, 1957.

———. Foreword to *Some Trees*, by John Ashbery, 11–16. Yale Series of Younger Poets. New Haven, CT: Yale University Press, 1956.

Bacigalupo, Massimo. "Wallace Stevens and the Firecat." *Wallace Stevens Journal* 21, no. 1 (Spring 1997): 94–98.

Bacon, Crystal. *Elegy with a Glass of Whiskey*. Rochester, NY: Boa Editions, 2004.

Baker, Houston A. *Afro-American Poetics: Revisions of Harlem and the Black Aesthetic*. Madison: University of Wisconsin Press, 1988.

Baraka, Amiri [LeRoi Jones]. *Preface to a Twenty Volume Suicide Note*. New York: Totem Press, 1961.

Barnstone, Aliki, Michael Tomasek Manson, and Carol J. Singley, eds. *The Calvinist Roots of the Modern Era*. Hanover, NH: University Press of New England, 1997.

———. "Mastering the Master: Emily Dickinson's Appropriation of Crisis Conversion." In Barnstone, Manson, and Singly, *Calvinist Roots of the Modern Era*, 145-61.

Bates, Milton J. *Wallace Stevens: A Mythology of Self.* Berkeley: University of California Press, 1985.

Beach, Christopher. *Poetic Culture: Contemporary American Poetry between Community and Institution.* Evanston, IL: Northwestern University Press, 1999.

Bell, Charles G. *Songs for a New America.* Indiana University Poetry Series. Bloomington: Indiana University Press, 1953.

Benamou, Michel. *Wallace Stevens and the Symbolist Imagination.* Princeton, NJ: Princeton University Press, 1972.

Benét, Stephen Vincent. Foreword to *The Deer Come Down*, by Edward Weismiller, 7–8. New Haven, CT: Yale University Press, 1936.

———. Foreword to *Theory of Flight*, by Murial Rukeyser, 5–6. Yale Series of Younger Poets. New Haven, CT: Yale University Press, 1935.

Bennet, Joseph. "Recent Verse." *Hudson Review* 7, no. 2 (Summer 1954): 302–8.

Bernstein, Charles. *Content's Dream: Essays 1975–1984.* Los Angeles: Sun and Moon Press, 1986.

Bevis, William W. "The Arrangement of *Harmonium.*" *English Literary History* 37, no. 3 (September 1970): 456–73.

Bidart, Frank. "Louise Glück." In Diehl, *On Louise Glück*, 23–25.

Blair, John. *The Green Girls.* Warrensburg, MO: Pleiades Press, 2003.

Blake, William. *The Selected Poems of William Blake.* Hertfordshire, UK: Wordsworth Editions, 1994.

Bledstein, Burton J. *The Culture of Professionalism: The Middle Class and the Development of Higher Education in America.* New York: W. W. Norton, 1976.

Blessing, Richard. *Wallace Stevens' "Whole Harmonium."* Syracuse, NY: Syracuse University Press, 1970.

Bloom, Harold. "Hart Crane's Gnosis." In *Agon: Towards a Theory of Revisionism*, 252–69. New York: Oxford University Press, 1982.

———. "John Ashbery: The Charity of the Hard Moments." In *Figures of Capable Imagination*, 169–208. New York: Seabury Press, 1976.

———. *A Map of Misreading.* New York: Oxford University Press, 1975.

———. *The Visionary Company.* Rev. ed. Ithaca, NY: Cornell University Press, 1974.

———. *Wallace Stevens: The Poems of Our Climate.* Ithaca, NY: Cornell University Press, 1977.

Bourdieu, Pierre. *The Field of Cultural Production.* Edited by Randal Johnson. New York: Columbia University Press, 1993.

Bradley, George. Introduction to *The Yale Younger Poets Anthology*, edited by George Bradley, xvii–ci. New Haven, CT: Yale University Press, 1998.

Breslin, Paul. *The Psycho-Political Muse: American Poetry since the Fifties.* Chicago: University of Chicago Press, 1987.

———. "Thanatos Turannos: The Poetry of Louise Glück." In Diehl, *On Louise Gluck*, 90–130.

Bromwich, David. *Hazlitt: The Mind of a Critic.* 1983. Reprint, New Haven, CT: Yale University Press, 1999.

———. *Skeptical Music: Essays on Modern Poetry.* Chicago: University of Chicago Press, 2001.

Brooks, Cleanth and Robert Penn Warren. *Understanding Poetry.* Rev. ed. New York: Henry Holt, 1950.

Brunner, Edward. *Cold War Poetry: The Social Text in the Fifties Poem*. Urbana: University of Illinois Press, 2000.

Buttel, Robert. "Teasing the Reader into *Harmonium*." *Texas Studies in Literature and Language* 25, no. 4 (Winter 1983): 79–86.

Carrier, Constance. *The Middle Voice*. New Poetry Series. Denver, CO: A. Swallow, 1955.

Carruth, Hayden. "Four New Books," *Poetry* 93, no. 2 (November 1958): 107–16.

Charvat, William. *The Profession of Authorship in America, 1800–1870*. Edited by Matthew J. Bruccoli. 1968. Reprint, New York: Columbia University Press, 1992.

Cheney, Patrick. "Did Shakespeare Have a Literary Career?" In Hardie and Moore, *Classical Literary Careers*, 160–78.

———. "'Jog On, Jog On': European Career Paths." In Cheney and de Armas, *European Literary Careers*, 3–23.

———. *Marlowe's Counterfeit Profession: Ovid, Spenser, and Counter-Nationhood*. Toronto: University of Toronto Press, 1997.

———. *Marlowe's Republican Authorship: Lucan, Liberty, and the Sublime*. Basingstoke, UK: Palgrave Macmillan, 2009.

———. *Shakespeare, National Poet-Playwright*. Cambridge: Cambridge University Press, 2004.

———. *Shakespeare's Literary Authorship*. Cambridge: Cambridge University Press, 2008.

———. "*The Shepheardes Calendar* and *Colin Clouts Come Home Againe*." In *The Cambridge Companion to Spenser*, edited by Andrew Hadfield, 79–105. Cambridge: Cambridge University Press, 2001.

———. *Spencer's Famous Flight: A Renaissance Idea of a Literary Career*. Toronto: University of Toronto Press, 1993.

———, and Frederick A. de Armas, eds. *European Literary Careers: The Author from Antiquity to the Renaissance*. Toronto: University of Toronto Press, 2002.

Christensen, Jerome. "Byron's Career: The Speculative Stage." *English Literary History* 52, no. 1 (Spring 1985): 59–84.

———. *Practicing Enlightenment: Hume and the Formation of a Literary Career*. Madison: University of Wisconsin Press, 1987.

Cifelli, Edward M. *John Ciardi: A Biography*. Fayetteville: University of Arkansas Press, 1997.

Coiro, Ann Baynes. "Fable and Old Song: *Samson Agonistes* and the Idea of a Poetic Career." *Milton Studies* 36 (1998): 123–52.

Coleridge, Samuel Taylor. *The Major Works*. Edited by H. J. Jackson. New York: Oxford University Press, 1985.

Conte, Joseph. *Unending Design: The Forms of Postmodern Poetry*. Ithaca, NY: Cornell University Press, 1991.

Cook, Eleanor. *Poetry, Word-Play, and Word-War in Wallace Stevens*. Princeton, NJ: Princeton University Press, 1988.

———. *A Reader's Guide to Wallace Stevens*. Princeton, NJ: Princeton University Press, 2007.

Corn, Alfred. *All Roads at Once*. New York: Viking, 1976.

Costello, Bonnie. "The 'Feminine' Language of Marianne Moore." In *Women and Language in Literature and Society*, edited by Sally McConnell-Ginet, Ruth Borker, and Nelly Furman, 222–38. New York: Praeger, 1980.

Costello, Bonnie. *Marianne Moore: Imaginary Possessions*. Cambridge, MA: Harvard University Press, 1981.

Crane, Hart. *Hart Crane: Collected Poems and Selected Letters*. Edited by Langdon Hammer. New York: Library of America, 2006.

———. *O My Land, My Friends: The Selected Letters of Hart Crane*. Edited by Langdon Hammer and Brom Weber. New York: Four Walls Eight Windows, 1997.

Creeley, Robert. Introduction to *Ivory Cradle*, by Anne Marie Macari, ix–xiv. Philadelphia: American Poetry Review, 2000.

Davidson, Michael. *Guys Like Us: Citing Masculinity in Cold War Poetics*. Chicago: University of Chicago Press, 2004.

———. *The Mutabilities & The Foul Papers*. Berkeley, CA: Sand Dollar Books, 1976.

———. *The San Francisco Renaissance: Poetics and Community at Mid-Century*. Cambridge: Cambridge University Press, 1989.

Davison, Peter. "Discovering Young Poets." *Atlantic Monthly*, June 1998.

Dickey, James. Foreword to *My Shining Archipelago*, by Talvikki Ansel, vii–x. Yale Series of Younger Poets. New Haven, CT: Yale University Press, 1997.

———. "Toward a Solitary Joy." *Hudson Review* 14, no. 4 (Winter 1961–2): 607–13.

Dickman, Matthew. *All-American Poem*. Philadelphia: American Poetry Review, 2008.

Diehl, Joanne Feit, ed. *On Louise Gluck: Change What You See*. Ann Arbor: University of Michigan Press, 2005.

DuBois, Andrew. *Ashbery's Forms of Attention*. Tuscaloosa: University of Alabama Press, 2006.

Eliot, T. S. *Collected Poems, 1909–1962*. London: Faber and Faber, 1963.

Emerson, Ralph Waldo. *Ralph Waldo Emerson: Essays and Poems*. Edited by Harold Bloom, Paul Kane, and Joel Porte. New York: Library of America, 1996.

English, James F. *The Economy of Prestige*. Cambridge, MA: Harvard University Press, 2005.

———. "Winning the Culture Game: Prizes, Awards, and the Rules of Art." *New Literary History* 33, no. 1 (Winter 2002): 109–35.

Epstein, Andrew. *Beautiful Enemies: Friendship and Postwar American Poetry*. New York: Oxford University Press, 2006.

Erickson, Lee. "The Egoism of Authorship: Wordsworth's Poetic Career." *Journal of English and Germanic Philology* 89, no. 1 (January 1990): 37–50.

Farber, Norma. *The Hatch: Poems*. Poets of Today 2. New York: Charles Scribner's Sons, 1955.

Farrell, Joseph. "Greek Lives and Roman Careers in the Classical *Vita* Tradition." In Cheney and de Armas, *European Literary Careers*, 24–46.

Finkel, Donald. *The Clothing's New Emperor and Other Poems*. Poets of Today 6. New York: Charles Scribner's Sons, 1959.

Fish, Stanley. "Anti-Professionalism." *New Literary History* 17, no. 1 (Autumn 1985): 89–108.

Fitts, Dudley. Foreword to *Views of Jeopardy*, by Jack Gilbert, vii–xi. Yale Series of Younger Poets. New Haven, CT: Yale University Press, 1962.

Forbes, Deborah. *Sincerity's Shadow: Self-Consciousness in British Romantic and Mid-Twentieth-Century American Poetry*. Cambridge, MA: Harvard University Press, 2004.

Foucault, Michel. "What Is an Author?" In *The Foucault Reader*. Edited by Paul Rabinow, 101–20. New York: Vintage, 2010.

Freedman, Jonathan. *Professions of Taste: Henry James, British Aestheticism, and Commodity Culture*. Stanford, CA: Stanford University Press, 1990.

Freidson, Eliot. *Professionalism: The Third Logic*. Chicago: University of Chicago Press, 2001.

———. *Professional Powers: A Study of the Institutionalization of Formal Knowledge*. Chicago: University of Chicago Press, 1988.

Fulton, Alice. *Dance Script with Electric Ballerina*. Philadelphia, PA: University of Pennsylvania Press, 1983.

Gangel, Sue. "John Ashbery." In *American Poetry Observed: Poets on Their Work*, edited by Joe David Bellamy, 9–20. Urbana: University of Illinois Press, 1988.

Gartner, Matthew. "Becoming Longfellow: Work, Manhood, and Poetry." *American Literature* 72, no. 1 (March 2000): 59–86.

Gates, Henry Louis. *The Signifying Monkey: A Theory of African-American Literary Criticism*. New York: Oxford University Press, 1988.

Genette, Gérard. *Paratexts: Thresholds of Interpretation*. Translated by Jane E. Lewin. Cambridge: Cambridge University Press, 1997.

Gibson, Roy, and Catherine Steel. "The Indistinct Literary Careers of Cicero and Pliny the Younger." In Hardie and Moore, *Classical Literary Careers,* 118-37.

Gibson, W. Walker. *Reckless Spenders*. Indiana University Poetry Series. Bloomington: Indiana University Press, 1954.

Gilbert, Jack. *Views of Jeopardy*. Yale Series of Younger Poets. New Haven, CT: Yale University Press, 1958.

Gilbert, Sandra M. "The Lamentations of the New." In Diehl, *On Louise Gluck*, 131–35.

———, and Susan Gubar. *Letters from the Front*. Vol. 3 of *No Man's Land: The Place of the Woman Writer in the Twentieth Century*. New Haven, CT: Yale University Press, 1994.

Gill, Jo. "*The Colossus* and *Crossing the Water*." In *The Cambridge Companion to Sylvia Plath*, edited by Jo Gill, 90–106. New York: Cambridge University Press, 2006.

Giovanni, Nikki. *Black Feeling Black Talk*. 1970. Reprint, Detroit, MI: Broadside Press, 1994

Glück, Louise. *Ararat*. New York: Ecco Press, 1990.

———. *Descending Figure*. New York: Ecco Press, 1980.

———. *Firstborn*. New York: New American Library, 1968.

———. *The House on the Marshland*. New York: Ecco Press, 1975.

———. Introduction to *In the Surgical Theatre*, by Dana Levin, vii–xi. Philadelphia: American Poetry Review, 1999.

———. *Meadowlands*. Hopewell, NJ: Ecco Press, 1996.

———. *Proofs and Theories: Essays on Poetry*. Hopewell, NJ: Ecco Press, 1994.

———. *The Triumph of Achilles*. New York: Ecco Press, 1985.

———. *Vita Nova*. Hopewell, NJ: Ecco Press, 1999.

———. *The Wild Iris*. Hopewell, NJ: Ecco Press, 1992.

Golding, Alan. *From Outlaw to Classic: Canons in American Poetry*. Madison: University of Wisconsin Press, 1995.

Goldstone, Andrew. *Fictions of Autonomy: Modernism from Wilde to de Man*. New York: Oxford University Press, 2013.

Graff, Gerald. *Professing Literature: An Institutional History*. Chicago: University of Chicago Press, 1987.

Graham, Jorie. Introduction to *Evidences*, by James McCorkle, xiii–xv.

Greenblatt, Stephen. *Renaissance Self-Fashioning: From More to Shakespeare*. Chicago: University of Chicago Press, 1980.

Grossman, Allen. "Hart Crane and Poetry: A Consideration of Crane's Intense Poetics." In *Modern Critical Views: Hart Crane*, edited by Harold Bloom, 221–54. New York: Chelsea House Publishers, 1986.

Guerrero, Laurie Ann. *A Tongue in the Mouth of the Dying*. Notre Dame, IN: University of Notre Dame Press, 2013.

Guillory, John. "Bourdieu's Refusal." *Modern Language Quarterly* 58, no. 5 (December 1997): 367-98.

———. *Cultural Capital: The Problem of Literary Canon Formation*. Chicago: University of Chicago Press, 1993.

———. "The Father's House: *Samson Agonistes* in its Historical Moment." In *Re-Membering Milton: Essays on the Texts and Traditions*, edited by Mary Nyquist and Margaret Ferguson, 148–76. New York: Methuen, 1987.

Hadas, Rachel. *Slow Transparency*. Middletown, CT: Wesleyan University Press, 1984.

Hall, Donald. "A Diet of Dissatisfaction." *Poetry* 87, no. 5 (February 1956): 299–302.

———. *Exiles and Marriages*. New York: Viking, 1956.

———. "Oddities and Sestinas." *Saturday Review*, June 16, 1956.

Halliday, Mark. *Little Star*. New York: William Morrow, 1987.

Hammer, Langdon. *Hart Crane and Allen Tate: Janus-Faced Modernism*. Princeton, NJ: Princeton University Press, 1993.

———. "Plath's Lives: Poetry, Professionalism, and the Culture of the School." *Representations* 75 (Summer 2001): 61–88.

Hanley, Alfred. *Hart Crane's Holy Vision: White Buildings*. Pittsburgh, PA: Duquesne University Press, 1981.

Hardie, Philip, and Helen Moore, eds. *Classical Literary Careers*. Cambridge: Cambridge University Press, 2010.

Harrison, Jim. *The Shape of the Journey: New and Collected Poems*. Port Townsend, WA: Copper Canyon Press, 1998.

Hedge Coke, Allison Adelle. *Dog Road Woman*. Minneapolis, MN: Coffee House Press, 1997.

Hejinian, Lyn. *The Language of Inquiry*. Berkeley: University of California Press, 2000.

———. *My Life and My Life in the Nineties*. Middletown, CT: Wesleyan University Press, 2013.

Helgerson, Richard. *Self-Crowned Laureates: Spenser, Jonson, Milton, and the Literary System*. Berkeley: University of California Press, 1983.

Henry, Brian. "To Speak of Woe." *Kenyon Review* (Winter 2001): 166–72

Herd, David. *John Ashbery and American Poetry*. New York: Palgrave, 2000.

Heyen, William. *Depth of Field*. Baton Rouge: Louisiana University Press, 1970.

Hoagland, Tony. *Sweet Ruin*. Madison: University of Wisconsin Press, 1993.

———. "Three Tenors: Glück, Hass, Pinsky, and the Deployment of Talent." *American Poetry Review* 32, no. 4 (July/August 2003): 37–42.

Hollander, John. *The Crackling of Thorns*. Yale Series of Younger Poets. New Haven, CT: Yale University Press, 1958.

———. *Melodious Guile: Fictive Pattern in Poetic Language*. New Haven, CT: Yale University Press, 1990.

Holmes, Theodore. *The Harvest and the Scythe: Poems*. Poets of Today 4. New York: Charles Scribner's Sons, 1957.

Howard, Richard. *Alone with America: Essays on the Art of Poetry in the United States since 1950*. 1969. Reprint, New York: Atheneum, 1980.

———. *Quantities / Damages: Early Poems*. Middletown, CT: Wesleyan University Press, 1984.

Imbriglio, Catherine. "'Our Days Put On Such Reticence': The Rhetoric of the Closet in John Ashbery's *Some Trees*." *Contemporary Literature* 36, no. 2 (Summer 1995): 249–88.

Irwin, John T. *Hart Crane's Poetry: Appolinaire Lived in Paris, I Live in Cleveland, Ohio*. Baltimore, MD: Johns Hopkins University Press, 2011.

Jackson, Virginia. *Dickinson's Misery: A Theory of Lyric Reading*. Princeton, NJ: Princeton University Press, 2005.

Jarrell, Randall. "Recent Poetry." *Yale Review* 45, no. 1 (September 1955): 122–32.

Justice, Donald. *Collected Poems*. New York: Alfred A. Knopf, 2006.

Kalaidjian, Walter. *Languages of Liberation: The Social Text in Contemporary American Poetry*. New York: Columbia University Press, 1989.

Kateb, George. *Emerson and Self-Reliance*. Lanham, MD: Rowman and Littlefield Publishers, 2002.

Keats, John. *Letters of John Keats*. Edited by Robert Gittings. New York: Oxford University Press, 1970.

Keller, Lynn. "'Free / of Blossom and Subterfuge': Louise Glück and the Language of Renunciation." In *World, Self, Poem: Essays on Contemporary Poetry from the "Jubilation of Poets,"* edited by Leonard M. Trawick, 120–29. Kent, OH: Kent State University Press, 1990.

Kennedy, X. J. *Nude Descending a Staircase*. Garden City, NY: Doubleday, 1961.

Kermani, David. *John Ashbery: A Comprehensive Bibliography*. New York: Garland Publishing, 1976.

Kimball, Bruce. *The "True Professional Ideal" in America: A History*. Lanham, MD: Rowman and Littlefield, 1992.

Kinnell, Galway. *What a Kingdom It Was*. Boston: Houghton Mifflin, 1960.

King, Everard H. *James Beattie's "The Minstrel" and the Origins of Romantic Autobiography*. Lewiston, NY: Edwin Mellen Press, 1992.

Koethe, John. "An Interview with John Ashbery." *SubStance* 37/38 (1983): 178–86.

Komunyakaa, Yusef. *The Pleasure Dome: New and Collected Poems*. Middletown, CT: Wesleyan University Press, 2001.

Kunitz, Stanley. Foreword to *Beginning with O*, by Olga Broumas, ix–xiii. New Haven, CT: Yale University Press, 1977.

———. Foreword to *Field Guide*, by Robert Hass, xi–xvii. New Haven, CT: Yale University Press, 1973.

Larson, Magalli Sarfatti. *The Rise of Professionalism: A Sociological Analysis*. Berkeley: University of California Press, 1977.

Leavell, Linda. *Holding On Upside Down: The Life and Work of Marianne Moore*. New York: Farrar, Straus, and Giroux, 2013.

LeGault, Paul. *The Madeleine Poems*. Richmond, CA: Omnidawn Publishing, 2010.

Leggett, B. J. *Early Stevens: The Nietzchean Intertext*. Durham, NC: Duke University Press, 1992.

Lehman, David. *The Last Avant-Garde: The Making of the New York School of Poets.* New York: Scribner's, 1998.

Lentricchia, Frank. *Modernist Quartet.* Cambridge: Cambridge University Press, 1994.

Levine, Philip. Foreword to *Late for Work*, by David Tucker, ix–x. New York: Houghton Mifflin, 2006.

Levy, Ellen. *Criminal Ingenuity: Moore, Cornell, Ashbery, and the Struggle between the Arts.* New York: Oxford University Press, 2011.

Lipking, Lawrence. *The Life of the Poet: Beginning and Ending Poetic Careers.* Chicago: University of Chicago Press, 1981.

———. "Inventing a Life – A Personal View of Literary Careers." In Hardie and Moore, *Classical Literary Careers,* 287-99.

Longenbach, James. "Louise Glück's Nine Lives." In Diehl, *On Louise Gluck,* 136–50.

———. *Modern Poetry after Modernism.* New York: Oxford University Press, 1997.

———. *Wallace Stevens: The Plain Sense of Things.* New York: Oxford University Press, 1991.

Longfellow, Henry Wadsworth. *Voices of the Night.* Cambridge, MA: John Owen, 1849.

Longfellow, Samuel, ed. *Life of Henry Wadsworth Longfellow.* Vol. 1. Boston: Ticknor and Company, 1886.

Lux, Thomas. Foreword to *Beautiful in the Mouth*, by Keetje Kuipers, 9–10. Brockport, NY: Boa Editions, 2010.

MacLeish, Archibald. Foreword to *Family Circle*, by Eve Merriam, 5–7. New Haven, CT: Yale University Press, 1946.

Markham, Melinda. *Ninety-Five Nights of Listening.* New York: Houghton Mifflin, 2002.

Martz, Louis L. " 'From the Journal of Crispin': An Early Version of 'The Comedian as the Letter C.' " In *Wallace Stevens: A Celebration*, edited by Frank Doggett and Robert Buttel, 3–45. Princeton, NJ: Princeton University Press, 1980.

Matthiessen, F. O. Introduction to *Fingerboard*, by Marshall Schacht, n.p. New York: Twayne, 1949.

McClatchy, J. D. *Scenes from Another Life.* New York: George Braziller, 1981.

McCorkle, James. *Evidences.* Port Townsend, WA: Copper Canyon Press, 2003.

McGurl, Mark. *The Program Era: Postwar Fiction and the Rise of Creative Writing.* Cambridge, MA: Harvard University Press, 2009.

Menand, Louis. *Discovering Modernism: T. S. Eliot and His Context.* 2nd ed. New York: Oxford University Press, 2007.

Meredith, George. *The Egoist.* 1879; Harmondsworth, UK: Penguin Books, 1987.

Meredith, William. "A Lot of Poems and a Bit of Theory." *Hudson Review* 7, no. 4 (Winter 1955): 594–601.

Merrin, Jeredith. "Sites of Struggle: Marianne Moore and American Calvinism." In Barnstone, Manson, and Singly, *The Calvinist Roots of the Modern Era,* 91–106.

Miller, Cristanne. *Cultures of Modernism: Marianne Moore, Mina Loy, and Else Lasker-Schüler.* Ann Arbor: University of Michigan Press, 2005.

Miller, Perry. *The New England Mind: The Seventeenth Century.* New York: Macmillan, 1939.

Milton, John. *An Apology for Smectymnuus.* In *John Milton: Selected Prose,* 61–65. Edited by C. A. Patrides. Columbia: University of Missouri Press, 1985.

Mintz, Alan. *George Eliot and the Novel of Vocation*. Cambridge, MA: Harvard University Press, 1978.

Molesworth, Charles. *Marianne Moore: A Literary Life*. Boston: Northeastern University Press, 1991.

Moore, Marianne. *Becoming Marianne Moore: The Early Poems, 1907–1924*. Edited by Robin G. Schulze. Berkeley: University of California Press, 2002.

———. *The Complete Prose of Marianne Moore*. Edited by Patricia C. Willis. New York: Viking, 1986.

———. "Interview with Donald Hall." In *A Marianne Moore Reader*, 253–73. New York: Viking, 1961.

———. *The Selected Letters of Marianne Moore*. Edited by Bonnie Costello. New York: Alfred A. Knopf, 1997.

Moramarco, Fred. "Coming Full Circle: John Ashbery's Later Poetry." In *The Tribe of John: Ashbery and Contemporary Poetry*, edited by Susan M. Schultz, 38–59. Tuscaloosa: University of Alabama Press, 1995.

Morgan, Edmund S. *Visible Saints: The History of a Puritan Idea*. Ithaca, NY: Cornell University Press, 1965.

Morris, Daniel. *The Poetry of Louise Glück: A Thematic Introduction*. Columbia: University of Missouri Press, 2006.

Moss, Thylias. *Hosiery Seams on a Bowlegged Woman*. Cleveland, OH: Cleveland State University Poetry Center, 1983.

Mossin, Andrew. *Male Subjectivity and Poetic Form in "New American" Poetry*. New York: Palgrave Macmillan, 2010.

Muske-Dukes, Carol. Foreword to *Swallow*, by Miranda Field, ix–x. New York: Houghton Mifflin, 2002.

Nealon, Christopher. *The Matter of Capital: Poetry and Crisis in the American Century*. Cambridge, MA: Harvard University Press, 2011.

New, Elisa. *The Regenerate Lyric: Theology and Innovation in American Poetry*. Cambridge: Cambridge University Press, 1993.

Newcomb, John Timberman. *Would Poetry Disappear? American Verse and the Crisis of Modernity*. Athens: University of Ohio Press, 2004.

Nicholson, Mervyn. "The Riddle of the Firecat." *The Wallace Stevens Journal* 22, no. 2 (Fall 1998): 133–48.

O'Hara, Frank. "Rare Modern." *Poetry* 89, no. 5 (February 1957): 307–16.

Ong, Walter. *The Barbarian Within*. New York: Macmillan, 1962.

Pack, Robert. *The Irony of Joy: Poems*. Poets of Today 2. New York: Charles Scriber's Sons, 1955.

Palmer, Michael. *Blake's Newton*. Los Angeles: Black Sparrow Press, 1972.

Pater, Walter. *The Renaissance: Studies in Art and Poetry*. Edited by Donald L. Hill. Berkeley: University of California Press, 1980.

Perelman, Bob. *Braille*. Ithaca, NY: Ithaca House, 1975.

Perloff, Marjorie. "Avant-Garde Tradition and the Individual Talent: The Case of Language Poetry," *Revue Française d'Études Américaines*, no. 103 (February 2005): 117–41.

———. *Differentials: Poetry, Poetics, Pedagogy*. Tuscaloosa: University of Alabama Press, 2004.

————. "'Fragments of a Buried Life': John Ashbery's Dream Songs." In *Beyond Amazement: New Essays on John Ashbery*, edited by David Lehman, 66–86. Ithaca, NY: Cornell University Press, 1980.

Perloff, Marjorie. *The Poetics of Indeterminacy.* Princeton, NJ: Princeton University Press, 1981. Reprint, Evanston, IL: Northwestern University Press, 1999.

Phillips, Siobhan. *The Poetics of the Everyday: Creative Repetition in Modern American Verse.* New York: Columbia University Press, 2010.

Plath, Sylvia. *The Colossus and Other Poems.* 1962. Reprint, New York: Vintage Books, 1968.

————. *Letters Home: Correspondence, 1950–1963.* Edited by Aurelia Schober Plath. London: Faber and Faber, 1975.

————. *The Unabridged Journals of Sylvia Plath.* Edited by Karen V. Kukil. New York: Anchor Books, 2000.

Plumly, Stanley. *In the Outer Dark.* Baton Rouge: Louisiana University Press, 1970.

Pope, Alexander. "A Discourse on Pastoral Poetry." *The Poems of Alexander Pope.* Edited by John Butt, 119–23. New Haven, CT: Yale University Press, 1963.

Pound, Ezra. *Selected Poems of Ezra Pound.* New York: New Directions, 1957.

Prunty, Wyatt. *The Times Between.* Baltimore, MD: Johns Hopkins University Press, 1982.

Ragg, Edward. *Wallace Stevens and the Aesthetics of Abstraction.* Cambridge: Cambridge University Press, 2010.

Rambuss, Scott. *Spencer's Secret Career.* Cambridge: Cambridge University Press, 1993.

Rampersad, Arnold. *The Life of Langston Hughes, Volume I: 1902–1941, I, Too, Sing America.* New York: Oxford University Press, 1986.

Rasula, Jed. *The American Poetry Wax Museum: Reality Effects, 1940–1990.* Urbana, IL: National Council of Teachers of English, 1996.

————. *Syncopations: The Stress of Innovation in Contemporary American Poetry.* Tuscaloosa: University of Alabama Press, 2004.

Rawson, Claude. "Bards, Boardrooms, and Blackboards: John Ashbery, Wallace Stevens, and the Academicization of Poetry." In *On Modern Poetry: Essays Presented to Donald Davie,* edited by Vereen Bell and Laurence Lerner, 181–91. Nashville, TN: Vanderbilt University Press, 1988.

Rector, Liam, ed. *The Day I Was Older: On the Poetry of Donald Hall.* Santa Cruz, CA: Storyline Press, 1989.

Reed, Brian. *Hart Crane: After His Lights.* Tuscaloosa: University of Alabama Press, 2007.

Richardson, Joan. *Wallace Stevens: The Early Years, 1879–1923.* New York: William Morrow, 1986.

Rifkin, Libbie. *Career Moves: Olson, Creeley, Zukofsky, Berrigan, and the American Avant-Garde.* Madison: University of Wisconsin Press, 2000.

Robbins, Bruce. *Secular Vocations: Intellectuals, Professionalism, Culture.* London: Verso, 1993.

Rosenfeld, Paul. "Another Pierrot." *Men Seen: Twenty-Four Modern Authors.* New York: Dial, 1925. In *Wallace Stevens: The Critical Heritage,* edited by Charles Doyle, 72–78. New York: Routledge, 1985.

Said, Edward. *Beginnings: Intention and Method.* New York: Basic, 1975. Reprint, New York: Columbia University Press, 1985.

Schulze, Robin G. *The Web of Friendship: Marianne Moore and Wallace Stevens.* Ann Arbor: University of Michigan Press, 1995.

Sewell, Lisa. "'In the End, the One Who Has Nothing Wins': Louise Glück and the Poetics of Anorexia." *Literature Interpretation Theory* 17 (2006): 49–76.

Shapiro, Harvey. *The Eye.* New Poetry Series. Denver, CO: Alan Swallow, 1953.

Shelley, Percy Bysshe. *Shelley's Poetry and Prose.* Edited by Donald H. Reiman and Sharon B. Powers. New York: W. W. Norton, 1977.

Shetley, Vernon. *After the Death of Poetry: Poet and Audience in Contemporary America.* Durham, NC: Duke University Press, 1993.

Shivani, Anis. *Against the Workshop: Provocations, Polemics, Controversies.* Huntsville: Texas Review Press, 2011.

Shoptaw, John. *On the Outside Looking Out: John Ashbery's Poetry.* Cambridge, MA: Harvard University Press, 1994.

Silverberg, Mark. *The New York School Poets and the Neo-Avant-Garde: Between Radical Art and Radical Chic.* Farnham, UK: Ashgate, 2010.

Simon, John. "More Brass Than Enduring." *Hudson Review* 15, no. 3 (Autumn 1962): 455–68.

Simpson, Louis. "Poets in Isolation." *Hudson Review* 6, no. 4 (Autumn 1957): 458–64.

Siskin, Clifford. *The Work of Writing: Literature and Social Change in Britain.* Baltimore: Johns Hopkins University Press, 1998.

Slatin, John. *The Savage's Romance: The Poetry of Marianne Moore.* University Park, PA: Penn State University Press, 1986.

Smith, Adam. *The Wealth of Nations.* (1776): 119. Quoted in Thomas Pfau, *Wordsworth's Profession: Form, Class, and the Logic of Early Romantic Cultural Production.* Stanford, CA: Stanford University Press, 1997.

Smith, Erin Elizabeth. *The Fear of Being Found.* Savage, MN: Three Candles Press, 2008.

Snyder, Gary. *Riprap and Cold Mountain Poems.* 1959. San Francisco, CA: North Point Press, 1990.

Spenser, Edmund. *The Faerie Queene.* Edited by Thomas P. Roche, Jr. Harmondsworth, UK: Penguin Books, 1978.

Spires, Elizabeth. Foreword to *Even the Hollow My Body Made Is Gone,* by Janice N. Harrington, 7–9. Brockport, NY: Boa Editions, 2007.

Stern, Gerald. Introduction to *Things Are Happening,* by Joshua Beckman, vii–xii. Philadelphia: American Poetry Review, 1998.

Stevens, Holly. *Souvenirs and Prophecies: The Young Wallace Stevens.* New York: Alfred A. Knopf, 1977.

Stevens, Wallace. *Letters of Wallace Stevens.* Edited by Holly Stevens. New York: Alfred A. Knopf, 1966. Reprint, Berkeley: University of California Press, 1996.

———. *Wallace Stevens: Collected Poetry and Prose.* Edited by Frank Kermode and Joan Richardson. New York: Library of America, 1997.

Stone, Walter. *Poems, 1955–1958.* Poets of Today 6. New York: Charles Scribner's Sons, 1959.

Strychacz, Thomas. *Modernism, Mass Culture, and Professionalism.* Cambridge: Cambridge University Press, 1993.

Svalina, Matthias. *Destruction Myth.* Cleveland, OH: Cleveland State University Press, 2010.

Taylor, Henry. *The Horse Show at Midnight.* Baton Rouge: Louisiana University Press, 1966.

Thompson, John. "A Catalogue of Poets." *Hudson Review* 13, no. 4 (Winter 1960–61): 618–25.

Trachtenberg, Alan. Introduction to *Hart Crane: A Collection of Critical Essays*. Englewood Cliffs, NJ: Prentice-Hall, 1982.

Valentine, Jean. *Dream Barker*. Yale Series of Younger Poets. New Haven, CT: Yale University Press, 1965.

Valenza, Robin. *Literature, Language, and the Rise of the Intellectual Disciplines in Britain, 1680–1820*. Cambridge: Cambridge University Press, 1993.

Vendler, Helen. *Coming of Age as a Poet*. Cambridge, MA: Harvard University Press, 2003.

———. *Part of Nature, Part of Us*. Cambridge, MA: Harvard University Press, 1980.

Wagner-Martin, Linda. *Sylvia Plath: A Biography*. New York: Simon and Schuster, 1987.

Wagoner, David. *Dry Sun, Dry Wind*. Indiana University Poetry Series. Bloomington: Indiana University Press, 1953.

Walton, Eda Lou. "Younger Voices." *Poetry* 43, no. 12 (March 1954): 343–47.

Wang, Dorothy. *Thinking Its Presence: Form, Race, and Subjectivity in Contemporary Asian Poetry*. Stanford, CA: Stanford University Press, 2014.

Weber, Max. *The Protestant Ethic and the "Spirit" of Capitalism and Other Writings*. Edited and translated by Peter Baehr and Gordon C. Wells. 1905. Reprint, New York: Penguin, 2002.

———. *The Vocation Lectures*. Edited by David Owen and Tracy B. Strong. Translated by Rodney Livingstone. Indianapolis, IN: Hackett, 2004.

Weiss, Neil. *Changes of Garments*. Indiana University Poetry Series. Bloomington: Indiana University Press, 1956.

White, Gillian. *Lyric Shame: The "Lyric" Subject of Contemporary American Poetry*. Cambridge, MA: Harvard University Press, 2014.

Whitman, Walt. *Walt Whitman: Complete Poetry and Collected Prose*. Edited by Justin Kaplan. New York: Library of America, 1982.

Williams, Raymond. *Culture and Society: 1780–1950*. 1958. Reprint, New York: Columbia University Press, 1983.

Williams, William Carlos. *Imaginations*. Edited by Webster Schott. New York: New Directions, 1970.

———. Introduction to *Howl and Other Poems*, by Allen Ginsberg, 7-8. 1956. San Francisco, CA: City Lights, 2000.

Woods, John. *Deaths at Paragon, Indiana*. Indiana University Poetry Series. Bloomington: Indiana University Press, 1955.

Yau, John. *Crossing Canal Street*. Binghamton, NY: Bellevue Press, 1976.

Yu, Timothy. *Race and the Avant-Garde: Experimental and Asian American Poetry since 1965*. Stanford, CA: Stanford University Press, 2011.

Zionkowski, Linda. *Men's Work: Gender, Class, and the Professionalization of Poetry, 1660–1784*. New York: Palgrave Macmillan, 2001.

Index